T0330984

Managing Human Resources in SMEs and Start-ups

International Challenges and Solutions

New Teaching Resources for Management in a Globalised World

Print ISSN: 2661-4774
Online ISSN: 2661-4782

Series Editor: Professor Léo-Paul Dana

The classic economic view of internationalisation was based on the theory of competitive advantage, and over the years, internationalisation was seen in various lights, as an expansion option. With the reduction of trade barriers, however, many local small enterprises face major international competitors in formerly protected domestic markets. Today, competitiveness in the global marketplace is no longer an option; it has become a necessity as the acceleration towards globalisation offers unprecedented challenges and opportunities.

This book series will bring together textbooks, monographs, edited collections and handbooks useful to postgraduates and researchers in the age of globalisation. Relevant topics include, but are not limited to: research methods, culture, entrepreneurship, globalisation, immigration, migrants, public policy, self-employment, sustainability, technological advances, emerging markets, demographic shifts, and innovation.

Published:

The complete list of the published volumes in the series can also be found at
https://www.worldscientific.com/series/ntrmgw

New Teaching
Resources for
Management in a
Globalised World
Volume 5

Managing Human Resources in SMEs and Start-ups

International Challenges and Solutions

Editors

Léo-Paul Dana
Dalhousie University, Halifax, Canada

Naman Sharma
Indian Institute of Foreign Trade, Kolkata, India

Vinod Kumar Singh
Gurukula Kangri Vishwavidyalaya, Haridwar, India

World Scientific

NEW JERSEY · LONDON · SINGAPORE · BEIJING · SHANGHAI · HONG KONG · TAIPEI · CHENNAI · TOKYO

Published by

World Scientific Publishing Co. Pte. Ltd.

5 Toh Tuck Link, Singapore 596224

USA office: 27 Warren Street, Suite 401-402, Hackensack, NJ 07601

UK office: 57 Shelton Street, Covent Garden, London WC2H 9HE

Library of Congress Cataloging-in-Publication Data
Names: Dana, Léo-Paul, editor. | Sharma, Naman, 1986–   editor. |
    Singh, V. K. (Vinod Kumar), 1969–   editor.
Title: Managing human resources in SMEs and start-ups : international challenges and solutions /
    editors, Léo-Paul Dana, Dalhousie University, Halifax, Canada,
    Naman Sharma, Indian Institute of Foreign Trade, Kolkata, India,
    Vinod Kumar Singh, Gurukula Kangri Vishwavidyalaya, Haridwar, India.
Description: New Jersey : World Scientific, [2022] | Series: New teaching resources for management
    in a globalised world, 2661-4774 ; vol. 5 | Includes bibliographical references and index.
Identifiers: LCCN 2021059119 | ISBN 9789811239205 (hardcover) |
    ISBN 9789811239212 (ebook) | ISBN 9789811239229 (ebook other)
Subjects: LCSH: Personnel management.
Classification: LCC HF5549 .M2238 2022 | DDC 658.3--dc23/eng/20211209
LC record available at https://lccn.loc.gov/2021059119

British Library Cataloguing-in-Publication Data
A catalogue record for this book is available from the British Library.

For any available supplementary material, please visit
https://www.worldscientific.com/worldscibooks/10.1142/12341#t=suppl

Desk Editors: Balamurugan Rajendran/Shi Ying Koe

Typeset by Stallion Press
Email: enquiries@stallionpress.com

Printed in Singapore

To Michelle, with infinite thanks
Léo-Paul Dana

About the Editors

Léo-Paul Dana is Professor at the Rowe School of Business of Dalhousie University, Canada. As well, he holds titles of Professor at Montpellier Business School, and Visiting Professor at Kingston University. He is also associated with the Chaire ETI at Sorbonne Business School. A graduate of McGill University and HEC-Montreal, he has served as Marie Curie Fellow at Princeton University and Visiting Professor at INSEAD.

Naman Sharma is currently affiliated with the Indian Institute of Foreign Trade, Kolkata (India) as an Assistant Professor, and has nearly five years of academic experience. He also has substantial research experience and his research has been published in ABDC ranked/Scopus-indexed journals and other reputable publishers such as the Emerald Publishing Group. He has also authored four books with publishers of international repute such as IGI-Global and is a serving guest editor for various journals.

 **Vinod Kumar Singh** is Professor of Marketing with 24 years of teaching experience. He has travelled to more than 14 countries on various teaching and research assignments. He is currently holding the responsibilities of Head & Dean at Faculty of Management Studies, Gurukula Kangri Vishwavidyalaya, Haridwar, India. He has supervised more than 20 PhD students and is currently guiding 5 scholars. He has published more than 10 books and more than 30 research papers in reputed journals indexed with SCOPUS, Web of Science and ABDC ranked journals. He has a teaching experience of more than 24 years.

https://doi.org/10.1142/9789811239212_fmatter

Contents

https://doi.org/10.1142/9789811239212_0001

Chapter 1

Management of Human Resources in SMEs and Start-ups: Introduction

Léo-Paul Dana

Dalhousie University, Canada

lp762359@dal.ca

Naman Sharma

Indian Institute of Foreign Trade, India

namanshandilya@gmail.com

Abstract: Management of human resources is a critical decision that organisations especially the small enterprises make after a lot of deliberation and careful analysis. The book addresses several issues and challenges that SMEs and start-ups face during the management of their workforce. This introductory chapter aims to set the premise of this discussion and shares the basic understanding of these issues and challenges, letting the readers know what they can expect from the rest of the book. The chapter also illustrates through real world images the involvement of human resources in the small business and the impact it has on their overall outcomes.

Keywords: Small business, Start-ups, Human resources, Workforce, Management.

Human resources are the most important and costliest assets in businesses of any nature and size. They also come with risks; in the airline sector, for example, pilot error can be deadly while mis-handling of freight (Figure 1.1) also has consequences.

Some jobs, such as data-entry, primarily require high accuracy (Figure 1.2); others require strength and stamina (Figure 1.3), and yet others require patience (Figure 1.4). Talent management is a key managerial function in MNCs (Figure 1.5) and other organisations with a global presence, but its importance in small businesses and start-ups cannot be overlooked. The purpose of this book is to give the reader an overview of human resources issues in SMEs and start-ups (Figure 1.6). Reflecting their importance around the world, the volume includes reflections from different country contexts. Chapters cover studies from Africa, Asia, and Europe, with a wide

Figure 1.1.   Unloading freight; photo © Léo-Paul Dana

Figure 1.2.   Typing documents requires precision; photo © Léo-Paul Dana

variety of jobs. Figure 1.7 features an elevator operator in North Africa, where automatic elevators have not replaced the need for elevator personnel. Figure 1.8 features men patiently waiting for directives. Figure 1.9 takes us to Europe. Culture is among many factors that affect human resources practices; for example, the role of women is perceived differently in different cultures (Figures 1.10 & 1.11).

Figure 1.3.   Physical labour; photo © Léo-Paul Dana

Figure 1.4.   Preparing food, just right; photo © Léo-Paul Dana

Figure 1.5. National Panasonic; photo © Léo-Paul Dana

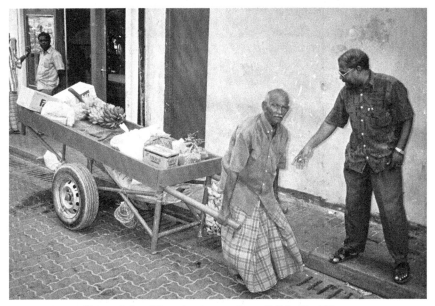

Figure 1.6. Micro-business; photo © Léo-Paul Dana

Figure 1.7.   Elevator operator; photo © Léo-Paul Dana

Figure 1.8.   India; photo © Léo-Paul Dana

Figure 1.9.   Eastern Europe; photo © Léo-Paul Dana

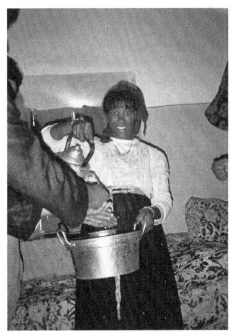

Figure 1.10.   Woman in North Africa; photo © Léo-Paul Dana

Figure 1.11.   Women in Europe; photo © Léo-Paul Dana

At its most basic level, managing employees encompasses compliance with the applicable labour laws, and these vary by country and sector. Some jurisdictions have child labour legislation while others do not (Figure 1.12). Health and safety regulations can have a great impact on the food sector (Figure 1.13). Working conditions also vary (Figure 1.14). Important issues include hiring and creating a channel for dealing with employee concerns. A happy employee (Figure 1.15) is good for business, and it is beneficial for team members to be compatible (Figure 1.16).

An important lesson from studying human resources is that a good fit is essential. Among front-line staff in the hospitality industry (Figure 1.17), for example, one does not want employees who do not like dealing with people. The price of not having the right employees can be extremely high, and this is aggravated in a smaller firm. Workers who are inefficient or in the wrong role can have critical consequences on the sustainability of a small business. While most entrepreneurs focus on marketing, finance, operations, and

Figure 1.12.   Child labour in coal mining sector; photo © Léo-Paul Dana

Figure 1.13.   Cleanliness standards vary; photo © Léo-Paul Dana

Figure 1.14.   Small-scale manufacturing; photo © Léo-Paul Dana

Figure 1.15.   Working with a smile; photo © Léo-Paul Dana

Figure 1.16.   Working as a team; photo © Léo-Paul Dana

Figure 1.17.   Front-line staff gives first impression; photo © Léo-Paul Dana

customers in their initial stages, they at times fail to establish and address their human resources function and the associated challenges that, if overcome, may help the organisation to meet all of its targets. This book aims to highlight these human resources challenges and shed new light on how to answer them.

Chapter 2

Different Water and in a Smaller Bottle: Understanding Motivations and Differences in Human Resources Management Needs of Small Firms — Common Systems to Unique Requirements

Mehmet Çetin

Istanbul Sabahattin Zaim University, Turkey

mehmet.cetin@izu.edu.tr

Abstract: Functions of human resources (HR) are often considered the most convenient issues to neglect or cancel in times of crisis or when there is a lack of resources by many organisations. This inaccurate approach is more common in start-ups and small scale firms where resources are more scarce. Good HR is good HR for both large and small firms. Evidence indicates that effective HR activities yield higher levels of performance in small firms as it does in large firms. Independent from the number of employees working in an organisation, the need for HR functions at the individual level remain same. Members of a small enterprise also need motivation, recognition, feedback training and development opportunities, and all other HR related efforts. Although the literature on strategic human resource management is dominantly focused on providing solutions for large scale organisations, there is still much to adapt from this knowledge for small firms. Besides, small firms may have unique conditions necessitating different solutions and investigations. This chapter aims to provide information regarding how small scale firms differ in their needs and conditions and further our knowledge on how we can create HR solutions specific to small firms or how best we can provide ways to adopt well-known systems and processes in small firms. A specific emphasis on the motivations for not adopting HR efforts will allow us to provide recommendations that would be easier and more motivating to adopt.

Keywords: HR, Small scale firms, Human resources, Employee motivation.

2.1 Introduction

Effective human resources (HR) is a critical need for both large and small firms. Evidence indicates that effective HR activities yield higher performance levels in small firms as it does in large firms (Kerr *et al.*, 2007). Independent from the number of employees working in an organisation, the significance of HR practices at the individual level remains the same. Members of a small enterprise also need motivation, recognition, feedback training and development opportunities, and other HR-related efforts. Addressing these needs requires a comprehensive understanding of HR-related factors in SMEs which can demonstrate unique characteristics.

Empirical evidence suggests that effective HR is a crucial determinant for the success of SMEs. For instance, Mear and Werner (2020) emphasise the role of high-performance HR systems that provide robust reinforcement and motivation for creativity in the competitiveness and innovativeness of German "Hidden Champion" SMEs. Despite the importance and dominance of small firms in many economies, very few studies attempt to explain the key for HR effectiveness in small firms (Williamson & Lynch-Wood, 2001). Although strategic human resource management (HRM) literature is dominantly focused on providing solutions for large-scale organisations, there is still much to adapt from this knowledge for small firms (Mayson & Barrett, 2006). On the other hand, despite the considerable research for making more sense of HR in family firms and small organisations (e.g., Combs *et al.*, 2018); the majority of the efforts for suggesting effective HR systems and practices address large scale organisations and what we know on how these solutions can be adapted to small scale companies is scarce (Cardon & Stevens, 2004). Besides, small firms may have unique conditions necessitating different solutions and investigations. Although some HR challenges are common among small, medium, and large scale companies, there is a substantial difference in the nature of these challenges, and effective HR functions may necessitate different processes (Deshpande & Golhar, 1994). All small firms demonstrate different characteristics; a general "one size fits at all" approach regarding the small firm employment relationships is not feasible (Atkinson, 2008). Still, we can create shared understandings and systems for small firms to adopt for their unique needs. We can clarify the differences between large-scale firms and small firms regarding their HR operations as well. Understanding the contingencies and factors moderating HR practices and their outcome can enhance our competence for creating practical recommendations for SMEs.

This chapter aims to provide information regarding how small-scale firms differ in their needs and conditions and further our knowledge of how we can create HR solutions specific to small firms or give the best ways to adapt well-known systems and processes to small firms. A particular emphasis on the motivations for not adopting HR efforts will allow us to provide recommendations that would be easier and more motivating to adopt. Elaborating the factors that can shape small firms differently from each other and the larger ones and understanding possible advantages and disadvantages (regarding HR) of being small can contribute to effective HR in small firms.

2.2 The Context for HR in SMEs

There are several reasons why SMEs tend to neglect HR functions and practices. Human resources functions are often considered the most convenient issues to ignore or cancel in crises or when there is a lack of resources by many organisations. This inaccurate approach is more common in start-ups and small-scale firms where resources are more scarce. One motivation to allocate more resources to other company functions instead of human resources is human resources functions. It usually gives feedback in the long run and requires more continuous effort. For instance, evidence suggests that HR investments can even be detrimental to employee and organisational outcomes in the short run if they are not implemented continuously and completely (Bryson & White, 2019).

Moreover, job owners or technical managers with no expertise or training in the field often take responsibility for HR. Empirical evidence suggests that owner-management has adverse effects on calculative human resources management practices (Wu, 2020). It is prevalent to see that human skills are mistaken for HR skills. Managers may be under an illusion regarding the need for HR practices. They may find them unnecessary or impossible for a small number of people or see themselves sufficient for all HR needs. One small pitfall firms may have about HR practices is that they may overestimate their HR capabilities and consider their HR processes and functions more powerful than they really are (McEvoy, 1984).

Who is responsible for HR-related functions is an essential determinant for HR practices in small firms (Cassell *et al.*, 2002). Combined with the perception regarding the importance and centrality of HR (HR norms), the responsible unit (or person) determines the power of HR in the firm. Organisations may attain various responsibilities and authority to HR units (Sarvaiya *et al.*, 2018). In small firms, the HR unit can be responsible for HR (among other duties). HR can both be perceived as a central strategic issue that is highly linked to the company's performance or a cost regarding supportive activities for other vital practices. The nature of this perception and understanding can yield to different structures of HR units and levels of importance given to HR functions.

2.3 Advantages and Disadvantages for Small Firms Regarding HRM

Understanding the possible advantages and disadvantages of small firms in general (with the notion that they can demonstrate unique characteristics) regarding HRM can help us provide strong recommendations on avoiding the weaknesses and using the strengths (Table 2.1).

One common disadvantage perceived by individuals working in small enterprises is the lack of systematic HR practices. HR functions in family firms are generally characterised by informality and lack of a systematic scientific approach (Mayson & Barrett, 2006). Beneficial training or career development opportunities, transparent and systematic compensation, performance management systems, or well-designed social activities can stand as motivations for talent to shift from small businesses to large corporate firms.

A resource-based approach predicts that it is much less possible to employ HR professionals for separate HR functions in small firms due to lack of resources. Top managers, who usually have no professional HR functions, take the initiative to manage HR-related operations. This has two negative consequences: first, the quality of HR policies and practices decrease due to lack of expertise and time, and second, managers struggling with HR problems (lacking the needed competence) can be distracted and kept away from the functions where they can be productive and effective (Klass *et al.*, 2002).

Recruitment of the best possible employees is a more challenging task and process for small firms compared to larger ones in many

Table 2.1. Possible advantages and disadvantages of being a smaller firm

Possible advantages	Possible disadvantages
More leadership support available per employee	Attraction of talent • Firm reputation
More customised HR practices tailored for each employee	• Riskiness • Ambiguity
Better opportunities to show self and take responsibility	Lack of resources Lack of know-how and formalisation Lack of economies of scale of HR systems

aspects. First, the talent attraction is more difficult given that small firms may not have the same opportunity and time to invest in their reputation as larger companies do. For instance, they have fewer resources or economies of scale to support advertisement, company-university relationships, or sizeable social responsibility projects. For example, SMEs invest less time and effort in attracting new graduates (McLarty, 1999). They usually do not build company recruitment websites where candidates can learn about the opportunities in the firm.

Second, even though they may provide better opportunities, small firms can initially be perceived as riskier endeavours by the candidates in the job market. Larger firms that have been in the market with higher market shares are more likely to be perceived as stable, sustainable, and reassuring. Another possible reason for employees not preferring small firms may be the generally negative perception regarding the institutionalisation of the companies. Legitimacy is a significant limitation for small firms (Cardon & Stevens, 2004). They are more prone to being perceived as workplaces with more role ambiguity or a power culture where managers make rules for each person and condition.

Another disadvantage for small firms is about the economies of scale. Building up HR systems and having a certain number of professionals just for HR functions are costly. These costs can run into large numbers, and the marginal cost or cost per employee would be smaller in large companies that can utilise economies of scale. For small firms, these investments are much costlier, considering the HR cost per employee.

On the other hand, although a formalised and systematic application of HR functions is less likely, more leader support and time per employee can be devoted in small firms. When groups are smaller in terms of leader-member exchange, leaders are less inclined to create in groups and out groups (Henderson *et al.*, 2009). For instance, leaders can invest more time for guidance, mentoring, coaching, or support for each employee's development.

Another possible strength for small firms regarding HR management can be the more profitable opportunities for tailoring HR practices to employee needs. Instead of structuring highly formalised and less flexible HR systems, employees may benefit from customised HR functions. For instance, training designed for a large group of people may contain some parts that are not relevant or necessary for all the participants. It is more possible to develop training which is just right for employee's needs for few people. Managing and monitoring HR metrics and tracking HR practices without human resources information systems (HRIS) is nearly impossible in large firms (Maamari & Osta, 2021). However, small firms do not demonstrate the same level of necessity for using HRIS. Although this can stand as an advantage in less investment required, it can also create difficulty in keeping track of HR metrics and practices. However, training and performance evaluation scores per employee can be controlled in separate files, and the change and development on these can be tracked through simpler technologies.

The "small is beautiful" approach suggests higher levels of quality leader-member exchange, higher loyalty, cohesiveness, effective (informal) communication, more value and goal alignment, and higher job identity in a small firm (Dundon & Wilkinson, 2018). According to this perspective, as there is a smaller number of employees, in-groups and out-groups are less likely to occur. Leaders can devote more time and concern for each employee, and employees can interact more frequently in a less formal environment. On the other hand, the "bleak house" approach presents small firms as having high power distance, autocracy, and illegitimacy, thus becoming a risky endeavour for prospective employees.

2.4 HR Functions in SMEs Compared to Large Companies

There is evidence that traditional HR, which is fundamentally designed for and studied in large firms, does not apply to small firms. For instance, although recruitment and selection processes present similar patterns for large and small organisations, they also show some differences in the methods and criteria. Hiring practices and job search behaviour are different (Barber *et al.*, 1999).

Generally, there are two primary criteria for selection and recruitment in organisations: person-job fit and person-organisation fit (Wuryaningrat *et al.*, 2019). Studies demonstrate that more emphasis is given to the latter in small companies (Deshpande & Golhar, 1994; Heneman *et al.*, 2000; Williamson *et al.*, 2002). There are several reasons for smaller firms to devote more importance to person-organisation fit, matching mindsets, values, or lifestyles. First, as fewer employees are working in the same unit, it is likely for small companies to have lower levels of job specialisation and broader job definitions. In larger firms, there is more opportunity for defining highly specialised jobs and less demand for multitasking.

On the other hand, in small firms, employees must be more multifunctional and adaptive to different roles, which necessitates a focus on personality traits and mindset. It is less likely to have a specialised employee for each task. Another reason for the personality focus in small firms can be the expected length of employment. Small firms and family firms tend to consider their long-term employees as family members if the agreement is full-time employment (Machek *et al.*, 2019). Lifetime careers in one organisation are more common in smaller firms.

Smaller firms employ more affordable and less sophisticated methods of selection and recruitment, such as direct applications or internal networks and more direct influence or involvement of managers in supervising the position (Heneman & Berkley, 1999). This nature of selection has its advantages and disadvantages. Members of the organisation are knowledgeable about the culture and characteristics of the organisation and the candidates they may suggest. This can provide a more affordable and less time-taking process. Still, this can also shape the organisation as one-sided and reduces cultural diversity. Limiting possible candidates with direct applications and members' network can leave the best-matching employees out.

In their meta-analysis, Cardon and Stevens (2004) list some recruitment options for small firms in light of the extant literature. Their list can be summarised under four main categories: (1) mimicking (imitating) large scale firms, (2) building their authentic (unique) ways, (3) outsourcing professional HR support, and (4) employing a contingent workforce. Although imitating large-scale firms can provide higher legitimacy for small firms in candidates' eyes, it may also create wrong expectations. A highly formalised approach in the selection process can signal to candidates high levels of institutionalisation, and they may expect the same in all other processes if they are hired. Creating realistic expectations is crucial for building healthy psychological contracts and longer retention of employees. Atkinson (2008) suggests a psychological contract framework for understanding the sophisticated nature of employment relationships in small firms. Building authentic (unique) methods for selection and recruitment may be more unconventional and a better fit with the expectations of Generation Z. Still, some candidates may favour more traditional methods of selection and recruitment.

SMEs also differ in some aspects regarding compensation. Evidence shows that positive perceptions on compensation strengthen the link between employee participation and retention (Khalid & Nawab, 2018). Thus compensation management is an essential determinant for employee attitudes and behaviours. Compared to larger firms, smaller ones more frequently use "at-risk pay" compensation tools such as stock sharing or incentives because their growth (even survival) bears uncertainty (Cardon & Stevens, 2004). Employees know that their compensation is highly related to the success and development of the firm. For employees who like risk-taking and entrepreneurial challenges more, SMEs with such a pay structure may serve as a better option.

On the other hand, this pay structure may not be the best option for employees who prefer stability and certainty more. Performance evaluation processes are more informal and less structured for SMEs (Cardon & Stevens, 2004). Performance appraisal is less frequent in smaller firms, and less systematic and formal than in larger ones (Kotey & Sheridan, 2004). A smaller number of employees allows paired comparison techniques in performance appraisal for small firms.

Although it has various critical positive outcomes, such as organisational citizenship behaviour and work engagement, talent management remains one of the most ignored functions in companies (Kuntonbutr & Sangperm, 2019). Organisations, big or small, often go through difficult periods where environmental factors are more demanding. Given the possible resource shortage in SMEs, it is highly critical for small firms to increase their capacities for resilience in the face of economic turbulence and various kinds of crises. Shortage of skilled labour and training facilities can be an essential barrier to organisational resilience in SMEs, which is crucial for corporate survival and success (Rahman & Mendy, 2019).

Training and development can be considered as the HR function that demonstrates the highest level of difference between SMEs and larger firms. Informal and unstructured training approaches and methods such as job training, pairing systems, mentoring, or modelling dominates SMEs (Cardon & Stevens, 2004). On the job training or close manager guidance is a general approach to training in small firms (Kotey, & Sheridan, 2004).

Utilising outsourced expert help on HR functions can provide positive outcomes. Klaas *et al.* (2002) indicate that small-scale companies using professional employer organisations report higher satisfaction levels in HR outcomes. Companies analysing each small firm as unique cases and providing specific solutions to their special needs may radically enhance HR performance.

Outsourcing support for the HR process is a common way small firms adopt. It can substitute professionals permanently working in the organisation and can serve as a more convenient and inexpensive alternative. In every decision for outsourcing or in-house production of services, the frequency of the need for the services and the importance of know-how in that field, in the long run, are critical. If the company uses a rich amount of HR support frequently, it may even cost more than having permanent professionals in the organisation. Another possible disadvantage can be that the firm cannot build know-how and culture on HR practices if they are always outsourced. Although outsourcing HR help can be seen as another option that small firms choose because of the lack of resources, research (Antcliff *et al.*, 2020) suggests that lack of resources is not the primary driver behind HR outsourcing, and change and demand are real motivators. What small firms look for in outsourcing is not strategic advice but information. HRM outsourcing is higher in larger firms and lower in family-owned ones. Another important finding of the study is that seeking outsourced support for HRM is not associated with the current shortage of talent or leadership but linked with the intentions and plans of the company.

2.5 Contingent Characteristics

There has been a contradiction between the "one size fits all" approach that suggests small firms prototype and follow the HRM policies and systems of larger firms and the "contingency and uniqueness" approach that offers ad hoc customised and reactive strategies tailored to the needs and nature variations among small firms in the literature (Nyamubarwa & Chipunza, 2019). Despite the assumptions of homogeneity of small firms, they may demonstrate critical differences in various aspects, and understanding the HRM practices in small firms necessitates investigation and comprehension of such heterogeneities and their possible outcomes (De Kok & Uhlaner, 2001). Table 2.2 provides a summary for the contingency factors and their possible outcomes.

Dabic *et al.* (2011) underscore the lack of theoretical frameworks combining HRM and entrepreneurial firms and describe the field as a newly emerging one with few attempts to explain the role of HR in start-ups. They also suggest differences between traditional HR and HRM in small entrepreneurial firms, such as the need for giving more importance to the relationship among employees and stakeholders.

The findings of Cassell *et al.* (2002) also support the contingency approach as small companies tend to adopt "pick and mix" methods under internal and external circumstances instead of a predetermined strategy-based system. Their findings demonstrate variations in determinants of HR practices among small firms in terms of the importance (centrality) of HR, the unit or person responsible for the HR, availability of resources, awareness of HR trends, and previous evaluations of HR practices.

Building on the findings of comprehensive meta-analysis and studies addressing the HRM in SMEs (Cardon & Stevens, 2004;

Table 2.2. Contingency factors for SMEs and their possible outcomes

Factor	Difference	Possible outcomes
Labour intensiveness	Small firms rely more on human effort and customisation; thus, the level of labour intensiveness can be higher than larger firms.	The more labour-intensive nature of the work can affect the centrality and characteristics of human resources functions such as talent management, training, and recruitment.
Multi-functionality (less job specialisation)	Employees in small firms are expected to be more multifunctional and have multiple roles due to number of employees who can be specialised on narrower job definitions.	Training designed in a more customised approach and addressing a more extensive scope of competencies can be more beneficial for small firms. More emphasis on multi-functionality, ability to substitute each other, learning focus, and mindset (or trait characteristics) over current competence and knowledge in selection and recruitment.
Legitimacy (employee candidates and customers)	Small firms may invest less in brand awareness, well-established HR systems, and their professional image. This can yield problems regarding candidates' as well as customers' perceptions of legitimacy.	Small firms can rely on the outcomes of professionalising their HR practices in order to benefit company legitimacy, which can attract more talent and answer the legitimacy concerns of customers with increased performance. Small firms can use larger associations by using or mimicking their HR practices, and they can adopt external professional help or create their own systems.

Need for adaptability and agility (flexibility and authenticity)	Strategically it is less possible for small firms to benefit from economies of scale, thus they concentrate on cost leadership strategies. Instead, they are more inclined to build on customisation and differentiation with more opportunities to deliver competencies such as more adaptability, flexibility, and agility.	Specific skills required for agility, adaptability, and flexibility can dominate the HR practices in small firms. Considered together with multi-functionality, employees should be selected and trained in high agility, flexibility and adaptability. These may require more authentic ways to shape HR practices.
Know-how and learning curve	Young small firms may lack the experience, know-how, and intellectual capital to deal with HR demands.	Lack of experience and know-how may cause small firms to make more mistakes. Considering the number of employees, a selection error can be less tolerable and critical to the performance even survival of the small firms. Awareness regarding this aspect can save time and resources for small firms.
Resources (lack of resources and stability)	Small firms can lack resources to make a significant investment in the building of HR systems.	Investments (relative to the total budget) may not allow small firms to recruit permanent HR professionals; hence owners (managers) take the HR responsibilities and manage them with less expertise and resources (such as time). Small firms can experience more fluctuations in resource availability, making it more challenging to structure sustainable HR functions.

Source: Cardon and Stevens (2004); Rauch and Hatak (2016); Harney and Alkhalaf (2021).

Rauch & Hatak, 2016; Harney and Alkhalaf, 2021), we listed essential factors that differentiate small firms from large firms and each other and how they shape the nature of HRM policies and practices.

Harney and Alkhalaf (2021) underscore the lack of studies addressing HRM in small firms through a contingency approach where contextual factors are taken into account. They also emphasise the need to overcome generalisations through labels such as "beautiful" or "bleak-house" that create overly positive or negative assumptions of small firms. The former stands for a positive view where small firms are flexible, cohesive, and agile (Tsai *et al.*, 2007). The latter depicts a negative picture where micromanagement, ambiguity, and randomness dominate the workplace (Wiesner & Innes, 2010). Some general suggestions can be provided for all SMEs. Still, sustainable, comprehensive, and effective solutions require an understanding of specific conditions of the firm regarding the market share, size, culture, sector, stakeholders, and the nature of the job. The roles and management philosophies of owners and managers, organisational resources, and environmental dynamics (if they provide autonomy and freedom for the firm to implement HR policies as they want) are listed by Harney and Alkhalaf (2021) as some of the factors that can shape the HRM uniquely for small firms. On these determinants and extant literature, they suggest a well-calculated cost/benefit analysis for formalising the HR functions as informality does not always hinder the HR performance, and a decision on the formalisation of HR that is not based on specific strategic goals can be detrimental to overall firm performance (p. 22).

A study conducted on 16 small firms demonstrates that company size, having a larger firm associate, and a growth-oriented corporate strategy are significant determinants for the nature of HRM functions (De Kok & Uhlaner, 2001). For instance, the study provides evidence for a positive association between company size and more formal and regular HRM practices. The same is applied to having a large associate (supplier, retailer, etc.) and strategic orientation for growth. If small firms have deliberate intentions and expansion plans, having formalised HR systems is more likely to be considered necessary as the number of human forces would be larger sooner or later. They can also risk making higher infrastructure building investments with the expectations of a high return on investment. Larger firm associates such as franchisers may necessitate and support the small firm's training and development, and recruitment process. At the least, exchanging know-how and best practices is more convenient when small firms operate closely with highly institutionalised stakeholders. Thus, having a pick-a-back approach and benefiting from the well-established formal HR practices of larger associates can serve as an option for small firms.

Tsai *et al.* (2007) report that although firm size is a determinant for employee-manager relationship and informality, factors such as autonomy and work pressure result from the nature of the sector that the firms operate in. The title of their study, "When and Why is Small Beautiful?" emphasises that firm size is not the only determinant, and many necessities such as effective leadership apply to small firms and large firms as well. Fabling and Grimes (2007) report that high-performance HR practices are more common in larger, younger, and more technology- and service-intensive companies. Huselid and Rau (1997) report that larger firms are more likely to apply high-performance work systems (regarding recruitment and development) compared to smaller ones. It is less frequent and possible for small and older companies to adopt high-performance HR practices (Fabling & Grimes, 2007).

HRM in small firms is characterised by informality, spontaneity, and reactivity, with differing aspects among firms (Harney & Alkhalaf, 2021). Larger firms operationalise a more planned, proactive, and formal nature for HR functions, while small firms react to urgencies with ad hoc solutions. However, creating more affordable solutions when necessary seems a more convenient way to deal with HR demands for SMEs; poor quality and late solutions can cost more than establishing proactive and planned systems in the long run. If the small firms can plan for the long run, for instance, if they have a growth orientation, they better reflect the suggestion mentioned above to their HRM policies and practices (De Kok & Uhlaner, 2001).

Through in-depth interviews, Nadin and Cassell (2007) reported that the HR practices in small firms are characterised by informality. Selection processes are less formal and structured, such as word of mouth; training is not built on systematic need analysis or long-term policies but conducted in an ad hoc style to fix problems in regular performance or answer individual needs. HR roles are usually just added to an existing employee role. Jobs are defined broadly and less clearly and roles get shaped by the requirements of the firm in time, and employees "fit in" the conditions (Nadin & Cassell, 2007).

Nolan (2002) describes the nature of HRM in small firms as characterised by owner-manager influence, ad hoc and reactive nature, and short-term perspective. Firms operating in service industries (such as finance and health) tend to adopt more extensive calculative human resources management, and this relationship is more robust for smaller firms (Wu, 2020). Psychological contracts are more tacit and intangible in small firms than large ones (Nadin & Cassell, 2007). More loyalty, flexibility, competence, and commitment are expected by employers in small firms and usually provide no tangible resources.

2.6 Growth, Change, and SMEs

Small firms do not remain the same and grow in time with their more substantial needs and requirements for sustainability. Human resource functions such as training and development, compensation, and communication are essential resources for the sustainability of small firms (Halberstadt & Johnson, 2014). On the other hand, small firms can also choose and desire to remain small (Nadin & Cassell, 2007). Considering the conditions and requirements of SMEs, Agile HRM can serve as a healthy option. Flexible work hours and arrangements, less hierarchical team structures, informality, less documentation, fast adaptation, and customisation are some of the features of Agile philosophy that can match SMEs' nature (Heilmann *et al.*, 2018). Transformation of HRM systems is faster in early growth phases in small firms than in the later stages (Kotey & Sheridan, 2004).

With rapid change and fast-developing technologies, organisations feel the pressure to constantly renewing themselves. Large or small, many companies today go through specific transitions with the need for adapting new management or production philosophies and methods such as Agile management, lean, and Kanban. These transformations require strong change management capacities and effective management of human resource practices. Many organisations utilise HR units as change agents where the responsibility of the communication and the management of the process is owned by HR. Roles and responsibilities of leaders and members can be reformed and require refreshment of job analysis and design. In addition, an adaptation of new methods and management philosophies necessitates thorough training and development needs and modification of incentive systems. Llinas Sala and Abad Puente (2019) underscore the role of the people management process as a key for success in the adaptation of Industry 4.0 in SMEs.

Based on Subramony's (2009) framework, Rauch and Hatak (2016) report that HR enhancing practices such as fostering talent, empowerment, and employee motivation are significantly and more robustly associated with SMEs performance compared to larger firms. Their findings oppose the view that companies require HR systems and professional practices only when they grow to a specific size and underscore the urgency of building HR practices when firms are young. Thus, the performance of young companies demonstrates higher associations with HR enhancing practices (motivation, training, and empowerment) than older ones. They list other moderators such as the intensity of technology and rigidity of labour regulations. The link between HR enhancing practices and firm performance is more potent in high-tech companies and contexts where labour regulations are more rigid and formalised. These findings on significant moderators are supportive of the contingency approach to understanding HR practices in SMEs. With the growth of the company, HR roles such as training and performance evaluation shift from the top manager (the owner) to the middle-level managers (Kotey & Sheridan, 2004).

Informality and a lower variety of selection methods shape the recruitment processes of small firms. Managers of small firms prefer working with familiar people, thus they use their and company members' networks to search for employee candidates (Kotey & Sheridan, 2004). This is also cheaper and less demanding on HR knowledge. On the other hand, using the network approach can lead to a smaller group of candidates, and best matching candidates in the external environment can be left out. This word of mouth and network dominant recruitment approach transforms to more formal and various ones when firms get bigger.

The scarcity of resources, informality, and absence of a professional HR unit can be some of the reasons for the significant relationship between the emotional intelligence of HR decision-makers and high-performance HR practices in SMEs (Cuéllar-Molina *et al.*, 2019).

Family firms have unique characteristics that can provide more sophisticated aspects that affect HR practices. For instance, in family firms, the perceived equality and justice of HR policies and applications among family and nonfamily members can stand as a strong moderator on the relationship between professionalisation of HR functions and firm performance (Madison *et al.*, 2018). In other words, the professionalisation of HR is vital to family firm success but how it is implemented is essential.

2.7 HRM: Performance Relationship in SMEs

Fabling and Grimes (2007) report that the adaptation of high-performance HR practices (such as performance management) is significantly related to firm performance regarding market share, profitability, and productivity. Lai *et al.*'s (2016) findings support the link between formalised HRM practices and financial and productive firm performance. Ogunyomi and Bruning (2015) provide evidence for positive and significant relationships between HRM practices (reward management, human capital development, performance management, occupational health, and safety) and nonfinancial and financial organisational performance in SMEs. Sheehan (2014) addresses the relationship between higher HR investment and firm performance in the chicken and egg situation. The direction of causality between firm performance and usage of formal HR practices can be debatable. Firms can increase their resources through higher performance levels, allowing them to invest in HR systems.

On the other hand, firms investing in formal HR functions can perform better due to this capacity improvement. Sheehan (2014) provides evidence for the positive link between formal human resources practices and SMEs' current performance and future performance (in terms of profitability, innovation, and turnover). They eliminate the other direction of causality through longitudinal statistical analysis.

The findings of Lai *et al.* (2016) support the link between formalised HRM practices and financial and productive firm performance. They also provide evidence that the link between professionalised HRM and firm performance is more vital in small firms with lower job satisfaction and organisational commitment. These findings indicate that formalised HRM is more critical in small firms where employee perceptions and attitudes towards the organisation and their job are more damaging.

A good question regarding the relationship between HR investment and positive returns is whether this relationship is linear. Bryson and White (2019) address these questions and report a U-shaped relationship between HRM investment and positive outcomes in small firms. The authors explain this as follows: small firms can benefit from intrinsically motivating conditions without formal HRM practices to a level. When formal HRM is implemented, this can reduce the motivation levels till more investments rebalance and go further on motivation levels. This raises the question, should small firms really invest in the necessary HRM resources? Would it yield them any productive results? Still, the introduction of such systems at low levels can be detrimental. This also warns practitioners about the risk that employees may react negatively in the initial stages of HRM implementation, but they respond positively if these efforts are continuous and intensive.

2.8 Conclusion

Although a talented, motivated, and high-performing human force is the primary determinant in the growth and success of small firms (Hornsby & Kuratko, 2003), academic and practical interest in this field is still growing. Small firms are not just smaller scale prototypes of large companies, and they demonstrate unique characteristics that may not follow the same attributes and patterns as larger institutions. Understanding the contingencies that characterise the small firms can further our understanding of how effective HRM can be implemented in SMEs.

References

Antcliff, V., Lupton, B., & Atkinson, C. (2020). Why do small businesses seek support for managing people? Implications for theory and policy from an analysis of UK small business survey data. *International Small Business Journal, 39*(6), 532–553.

Atkinson, C. (2008). An exploration of small firm psychological contracts. *Work, Employment and Society, 22*(3), 447–465.

Barber, A. E., Wesson, M. J., Roberson, Q. M., & Taylor, M. S. (1999). A tale of two job markets: Organizational size and its effects on hiring practices and job search behavior. *Personnel Psychology, 52*, 841–867.

Bryson, A., & White, M. (2019). HRM and small-firm employee motivation: Before and after the great recession. *ILR Review, 72*(3), 749–773.

Cardon, M. S., & Stevens, C. E. (2004). Managing human resources in small organizations: What do we know? *Human Resource Management Review, 14*(3), 295–323. https://doi.org/10.1016/j.hrmr.2004.06.001

Cassell, C., Nadin, S., Gray, M., & Clegg, C. (2002). Exploring human resource management practices in small and medium sized enterprises. *Personnel Review, 31*(6), 671–692.

Combs, J. G., Jaskiewicz, P., Shanine, K. K., & Balkin, D. B. (2018). Making sense of HR in family firms: Antecedents, moderators, and outcomes. *Human Resource Management Review, 28*(1), 1–4. https://doi.org/10.1016/j.hrmr.2017.05.001

Cuéllar-Molina, D., García-Cabrera, A. M., & de la Cruz Déniz-Déniz, M. (2019). Emotional intelligence of the HR decision-maker and high-performance HR practices in SMEs. *European Journal of Management and Business Economics, 28*(1), 52–89.

Dabic, M., Ortiz-De-Urbina-Criado, M., & Romero-Martínez, A. M. (2011). Human resource management in entrepreneurial firms: a literature review. *International Journal of Manpower, 32*(1), 14–33.

De Kok, J., & Uhlaner, L. M. (2001). Organization context and human resource management in the small firm. *Small Business Economics, 17*(4), 273–291.

Deshpande, S. P., & Golhar, D. Y. (1994). HRM practices in large and small manufacturing firms: A comparative study. *Journal of Small Business Management, 32*(2), 49–56.

Dundon, T., & Wilkinson, A. (2018). HRM in small and mediumsized enterprises (SMEs). In *Human resource management: A Critical Approach,* (pp. 194–211). Routledge.

Fabling, R., & Grimes, A. (2007). *HR Practices and Firm Performance: What Matters and Who Does It?* (No. 1124-2019-3295).

Halberstadt, J., & Johnson, M. (2014). Sustainability Management for Startups and Micro-Enterprises: Development of a Sustainability-Quick-Check and Reporting Scheme. In *EnviroInfo* (pp. 17–24). Proceedings of the 28th EnviroInfo 2014 Conference, Oldenburg, Germany September 10–12, 2014 (Conference proceeding).

Harney, B., & Alkhalaf, H. (2021). A quarter-century review of HRM in small and medium-sized enterprises: Capturing what we know, exploring where we need to go. *Human Resource Management, 60*(1), 5–29.

Heilmann, P., Forsten-Astikainen, R., Kultalahti, S. (2018). Agile HRM Practices of SMEs. *Journal of Small Business Management, 58*(6), 1291–1306. DOI: 10.1111/jsbm.12483

Henderson, D. J., Liden, R. C., Glibkowski, B. C., & Chaudhry, A. (2009). LMX differentiation: A multilevel review and examination of its antecedents and outcomes. *The Leadership Quarterly, 20*(4), 517–534.

Heneman, H. G., & Berkley, R. A. (1999). Applicant attraction practices and outcomes among small businesses. *Journal of Small Business Management, 37*, 53–74.

Heneman, R. L., Tansky, J. W., & Camp, S. M. (2000). Human resource management practices in small and medium-sized enterprises: Unanswered questions and future research perspectives. *Entrepreneurship Theory and Practice, 25*, 11–26.

Hornsby, J. S., & Kuratko, D. F. (2003). Human resource management in US small businesses: A replication and extension. *Journal of Developmental Entrepreneurship, 8*(1), 73.

Huselid, M. A., & Rau, B. L. (1997). The determinants of high performance work systems: Cross-sectional and longitudinal analyses. In *Academy of Management Annual Meetings* (pp. 255–276). Submitted to the 1997 Academy of Management Annual Meetings, Human Resource Management Division.

Kerr, G., Way, S. A., & Thacker, J. (2007). Performance, HR practices and the HR manager in small entrepreneurial firms. *Journal of Small Business & Entrepreneurship, 20*(1), 55–68. https://doi.org/10.1080/08 276331.2007.10593386

Khalid, K., & Nawab, S. (2018). Employee participation and employee retention in view of compensation. *SAGE Open, 8*(4), 2158244018810067.

Klass, B. S., McClendon, J., & Gainey, T. W. (2002). Trust and the role of professional employer organizations: Managing HR in small and medium enterprises. *Journal of Managerial Issues, 14*(1), 31.

Kotey, B., & Sheridan, A. (2004). Changing HRM practices with firm growth. *Journal of Small Business and Enterprise Development, 11*(4), 474–485.

Kuntonbutr, C., & Sangperm, N. (2019). Study on talent management influence on customer satisfaction. *Polish Journal of Management Studies, 20*(2), 334–344.

Lai, Y., Saridakis, G., & Johnstone, S. (2016). Human resource practices, employee attitudes and small firm performance. *International Small Business Journal, 35*(4), 470–494.

Llinas Sala, D., & Abad Puente, J. (2019). The role of high-performance people management practices in Industry 4.0: The case of medium-sized Spanish firms. *Intangible Capital, 15*(3), 190–207.

Maamari, B. E., & Osta, A. (2021). The effect of HRIS implementation success on job involvement, job satisfaction and work engagement in SMEs. *International Journal of Organizational Analysis, 29*(5), 1269–1286. https://doi.org/10.1108/IJOA-07-2020-2298.

Machek, O., Hnilica, J., & Lukeš, M. (2019). Stability of family firms during economic downturn and recovery. *JEEMS Journal of East European Management Studies, 24*(4), 566–588.

Madison, K., Daspit, J. J., Turner, K., & Kellermanns, F. W. (2018). Family firm human resource practices: Investigating the effects of professionalization and bifurcation bias on performance. *Journal of Business Research, 84*, 327–336.

Mayson, S., & Barrett, R. (2006). The "science" and "practice" of HRM in small firms. *Human Resource Management Review, 16*(4), 447–455. https://doi.org/10.1016/j.hrmr.2006.08.002

McEvoy, G. M. (1984). Small business personnel practices. *Journal of Small Business Management, 22*(4), 1–9.

McLarty, R. (1999). The skills development needs of SMEs and focus on graduate skills application. *Journal of Applied Management Studies, 8*(1), 103–111.

Mear, F., & Werner, R. A. (2020). Subsidiarity as secret of success: "Hidden Champion" SMEs and subsidiarity as winning HRM configuration in interdisciplinary case studies. *Employee Relations: The International Journal, 43*(2).

Nadin, S., & Cassell, C. (2007). New deal for old? Exploring the psychological contract in a small firm environment. *International Small Business Journal, 25*(4), 417–443.

Nolan, C. (2002). Human resource development in the Irish hotel industry: The case of the small firm. *European Journal of Training and Development, 26*(2–4), 88.

Nyamubarwa, W., & Chipunza, C. (2019). Debunking the one-size-fits-all approach to human resource management: A review of human resource practices in small and medium-sized enterprise firms. *SA Journal of Human Resource Management, 17*(1), 1–6.

Ogunyomi, P., & Bruning, N. S. (2016). Human resource management and organizational performance of small and medium enterprises (SMEs) in Nigeria. *The International Journal of Human Resource Management, 27*(6), 612–634.

Rahman, M., & Mendy, J. (2019). Evaluating people-related resilience and non-resilience barriers of SMEs' internationalisation. *International Journal of Organizational Analysis, 27*(2), 225–240.

Rauch, A., & Hatak, I. (2016). A meta-analysis of different HR-enhancing practices and performance of small and medium sized firms. *Journal of Business Venturing, 31*(5), 485–504.

Sarvaiya, H., Eweje, G., & Arrowsmith, J. (2018). The roles of HRM in CSR: Strategic partnership or operational support?. *Journal of Business Ethics, 153*(3), 825–837.

Sheehan, M. (2014). Human resource management and performance: Evidence from small and medium-sized firms. *International Small Business Journal, 32*(5), 545–570.

Subramony, M. (2009). A meta-analytic investigation of the relationship between HRM bundles and firm performance. *Human Resource Management, 48*(5), 745–768.

Tsai, C. J., Sengupta, S., & Edwards, P. (2007). When and why is small beautiful? The experience of work in the small firm. *Human Relations, 60*(12), 1779–1807.

Wiesner, R., & Innes, P. (2010). Bleak house or bright prospect?: HRM in Australian SMEs over 1998-2008. *Asia Pacific Journal of Human Resources, 48*(2), 151–184.

Williamson, I. O., Cable, D. M., & Aldrich, H. E. (2002). Smaller but not necessarily weaker: How small businesses can overcome barriers to recruitment. In J. Katz, & T. M. Welbourne (Eds.), *Managing People In Entrepreneurial Organizations: Learning from the Merger of Entrepreneurship and Human Resource Management* (pp. 83–106). Amsterdam: JAI Press.

Williamson, D., & Lynch-Wood, G. (2001). A new paradigm for SME environmental practice. *The TQM Magazine, 13*(6), 424–433.

Wu, N. (2020). Small Is Beautiful or Big Is Better: How much do industry and family ownership matter in firms of different sizes? *European Management Review, 17*(4), 977–991.

Wuryaningrat, N. F., Kindangen, P., Sendouw, G., & Lumanouw, B. (2019). The role of person job fit and person organization fit on the development of innovation capabilities at Indonesia creative industry. *International Journal of Engineering and Advanced Technology, 8*(5C), 80–85.

Chapter 3

A Global Review of the Impact of Human Resource Management Practices on SMEs and Start-ups

Neerja Aswale* and Rahul Waghmare†

Vishwakarma University, Pune, India

*neerjaaswale@gmail.com

†Rahul.waghmare@vupune.ac.in

Abstract: This chapter explores the best practices used by SMEs and start-ups from a global perspective. Human Resources is an asset and the backbone of any organisation. For an organisation to survive and excel the Human Resources personnel should put in place the best practices so that the goals can be achieved. The objective of this chapter is to assess the Human Resources functions and its best practices used in small and medium-sized enterprises. The components of human resources management reviewed in this chapter are talent management, learning and development, talent acquisition, and performance management system. A combination of comprehensive literature review through journals, articles, observations, and SME surveys were used to achieve the objectives of this study. The result will show the impact of best practices on the overall effectiveness and productivity of employees. However, we are focusing on the factors that will lead to success and other blending factors which will enhance the organisation's performance.

These, in turn, can be easily adapted into elements of organisational structure, organisational culture, and workforce training. These results can also be applied to other small businesses. This is one of the first studies to investigate HR factors and best practices through organisational structure, talent development and promotions, and the organisational culture of small businesses.

Keywords: Human resource practices, SMEs, Best practices, Start-ups.

3.1 Introduction

Despite significant literature on human resource management (HRM) and small and medium enterprises (SMEs) and start-ups, the two domains have seldom been studied together. There exists very little research on HRM in SMEs and start-up companies. HRM, however, is essential to expertise the agency of entrepreneurial companies. The SMEs and start-ups require a critical amount of innovation and strategic thinking to counter the competition from more successful firms and larger enterprises and talented employees are a significant tool to attain that.

While innovation is also the merchandise of a great mind, the method of design, production, and distribution depends on effectively managing the work, effort, and commitment of people within the organisation. It is important to learn the role of human resources in the development of small and medium enterprises and start-ups. The analysis on the role of HRM in the entrepreneurial process, however, is currently down trending.

The current research literature on HRM in small and medium enterprises and start-ups "appears to be restricted in descriptive surveys, and distributed in analytical research". The study of the role of HRM in small and medium enterprises and start-ups needs a holistic approach. Previous comprehensive reviews of analysis on HRM and small and medium enterprises and start-ups are almost non-existent. Given the importance of best practices in HRM for small and medium enterprises and start-ups, this chapter analyses the literature relating to these two areas.

The dominant purpose of the chapter is to find out how much this line of research has progressed and what areas are still unexplored. This chapter has three objectives. Firstly, to explain the literature in general. Second, to analyse the topics studied within the papers. And lastly, to spot the limitations of these papers and emergence of future areas of analysis during this field.

This chapter, then, serves not solely to assess the structure and evolution of the link between these two research areas. It intends to add new concepts for brand new research and facilitate student-oriented future research by enabling them to know the direction the sector is heading and what gaps remain.

With these objectives in mind, this chapter is divided into four sections. Section 3.2 includes the theoretical background on HRM and small and medium enterprises and start-ups and their relationship. Section 3.3 describes the papers published thus far on HRM and small and medium enterprises and start-ups. Section 3.4 covers topics in the published papers, and the final section contains a discussion of the findings, with special regard to the limitations of the literature and future areas of research.

3.2 Theoretical Background

3.2.1 *Human Resource Management and Its Best Practices*

Human resource management (HRM) is the process of hiring, training, compensating, setting policies, as well as devising retention tactics for human resources. HRM has evolved significantly during the previous two decades, allowing it to play an even more critical role in today's enterprises. HRM used to imply handling payroll, giving birthday gifts to employees, and so on.

What is the essence of a positive relationship between best practices in HRM and organisational performance and competitiveness? It is the optimal human resource management system, based on proven best practices in job design, employee selection, performance management, employee compensation, or employee training, which enables executives to achieve the expected business performance and competitiveness by achieving desired employee's skills, motivation, and productivity (Šikýř, 2013).

Research shows that performance evaluation, internal communication, organisational HRM consistency, and career planning are the best practices for personnel management (Beh & Loo, 2013). It was found that this was a strong relationship and development, training, coaching, and compensation plans had an impact on worker performance whereas employee participation had less impact on employee performance (Mahadevan & Mohamed, 2014).

The relationship between human resource management practices (HRMP) and innovation is described as a black box with much to explore. There is a positive relationship between HRMP and innovation in various organisations of different countries (Easa & Orra, 2020).

3.2.2 *Small and Medium Enterprises*

SMEs are non-subsidiary, independent firms that employ less than a given number of employees. This number varies across countries. The most frequent upper limit designating an SME is 250 employees in the European Union. However, some countries set the limit at 200 employees, while the United States considers SMEs to include firms with fewer than 500 employees. Small firms are generally those with fewer than 50 employees, while micro-enterprises have at most 10, or in some cases, 5 workers (OECD, 2005).

Although the definition of SMEs varies according to legal and institutional frameworks, public evidence shows that SMEs continue to constitute the vast majority of global trade organisations.

According to the US Small Business Administration (2016), there are 29.6 million companies that have fewer than 500 employees, which show that SMEs account for 99.9% and 47.8% of all companies in the private sector in the United States. The European Commission defines an SME as a company with fewer than 250 employees, an annual turnover of no more than 50 million euros, or a total balance of no more than 43 million euros. According to this definition, SMEs account for 99% of all European companies, employ 66.7% of the European workforce, and contribute 58.6% of the value-added in the non-financial sector. In emerging and transition countries, the proportion of SMEs and their economic impact is even higher. This quantitative advantage of SMEs means that it has a greater contributions towards the growth of the financial sector of the company (Kull *et al.*, 2017).

The definition of SMEs in the European Union (EU) (OECD, 2005) that came into effect on January 1, 2005, together with the standards for annual turnover and number of employees, defines the "independent" dimension, which describes the independent SMEs as "the only company where 25% or more of the capital (or equity) is not owned by the company, or its capital is not owned by a company that has not been identified as an SME". The quantitative factors that determine whether the company is an SME, namely, the number of employees, sales, and the overall balance sheet, are shown in Table 3.1 (Karadag, 2015).

3.2.3 *Human Resource Management and Small and Medium Enterprises*

The HR practices SMEs implemented were more effective in increasing the sustainable employability of employees, as a greater number of the HR practices were implemented, the more employees used the implemented practices and were involved in shaping those practices (Ybema *et al.*, 2020; Sharma, 2020).

Start-ups and small and medium enterprises are different from massive corporates in several factors, such as team size, uncertainty, worker money security: Social and financial security of workers, employee satisfaction level, and communication openness between

Table 3.1.   Quantitative categorisation of SMEs in the EU

Company categories	No. of employees	Turnover	Balance sheet total
Medium	<250	≤EUR 50 million	≤EUR 43 million
Small	<50	≤EUR 10 million	≤EUR 10 million
Micro	<10	≤EUR 2 million	≤EUR 2 million

workers and managers. Hence human resources play an important role (Youssif Abo Keir, 2019).

The study of human resource practices in SMEs remains under-theorised and under-researched. Very little literature has attempted to examine the role of HRM through organisational structure, personnel training and promotion, and organisational culture. This is one of the first studies to examine HRM through organisational structure, personnel training and promotion, and organisational culture of SMEs. The purpose of this study is to assess and understand the nature of human resource factors in SMEs as well as to study their impact on improving organisational performance (Shafeek, 2016).

3.3 Methodology

Various types of raw data, including scientific articles on SMEs and HRM, are used to describe these studies. Porter and Cunningham reported that it is possible to identify abstracts for text mining data by identifying keywords. We search NPD-related abstracts, use scientific databases such as EBSCO, Elsevier Science Direct, ProQuest, Scopus, Emerald, etc., and use search engines such as Google Scholar to find relevant scientific articles.

These are the most widely used databases by researchers in the fields of business, economics, administration, and finance. All years available in these databases are included in the study. The search uses terms such as "small and medium enterprises", "start-up company" across the search term "human resources management", and "best practices in human resources management". A total of 278 articles were found in the search; 162 of them came from the questions of "human resource management" and "small and medium enterprises"; 47 were the results of searching for the words "start-ups" and "human resource management", while remaining articles fell into the category of other related themes.

Screening the articles reduced the sample to 51 papers. The article analysis is as follows: Articles that appear more than once are limited to one entry, and similar terms in the title or abstract are deleted for those that do not involve human resource manage-ment and small and medium enterprises and start-ups at the same time, and other areas are not checked. More common is the practice of automatically classifying data organised by small and medium enterprises (SMEs) as start-ups. In addition, literature is often used in articles regarding the theoretical analysis and hypothesis of SMEs, then conduct empirical research based on samples of SMEs, which may or may not be related.

3.4 Results

This section contains the results of the descriptive and topic analyses of the literature in the sample.

3.4.1 *Descriptive Analysis*

As Figure 3.1 shows, most papers in the combined area of HRM and SMEs and start-ups have been published since 1990, with 2016, 2019, and 2020 being peak years. Comparing the period of 1990 to 1999

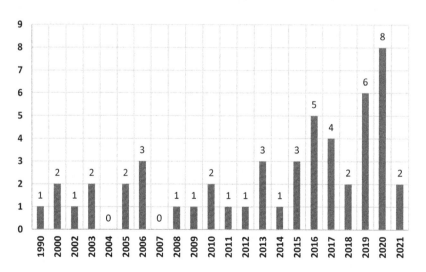

Figure 3.1. Year-wise classification of articles

with the period of 2000 to 2021 reveals how much this dual area of research has grown in recent years.

A year-wise analysis is shown in Figure 3.1. It can be seen that in the initial years in the 1990s, research was not a priority, especially among scholars in the area of SMEs and start-ups. However, with time, scholarly contributions to SMEs and start-ups began to grow and expand from 2000. This could be due to favourable economic policies that boosted the emergence of new start-ups and SMEs globally.

A research-wise analysis is shown in Figure 3.2. It can be seen from the graph that 65% of research is empirical in nature, whereas 31% is descriptive and very few papers are exploratory, quantitative, and qualitative in nature. We can see that the research in this area done by the scholars is mostly empirical and descriptive. This study also scanned research papers to determine the prominent research approaches used by researchers. Most researchers preferred empirical research methods, and this trend was consistent across all 3 decades. Descriptive and exploratory research methods were the second and third most popular research methods.

A country-wise/region-wise analysis is shown in Figure 3.3. To understand the geographical spread of our research, this study

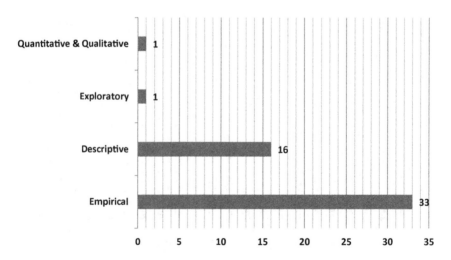

Figure 3.2.   Research wise classification

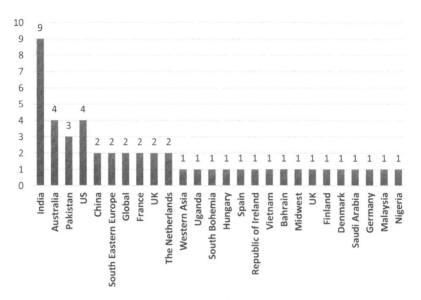

Figure 3.3.   Country-wise/region-wise classification

investigated the origins of the publications and the density of publication by region. We found that the density of research was highest in India and then in Australia and the US. The top ten countries accounted for approximately 63% of the total articles published. India alone contributed 18% to the research conducted in the top ten countries, followed by the Australia and US at 8% each. The majority of the research on the impact of HRM practices on SMEs and start-ups is concentrated in developed and developing countries. The research on the impact of HRM practices on SMEs and start-ups is in its nascent stages in other countries.

As seen from Table 3.2, almost 51% of the articles were published in general journals such as *European Scientific Journal, International Journal of Engineering, Journal of Small Business Management,* etc. The remaining of the articles were published in human resource journals such as *Employee Relations: The International Journal* and *The International Journal of Human Resource Management.* Some universities and SME journals also made contributions to the research in this domain.

Table 3.3 lists the topics that were analysed by the papers.

Table 3.2. Frequency of articles per journal

Topics	Journals	Frequency
Human resource	Human Resource Management Review	2
	Journal of Management Informatics and Human Resource	1
	Employee Relations: The International Journal	2
	Journal of Employee Relations	1
	Advances in Industrial and Labor Relations	1
	Personnel Review	1
	Education and Training	1
	Human Resource Management	1
	The International Journal of Human Resource Management	2
SMEs/ start-ups	Entrepreneurship — Development Tendencies and Empirical Approach	1
	Journal of Developmental Entrepreneurship	1
	Small Enterprise Association of Australia and New Zealand	1
	Journal of Small Business and Enterprise Management	3
	ET & P	1
General/ others	European Scientific Journal	2
	International Journal of Engineering	1
	Indian Journal of Research	1
	Arts & Humanities Open Access Journal	1
	Shanlax International Journal of Management	1
	Global Journal of Management and Business Research	1
	International Journal of Business Administration and Management	1
	Journal of Small Business Management	1
	International Journal of Management and Applied Science	1
	International Journal of Management, Accounting, and Economics	1
	Zeichen Journal	1
	Information Sciences Letters	1
	People and Strategy Journal	1
	American Journal of Business	1
	International Journal of Management (IJM)	1

Table 3.2.   (*Continued*)

Topics	Journals	Frequency
	International Journal of Advance and Innovative Research	1
	RKG Journal of Management	1
	Journal of Evolutionary Economics	1
	PalArch's Journal of Archaeology of Egypt/Egyptology	1
	Procedia — Social and Behavioural Sciences	1
	LogForum Scientific Journal of Logistics	1
	Service Business	1
University/	University of Wollongong	1
schools	University of Baylor	1
	University of Lahore	1
	University of Rowan	1
	Hanken School of Economics	1
	Total	47

Table 3.3.   Analysis of topics

SMEs and start-ups and functions of HRM	
HRM and the creation of start-ups in different geographical areas	Chandrakumara (2013), Ahmeti and Marmullaku (2015), Newman and Sheikh (2015)
Role/impact HRM in SMEs and start-up firms	Shafeek (2016), Singh *et al.* (2020)
HRM practices and firm performance	Lai *et al.* (2016), Bendickson *et al.* (2017), Hayton (2003)

SMEs and start-ups and specific functions of HRM	
HRM and retention in SMEs	Padmaja *et al.* (2020), Hussien (2017)
HRM and other functions	King-Kauanui *et al.* (2016), Khan *et al.* (2013)

Theoretical development and models in SMEs and start-ups	
Functional models	Al-Tal and Emeagwali (2019), Bajpai and Gandhi (2016), Ybema *et al.* (2020)
Future research perspectives	Heneman *et al.* (2000), Kaushik and Bakre (2020)
Theories and case studies in SMEs	Mutumba *et al.* (2021), Holátová and Březinová (2018), Hussien (2017), Fabi *et al.* (2019)

3.5 Discussion

Although HRM and SMEs and start-ups are well-developed and self-proclaimed disciplines, the combination of these two studies is a relatively new development. Since 2019, interest in this field of combining human resource management and entrepreneurship has reached its peak. In fact, since then, with the emergence of more rigorous empirical research with robust and diverse theoretical foundations, the literature in this field has increased significantly. Why is this field only attractive now? These include the difficulty of obtaining data on HRM and SMEs and start-ups, and the lack of complete and rigorous theoretical models to link these two fields, mainly due to the very vague definitions.

Most of the 51 papers in our analysis are empirical. Future analysis ought to outline comprehensive theoretical models that integrate each research area; this research should look to develop strong theories of HRM in organisations. This approach would additionally pave the way for the advent of more empirical research. Previous research on the role of HRM practices in start-ups and SMEs in very general. Future work should focus more on HRM and start-ups in aspects of theoretical models as well as specific functional aspects. It should also study entrepreneurship from a more holistic point of view, together with both start-ups as well, because of the entrepreneurial behaviour of established firms. New studies on specific aspects of human resources would be interesting.

A high percentage of the papers study Indian firms. India is the nation with the youngest population, with 64% of its population within the working age group. It is no secret that the start-up ecosystem in India has evolved exponentially in recent years. Per a recent NASSCOM report, India is the third largest start-up ecosystem in the world and is increasingly becoming more global (Adhana & Kumar, 2020).

Most of the empirical articles are exploratory, cross-sectional, and include the company as a unit of analysis, thus showing the current character of this combined research area. Most studies also rely exclusively on primary sources of information, i.e., the case study approach of most empirical articles. Case studies play an important role in investigating the effectiveness of human studies, resource practice, and entrepreneurship. However, future studies should go a step further and use different analytical techniques for explanatory and longitudinal studies. As far as possible, they should also try to combine qualitative and quantitative information. This perspective should be used to study the relationship between HRM and SMEs and start-ups. In addition, future studies could also adopt the group as the unit of analysis, as is common in HRM literature.

Future researchers may use this review paper as a reference point for their work and for grounding new theories. Academicians proposing new theories and methodologies for researching the role of HRM in SMEs and start-ups should consider publishing their works in the leading refereed journals so that new knowledge related to this domain is disseminated widely and used by academics and practitioners. Lastly, this review may help managers identify sources of valuable information on the impact of HRM on SMEs and start-ups.

References

Adhana, D., & Kumar, A. (2020). Start-up ecosystem in India: A study with focus on entrepreneurship and university business incubators. *Aegaeum Journal, 8*(9), 754–772.

Ahmeti, F., & Marmullaku, B. (2015). Human resource management and practices in SMEs in developing countries: Practices in Kosovo. *European Scientific Journal, 11*(7), 416–428.

Al-Tal, M., & Emeagwali, O. (2019). Knowledge-based HR practices and innovation in SMEs. *Organizacija, 52*(1), 6–21. doi:10.2478/orga-2019-0002

Bajpai, D., & Gandhi, R. (2020). The study of HR practices in SMEs during the buffeted COVID-19 times in India. *Paripex Indian Journal of Research, 9*(9), 25–30. doi:10.36106/paripex

Beh, L.-S., & Loo, L. H. (2013). Human resource management best practices and firm performance: A universalistic perspective approach. *Serbian Journal of Management, 8*, 155–167. doi:10.5937/sjm8-4573

Bendickson, J., Muldoon, J., Liguori, E., & Midgett, C. (2017). High performance work systems: A necessity for startups. *Journal of Small Business Strategy, 27*(2), 112.

Chandrakumara, P. (2013). Human resources management practices in small and medium enterprises in two emerging economies in Asia: Indonesia and South Korea. *Annual SEAANZ Conference* (pp. 1–15). Small Enterprise Association of Australia and New Zealand.

Easa, N., & Orra, H. (2020). HRM practices and innovation: An empirical systematic review. *International Journal of Disruptive Innovation in Government, 1*(1), 15–35. doi:10.1108/ijdig-11-2019-0005

Fabi, B., Raymond, L., & Lacoursière, R. (2009). Strategic alignment of HRM practices in manufacturing SMEs: A Gestalts perspective. *Journal of Small Business and Enterprise Development, 16*(1), 7–25. doi:10.1108/14626000910932854

Hayton, J. (2003). Strategic human capital management in SMEs: An empirical study of entrepreneurial performance. *Human Resource Management, 42*(4), 375–391. doi:10.1002/hrm.10096

Heneman, R., Tansky, J., & Camp, M. (2000). Human resource management practices in small and medium-sized enterprises: Unanswered questions and future research perspectives. *Entrepreneurship Theory and Practice, 25*(1), 11–26.

Hussien, F. (2017). A multiple case study on employee engagement and retention at startup companies. Master's thesis, Hanken School of Economics.

Karadag, H. (2015). The role and challenges of small and medium-sized enterprises (SMEs) in emerging economies: An analysis from Turkey. *Business And Management Studies, 1*(2), 179. doi:10.11114/bms.v1i2.1049

Kaushik, O., & Bakre, P. (2020). The future of HR in startups. *Zeichen Journal, 6*(12), 11.

Khan N. R., Taha S., Ghouri, A. M., Khan, M. R., & Yong, C. K. (2013). The impact of HRM practices on supply chain management success in SME. *LogForum, 9*(3), 177–189.

King-Kauanui, S., Ngoc, S., & Ashley-Cotleur, C. (2006). Impact of human resource management: SME performance in Vietnam. *Journal Of Developmental Entrepreneurship, 11*(01), 79–95. doi:10.1142/s1084946706000271

Kull, T. J., Kotlar, J., & Spring, M. (2017). Small and medium enterprise research in supply chain management: The case for single-respondent research designs. *Journal of Supply Chain Management, 54*(1), 23–24. doi:10.1111/jscm.12157

Lai, Y., Saridakis, G., & Johnstone, S. (2016). Human resource practices, employee attitudes and small firm performance. *International Small Business Journal: Researching Entrepreneurship, 35*(4), 470–494. doi:10.1177/0266242616637415

Mahadevan, A., & Mohamed, F. (2014). Impact of human resource management (HRM) practices on employee performance (A case of Telekom Malaysia): Introduction. *International Journal of Accounting & Business Management, 2*(2), 29–42.

Mayson, S., & Barrett, R. (2006). The "science" and "practice" of HRM in small firms. *Human Resource Management Review, 16*(4), 447–455. doi:10.1016/j.hrmr.2006.08.002

Mutumba, R., Basik, E., & Menya, J., *et al.* (2021). A review of the human resource management dilemma for SMEs: Case of central Uganda. *Art Human Open Access Journal, 5*(1), 1–7. doi:10.15406/ahoaj.2021.05.00178

Newman, A., & Sheikh, A. (2014). Determinants of best HR practices in Chinese SMEs. *Journal of Small Business and Enterprise Development, 21*(3), 414–430. doi:10.1108/jsbed-05-2014-0082

OECD, (2005). Annual report Organisation for Economic Co-operation and Development OECD https://www.oecd.org

Padmaja, P., Koteswari, B., Dhanalakashmi, R. V., & Tiwari, R. (2020). The role of training and work environment on retention and job satisfaction as a mediator at startups, Bangalore. *International Journal of Management, 11*(9), 2020, 1181–1191.

Shafeek, H. (2016). The impact of human resources management practices in SMEs. *International Journal of Engineering, 14*, 91–102.

Sharma, N. (2020). Fostering positive deviance: A potential strategy to an engaged workforce. *Strategic Direction, 36*(8), 1–3.

Šikýř, M. (2013). Best practices in human resource management: The source of excellent performance and sustained competitiveness. *Central European Business Review, 2*(1), 43–48. doi:10.18267/j.cebr.38

Singh, L., Mondal, S., & Das, S. (2020). Human resource practices & their observed significance for Indian SMEs. *Espacious, 41*(7), 15.

US Small Business Administration (2016). Independent agency of the Federal Government https://www.sba.gov/advocacy/small-business-profiles-states-and-territories-2016

Ybema, J. F., van Vuuren, T., & van Dam, K. (2020). HR practices for enhancing sustainable employability: Implementation, use, and outcomes. *The International Journal of Human Resource Management, 31*(7), 886–907. doi: 10.1080/09585192.2017.1387865

Youssif Abo Keir, M. (2019). Prospective on human resources management in startups. *Information Sciences Letters,* 8(3), 81–88.

https://doi.org/10.1142/9789811239212_0004

Chapter 4

What Makes Small Businesses Better? Innovation, Innovative Work Climate, Readiness for Change and Entrepreneurial Leadership

Meltem Akca

Alanya Alaaddin Keykubat University, Antalya, Turkey

meltem.akca@alanya.edu.tr

İhsan Akca

State Airports Authority, Antalya, Turkey

ihsanakca@outlook.com

Ferruh Tuzcuoğlu

Sakarya University, Sakarya, Turkey

tuzcuoglu@sakarya.edu.tr

Abstract: In today's business life, known as Industry 4.0, intensive research and development studies are carried out, and technological applications from the use of artificial intelligence to automation are preferred. During this process, the expectations of the enterprises can create sustainable innovations that will have a competitive advantage in the market in which they play a role. From this point of view, innovation is considered an important resource that will bring high returns and competitiveness to businesses. Moreover, innovation is also evaluated as a rapid development indicator of small businesses and family businesses. Entrepreneurial leaders have the ability to analyse the environment well, and are role models for employees. Entrepreneurial leaders ensure that innovation is a sustainable competence within the organisation. On the other hand, making the necessary preparations for the adaptation of the employees who resist in situations where change is needed, and explaining the necessity of change are an issue that entrepreneurial leaders emphasise. In addition, the concept of innovation climate, which enables innovation to be an organisational element, is also significant for the evolvement of the innovation in the workplace. The role of leadership in creating an innovation climate and adapting it to the organisational structure has a major role on businesses performance. In this chapter, the subject of how small businesses will survive in the perspective of innovation in today's competitive business life is examined theoretically in the context of entrepreneurial leadership, innovation climate, and readiness to change variables. Suggestions were made for small businesses and the relations between variables were examined within the scope of the theoretical framework.

Keywords: Industry 4.0, Entrepreneurship, Organisations, Small business, Innovation.

4.1 Introduction

Businesses are units that produce goods and services for the purpose of meeting human needs and solving problems. If a value is created by the consumer in this production (product-service) stage or if a benefit is provided to the consumer in meeting the need, the price for the product-service will be paid and the commercial relationship will continue in a strong way. In this context, it is necessary to manage the entire process effectively, from the innovation of the enterprise to the planning, organisation, execution, and control of innovations. In addition, the prerequisite for innovation is that, it starts with an idea and must be carried out with investment. For this reason, the success of innovation management in businesses also affects the rational use of investments to achieve goals.

Atkins and Lowe (1997) stated that there are various definitions of small businesses in the literature. In the European Union, in addition to the condition of having less than 50 employees, businesses with annual sales of less than €10 million are also considered as small business. In Turkey, businesses with a maximum of 50 employees and annual sales of less than 25 million Turkish Lira are also considered small businesses (Yiğitoğlu & Şirin, 2020).

There are various types of definition about innovation in literature. Firstly, Schumpeter and Nichol (1934) used the concept as the magnitude element of the development of economies. Schumpeter (1934) also explained that integration of innovation and entreprencurship leads an economical change that triggers better outcomes for nations. Later, Baker and Thomspon (1995) stated innovation definition as "generation, acceptance and implementation of new ideas, product, processes and services". With reference to the OECD, innovation is identified as the introduction of new products, process, or service or significantly improved products, services, or processes (OECD, 2005). In this context, innovation is considered as a major factor for organisational performance and requires changes both in minds and everything in implementation (Harel *et al.*, 2020). However, every change may meet with resistance not only by employees in organisations but also society in governments. For that reason, innovation-based changes that expect to enhance organisational performance should be planned in details with orientation and training programs. Besides, in today's business area, innovation is considered with the usage of technology. Moreover, entrepreneurship leadership, employee support, and formulation of innovation based organisational climate have significant roles for adaptation of innovation practices in organisation.

In this chapter, we aim to discuss entrepreneur leadership, innovation, and innovation climate and readiness to change in small businesses that is expected to lead to better outcomes in having a sustainable competitive advantage. In accordance with the aim, related variables are mentioned.

4.2 Innovation

Today, innovation has become an important competence that businesses use in cost minimisation or differentiation strategies to gain strategic advantage and increase their market share against their competitors. Approaches such as developing new products, developing production methods, and innovating in business functions create value for the consumer and as a result, initiatives that will pave the way for a commercial increase are defined as innovation (Çakir, 2012).

Many things that are perceived as new are considered innovations today. Of course, things that are new in product-service-process and functions should have a commercial counterpart when considered on a business basis. This is where the concepts of invention and innovation differ from each other. Entrepreneurs, not the inventor of that product, come to the fore in the fact that many inventions take place in the market as innovation. For this reason, not every invention is an innovation, and not every inventor is an entrepreneur. When the invention that emerges with the invention turns into a commercial value, it becomes an innovation. However, with the spread, it is seen that the innovations in the commercial field have started to expand (Oğuztürk, 2003).

Schumpeter (1934) explained innovation as the introduction of new products, the introduction of new production methods, the opening of new markets, the development of new sources of supply for raw materials and other inputs, and the creation of new market structures in a sector (Çakir, 2012). Innovations that are intended to increase organisational performance may differ according to the types of performance measurement, size of the enterprise, economic levels, and the sector (Chuang & Lin, 2015). For that reason, not only international companies but also small businesses need to focus on innovation related transformation practices to survive in volatile and competitive environment. In this perspective innovation is generally classified under six types (see Table 4.1). Product innovation, service innovation, process

Table 4.1. Types of innovations

Innovation type	Definition
Product innovation	It is the improvement of the product manufactured by the enterprise and the features of that product or the creation of a new area according to the usage area. From the design of the product to its technical features, minor or radical improvements are considered to be within product innovation.
Process innovation	Reducing costs, increasing quality, and producing and delivering improved products are listed as the main aims of innovation made on processes. Generally, business process re-engineering technique is among the applications used to provide process innovation. It is aimed to ensure innovation in products and services by going through improvement and change on processes (Erdil *et al.*, 2016; Niewöhner *et al.*, 2020; Oğuztürk, 2003). Process innovation techniques has begun to be used in organisation as a post-modern management approach.
Service innovation	The concept of service innovation was first used by Barras (1986) and started to become popular in the literature. Service innovation refers to the application of new concepts and technologies for change in the service process. By innovating service, it is aimed to improve existing services and products, increase service quality and efficiency, enrich the scope and content of services, create value for customers, and provide sustainable competitive advantage (Oke, 2007; Kheng *et al.*, 2013).
Marketing innovation	The concept of marketing innovation defines significant improvements in marketing activities. Changes or improvement in marketing activities for products and services, from product packaging to pricing, from positioning to promotion, are considered as marketing innovations. Increasing sales, ensuring customer loyalty and commitment, accessing new markets, repositioning the product in the current market, and responding to customer requests and needs more powerfully and quickly are among the objectives of marketing innovation.

(Continued)

Table 4.1.   (*Continued*)

Innovation type	Definition
Organisational innovation	Organisational innovation describes the application of new and improved methods in the business practices of enterprises. Organisational innovations are significantly improved practices aimed at reducing costs for administrative activities, ensuring internal and external customer satisfaction, and increasing business performance.
Social innovation	It is the use of improved and radical changes in order to eliminate social problems. New practices for solving environmental problems, creating employment for disadvantaged groups, and ensuring equality in labour and education can also be considered as innovations. It is aimed to produce social and innovative solutions. Rather than providing commercial gains on the basis of the enterprise, social gain and reciprocity come to the fore (Erdil *et al.*, 2016).

Source: Çakir (2012); Oğuztürk (2003); Chuang and Lin (2015); Erdil *et al.* (2016).

innovation, marketing innovation, organisational innovation and social innovation are considered as types of innovation.

4.3 Innovative Work Climate

Toivonen and Tuominen (2009) state that the essence of innovation is hidden in the ability of organisations to use developments in their application competence by creating new product-service-process areas or improving existing ones. Achieving competitive advantage by keeping up with the ever-changing environmental conditions is possible by transformation of intellectual capital into the innovation process. Intellectual capital and competencies accelerate the innovation process and increase the sharing of information within the organisation, providing the formation of a more innovative culture. Isaksen and Akkermans (2011) state that more innovative results will emerge in an innovative work environment. A supportive work climate, where employees can develop and implement innovative ideas, has an impact on innovation performance (Sharma, 2020). In this context, innovative climate is described as an open organisational atmosphere that includes working independently, developing ideas, feedback, continuous training and development, and preventing the formation of problems (Hartmann, 2006; cited in Özer, 2017). The establishment of this climate emerges in subordinate-superior-colleague relations. Moreover, the innovative organisational climate that will nurture innovative behaviours plays a critical role for businesses that want to respond to customer demands in the fastest way, keep up with the requirements of the age, and always be ahead by acting before their competitors (Okan, 2018; Yorgancılar, 2011). Besides, an innovative work climate is the type of organisational climate that motivates entrepreneurship and risk-taking behaviour, provides the necessary resources for creativity, and supports the development of employees (Jaiswal & Dhar, 2015). On the other hand, the innovative work climate can also be explained by the innovation support shaped by the perceptions of the employers of the organisation about the extent to which they see their businesses as an open organisation and to what extent they support the creative and innovative thoughts of the employees (Sharma, 2020). In addition, resource support that explains how and in what way internal resources can be sufficient on innovation also has an impact on climate (Scott & Bruce, 1994; Sarros *et al.*, 2008; cited in Kılıç, 2018). It is also assumed that organisational work environment features such as future vision, collaborative, extrovert, exploratory, value-oriented, open to all ideas, flexibility, and supporting teamwork enrich the innovative capabilities of the enterprise (Bate & Johston, 2003; Yaman Kahyaoğlu, 2019).

4.4 Entrepreneur Leadership

Innovation is the process of transforming a new idea or business model into a commercial value (Aydoğar & Yirci, 2020). Not everything new can be defined as innovation. Not every invention can turn into innovation. In order for something new to be accepted as innovation, it must meet human needs, find solutions to problems, and create value in social and economic perspective, and as a result, it must be expressed in monetary terms for the benefit provided. From this perspective, inventors who create a new product or service cannot always transform their products into innovations. Sometimes, entrepreneurs who manage the process come to the fore in the innovative evaluation of these products. At this point, managing innovation by considering environmental changes will reveal organisational success. Innovation management is also strengthened by the integration of the entire innovation process with managerial functions.

Organisations want to keep the innovation strategies that are desired constantly updated with leaders who can direct innovation management. For this reason, the evaluation of the performance of innovations is considered a phenomenon that will add value to the organisation in determining the success of the variables associated with the innovation process (Oğuztürk, 2003; Adıgüzel, 2012; Gökçek, 2007; Aydoğar & Yirci, 2020).

Today, with the huge competition and rapid change in businesses environment, organisations need to gain sustainable performance. Entrepreneurial activities trigger innovations to have a better organisational success. This trend is accompanied by new business formations. In this context, entrepreneurial leaders play a major role in the implementation of innovative applications for existing businesses and innovative work behaviours of employees (Akkoç *et al.*, 2019; Sharma & Singh, 2016). Furthermore, flexible and proactive opportunities on business activities shaped by capturing and transforming them into outputs to create value is actualised by entrepreneurial leaders leading. This change and transformation only emerge as a result of the integration of efforts with entrepreneurship philosophy and individual efforts in the workplace with high quality of leader-member exchange (Ensley *et al.*, 2006).

Entrepreneurial leadership gets popular day by day in establishing a new business as well as in existing business activities and restructuring processes in the axis of environment and competition.

In small businesses, competition with entrepreneurial strategies relates to the entrepreneurial characteristics of leaders who want to create an innovative work atmosphere and work behaviours to contribute to organisational outcomes. When considered from this point, entrepreneurial leadership is a term that integrates entrepreneurship and leadership concepts (Abdelgawad *et al.*, 2013; Harrison *et al.*, 2015; Al Mamun *et al.*, 2018).

Entrepreneurial leadership is considered a leadership style that identifies, values, and exploits opportunities. In organisations with the direction of entrepreneurial leaders, employees understand social transformation in the environment and generally act according to the requirements (Tlaiss & Kauser, 2019). Moreover, entrepreneurial leadership focuses on (i) empowerment of employees to increase innovative capabilities, and (ii) decentralisation to create value within the organisation (Gupta *et al.*, 2004). Entrepreneurial leaders aim to maintain organisation success with the usage of innovation, technology, and opportunities (Zainol *et al.*, 2018). Entrepreneurial leadership also tends to employee creativity that will increase employee performance. For that reason, formation of innovative work climate by entrepreneurial leaders has a significant influence on the existence of innovation-based practices in organisation (Ximenes *et al.*, 2019).

Innovation, creativity, and change related to the leadership characteristics of entrepreneurial leaders are aimed at gaining a competitive advantage in today's business world (Lee & Venkataraman, 2006). In addition to traditional management functions, entrepreneurial leaders focus on flexible and innovative job practices in the workplace (Gupta *et al.*, 2004). Entrepreneurial leaders also motivate employees' work behaviours to increase innovative capabilities that provide competitive advantage (Surie & Ashley, 2008). Because of the positive relations between leadership and organisational innovativeness, entrepreneurial leaders support creative thinking in the organisation (Chen, 2007; Morris & Sexton, 1996; Scheepers *et al.*, 2008; Leitch *et al.*, 2013).

Sarabi and colleagues (2020) also noticed that innovative and technology-oriented leadership has a major role in today's work environment. In addition, not only big companies but also small and medium enterprises are required to equip their employees with technology adaptable skills. For that reason, entrepreneurial leaders trigger the adaptation of digital transformation between organisation and outside with a readiness to change implementations (Roesminingsih & Suyanto, 2019).

4.5 Readiness for Change

The phenomenon of change is an indispensable element of human beings and is accepted as a social situation. Reflections of social change movements also affect organisations. In this context, a systematic and disciplined evaluation of change is important in ensuring organisational performance. On the other hand, organisational products and processes can also guide social change. In today's information society, the value creation of bilateral change movements paves the way for the acceleration of innovative practices (Aydoğar & Yirci, 2020). However, readiness for changes in small businesses are not perceived as easy by employees. Because of traditional management applications, it is generally adapted from classical and manual practices. On the other hand, small businesses that want to be sustainable need to gain competitive advantages to survive in the dynamic work environment. In this context, small businesses should adapt to environmental and technological requirements in today's digital era. Readiness for technology shows the tendency of individuals to use new technology for different purposes (Parasuraman & Colby, 2015). Technology readiness is closely related to the changes in the field of information technologies carried out by organisations that can compete in the axis of Industry 4.0. The combination of positive and negative feelings about technology forms the basis of the technological readiness field

(Parasuraman, 2000; Mahendrati & Mangundjaya, 2019). Small businesses, related to Industry 4.0 or not, need to benefit from information and communication technologies that lead them to a higher level in the market. This transformation will be actualised by investments of technological implementations in organisations. These implementations aim to increase employee efforts that enhance individual and organisational performance. Although there are expected advantages of new technological practices, it is not so easy, particularly in family and small businesses because of the resistance. It is important to solve the resistance problems with change related explanations and orientations. Thus, readiness for change occurs and leads the organisation to success. In this context, readiness for change is considered as beliefs, attitudes, and intentions of employees that reveal the level of readiness of the members in the organisation within the scope of the content, process, and features included in the change process (DeLong Goldman, 2009; Holt *et al.*, 2007).

It is emphasised that the organisations' success in change is that employees are ready for change rather than implementing change (Holt *et al.*, 2007; Kirrane *et al.*, 2017). According to the dynamics of Information Processing Theory, an organisation's readiness for change is affected by the level of readiness for change of its employees (Armenakis *et al.*, 2007). It is important for employees to be ready because it has been determined that readiness plays a vital role in every organisational change and transformation and is a significant driver of change success (Armenakis *et al.*, 1993; Oreg *et al.*, 2011; Vakola, 2014). Because, if employees do not believe that change is necessary, change initiatives may ultimately fail (Rafferty & Simons, 2006; Myklebust *et al.*, 2020).

Readiness for change is seen as a vital factor in organisational change processes (Myklebust *et al.*, 2020). In addition, the level of readiness for change can be affected by individual, organisational, and situational factors (Kirrane *et al.*, 2017; Oreg *et al.*, 2011; Vakola, 2014). In this context, the level of readiness of the organisations and the human resources, which make the most important contribution to the continuation of their existence during the COVID-19 pandemic we are struggling with, also determines the acceptance and targeted applicability of digital transformation. For that reason, small businesses, particularly after COVID-19, will pay more attention to innovation, change management, flexibility, and technology usage when necessary.

4.6 Studies About Small Businesses

International studies emphasise the need to increase the readiness of employees to change in order to increase the possibility of organisations to implement such changes successfully (Holt *et al.*, 2007; Kirrane *et al.*, 2017; Myklebust *et al.*, 2020). For this reason, it is necessary to support individuals with innovative training programs in order to ensure and continuously improve their level of readiness for this change.

Hsu and Fang (2009) define innovation capital as the structure that enables employees to reveal their valuable ideas and transform these ideas into new products. This structure lays the groundwork for creating an environment that will enable the learning of new competencies by sharing new ideas within the organisation (Agostini *et al.*, 2017). However, Carmona-Lavado *et al.* (2013) state that human capital and employee competencies have a positive impact on service innovation. Wu and colleagues (2008) found a positive relationship between human capital and innovation. Hsu and Fang (2009) also emphasised that intellectual capital will increase the performance of new product generation by improving organisational learning abilities. Besides, Agostini and colleagues (2017) concluded in their empirical study that intellectual capital and innovation capital are effective on innovation performance. Studies show that knowledge, experience, skills, and competencies of the human factor also have positive effects on the innovation performance of organisations. With reference to previous explanations, employee-related talent and capability-based improvements have a major role in today's work approaches due to their intangible impact on work outcomes.

Furthermore, research conducted by Bowen *et al.* (2010) and Martínez-Román *et al.* (2011) found positive relationships between innovation competencies and performance, and innovation competencies and innovation outputs. In addition, Ren and Zhang (2015) state that the innovative climate that permeates the organisation can have an impact on employee behaviour and lead individuals to innovative behaviours (cited in Kılıç, 2018). Taşgit and Torun (2016) also emphasised that organisational culture can be effective on innovation performance. However, Yiğit (2014) underlined that the culture of innovation positively affects organisational performance. Klein and Knight (2005), on the other hand, stated that the innovative organisational climate can spread to employees in a positive way only if there is strong management support. In this context, establishing suitable environments where innovations can be developed will increase the success and effectiveness of innovations and contribute to the development of quality (Singh *et al.*, 2020).

Small enterprises are required to be innovative and more entrepreneurial to survive (Cefis & Marsili, 2005). In this perspective, leadership has a major role on the transformation of small businesses into inno-preneur organisations (Dunne & Dougherty, 2016; Meri, 2020). Dunne and Dougherty (2016) obtained that leadership is an important antecedent of innovativeness in small businesses. Moreover, inno-preneur leaders in small businesses may i) provide required funds, consultancy programs ii) enhance marketing capabilities, and iii) support information and communication technology usage to increase employee efficiency (Dunne & Dougherty, 2016; Meri, 2020). Because small businesses are more sensitive about resource and capability issues (Dunne & Dougherty, 2016), leadership and organisational climate are much more essential for small businesses' existence.

4.7 Conclusion

The industrial revolution and the rapid transformation after the Second World War triggered an innovation paradigm that leads today's business environment. The change and technological evolution that took place within a century has triggered the concept of innovation to become a competency-based superiority tool. Research and development and innovation initiatives aimed at creating social value and demand in line with the increase in production played an important role in markets dominated by more than one player. Especially in the transition period from traditional management to strategic management, innovation has become one of the most valuable dynamics of the 21st century.

In today's business life, called Industry 4.0, intensive research and development studies are carried out, and technological applications from the use of artificial intelligence to automation are preferred by businesses. In all these processes, the expectations of the enterprises can create sustainable innovations that will have a competitive advantage in the market in which they play a role. From this point of view, innovation is considered as an important resource that will bring high returns and competitiveness to businesses.

It is essential to conduct research on a new topic that leads to the development of particularly small businesses as inno-preneurs (Meri, 2020). Inno-preneurs are entrepreneurs and leaders who focus on change, dynamism, innovation, creation, automation, and competition to establish and survive an organisation with new implementations to operate in the long run. Furthermore, it should enhance the innovation capabilities in small businesses so as to transform employee behaviours to innovative behaviours that triggers increase of efforts and performance (Saunila, 2020).

Innovative capabilities in a business are explained by the power of organisational culture to transform ideas into innovation (Okan, 2018). Organisations need a working climate that will develop their innovation capabilities and support the creation and sharing of ideas to gain a strategic advantage. Employees' perceptions of their organisation's climate are the result of the implementation of a particular innovation, shared experiences, and observations of employees (Klein & Sorra, 1996). Innovative climate is evaluated as an organisational environment where employees can take risks and realise innovative and creative practices. Besides, the innovative climate triggers working collectively, supports research-development, and leads suitable structure for the use of technology (Yaman

Kahyaoğlu, 2019). Furthermore, Prima Lita *et al.* (2020) found that organisational culture and entrepreneurial orientation have important impact on innovation that leads performance increase in small and medium enterprises.

On the other hand, Zaltman *et al.* (1973) stated that innovation consists of the stages of generating a new idea and applying the new idea. Mumford and Licuanan (2004) defined the elements that shape innovation within the organisation as work climate, interpersonal relations, organisational structure, strategies, and individual abilities. Intellectual capital is also expressed as the combination of knowledge, skills, experiences, and individual abilities of organisational employees (Edvinsson & Malone, 1997). Intellectual accumulation and experience created by intellectual capital in enterprises should be brought together in the innovation process. The presence of intellectual capital strengthens the interest and desire for innovation (Konyalılar, 2020). Innovative behaviours of employees are related to their creativity as well as their innovative competencies and skills. Innovative behaviours are behaviours that can be motivated and play an important role in organisational performance (Shin & Zhou, 2007; Pieterse *et al.*, 2010; cited in Kılıç, 2018). For that reason, to make a small business better, it is necessary to equip employees with innovation capabilities to demonstrate innovative behaviours to gain qualified work outcomes. This situation can be easily obtained when organisational work environment is formulated as innovative by visionary and implementer leaders who are also called as entrepreneurial leaders.

Finally, it is considered that organisations that want to earn high returns in the 21st century should conduct behaviours that can transform their ability to innovate into competitive advantage. Organisational abilities are formed by employees' capabilities. The realisation of these behaviours will emerge more easily and quickly in the presence of entrepreneurial leaders (Kuratko, 2007).

References

Abdelgawad, S. G., Zahra, S. A., Svejenova, S., & Sapienza, H. J. (2013). Strategic leadership and entrepreneurial capability for game change. *Journal of Leadership & Organizational Studies, 20*(4), 394–407.

Adıgüzel, B. (2012). *İnovasyon ve inovasyon yönetimi: Steve Jobs örneği.* Gazi Üniversitesi Sosyal Bilimler Enstitüsü Yayınlanmamış Yüksek Lisans Tezi, Ankara.

Agostini, L., Nosella, A., & Filippini, R. (2017). Does intellectual capital allow improving innovation performance? A quantitative analysis in the SME context. *Journal of Intellectual Capital, 18*(2), 400–418.

Akkoç, İ., Çalişkan, A., & Turunç, Ö. (2012). Örgütlerde gelişim kültürü ve algılanan örgütsel desteğin iş tatmini ve iş performansına etkisi: Güvenin aracılık rolü. *Yönetim ve Ekonomi: Celal Bayar Üniversitesi İktisadi ve İdari Bilimler Fakültesi Dergisi, 19*(1), 105–135.

Al Mamun, A., Ibrahim, M. D., Yusoff, M. N. H. B., & Fazal, S. A. (2018). Entrepreneurial leadership, performance, and sustainability of micro-enterprises in Malaysia. *Sustainability, 10*(5), 1–23.

Armenakis, A., Jeremy B., Jennifer P., & Walker, H. J. (2007). Organizational change recipients' beliefs scale: Development of an assessment instrument. *Journal of Applied Behavioral Science, 43*, 481–505.

Armenakis, A., Stanley H., & Mossholder, K. (1993). Creating readiness for organizational change. *Human Relations, 46*, 681–703.

Atkins, M. H., & Lowe, J. F. (1997). Sizing up the small firm: UK and Australian experience. *International Small Business Journal, 15*(3), 42–55.

Aydoğar, N., & Yirci, R. (2020). Devlet ve özel okul yöneticilerinin yenilik yönetimi becerilerinin karşılaştırılması: Nicel bir araştırma. *İstanbul Ticaret Üniversitesi Sosyal Bilimler Dergisi, 19*(39), 1286–1308.

Baker, R., & Thompson, J. (1995). Innovation in general practice: is the gap between training and non-training practices getting wider? *British Journal of General Practice, 45*(395), 297–300.

Barras, R. (1986). Towards a theory of innovation in services. *Research Policy, 15*(4), 161–173.

Bate, J. D., & Johnston, R. E. (2003). Strategic frontiers: The starting-point for innovative growth. *Strategy & Leadership, 33*(1), 12–18–35.

Bowen, F. E., Rostami, M., & Steel, P. (2010). Timing is everything: A meta-analysis of the relationships between organizational performance and innovation. *Journal of Business Research, 63*(11), 1179–1185.

Çakır, S. (2012). *Ar-ge ve Yenilik Ders Notları.* Ortadoğu Teknik Üniversitesi.

Carmona-Lavado, A., Cuevas-Rodríguez, G., & Cabello-Medina, C. (2013). Service innovativeness and innovation success in technology-based knowledge-intensive business services: An intellectual capital approach. *Industry and Innovation, 20*(2), 133–156.

Cefis, E., & Marsili, O. (2005). A matter of life and death: Innovation and firm survival. *Industrial and Corporate Change, 14*(6), 1167–1192.

Chen, M. H. (2007). Entrepreneurial leadership and new ventures: Creativity in entrepreneurial teams. *Creativity and Innovation Management, 16*(3), 239–249.

Chuang, S. H., & Lin, H. N. (2015). Co-creating e-service innovations: Theory, practice, and impact on firm performance. *International Journal of Information Management, 35*(3), 277–291.

DeLong Goldman, G. (2009). Initial validation of a brief individual readiness for change scale (BIRCS) for use with addiction program staff practitioners. *Journal of Social Work Practice in the Addictions, 9*(2), 184–203.

Dunne, D. D., & Dougherty, D. (2016). Abductive reasoning: How innovators navigate in the labyrinth of complex product innovation. *Organization Studies, 37*(2), 131–159.

Edvinsson, L., & Malone, M. S. (1997). *Intellectual Capital: Realizing Your Company's True Value by Finding Its Hidden Roots.* HarperCollins Publishers, Inc., New York.

Ensley, M. D., Hmieleski, K. M., & Pearce, C. L. (2006). The importance of vertical and shared leadership within new venture top management teams: Implications for the performance of start-ups. *The Leadership Quarterly, 17*(3), 217–231.

Erdil, E., Pamukçu, M. T., Akçomak, İ. S., & Tiryakioğlu, M. (2016). Bilgi, bilim, teknoloji ve yenilik: Kavramsal tartışma. Science and Technology Policies Research Center Tekpol, Working Paper Series STPS-WP-16, 1.

Gökçek, O. (2007). *Yenilik Yönetimi Süreci ve Yenilik Stratejileri: Otomotiv Sektöründe Bir Alan Çalışması.* İstanbul Üniversitesi Sosyal Bilimler Enstitüsü Yayımlanmamış Yüksek Lisans Tezi, İstanbul.

Gupta, V., MacMillan, I. C., & Surie, G. (2004). Entrepreneurial leadership: Developing and measuring a cross-cultural construct. *Journal of Business Venturing, 19*(2), 241–260.

Harel, R., Schwartz, D., & Kaufmann, D. (2020). Organizational culture processes for promoting innovation in small businesses. *EuroMed Journal of Business, 16*(2), 218–240.

Harrison, R. T., Leitch, C. M., & McAdam, M. (2018). Breaking glass: Towards a gendered analysis of entrepreneurial leadership. In *Research Handbook on Entrepreneurship and Leadership.* Edward Elgar Publishing.

Hartmann, A. (2006). The context of innovation management in construction firms. *Construction Management and Economics, 24*(6), 567–578.

Holt, D. T., Armenakis, A. A., Feild, H. S., & Harris, S. G. (2007). Readiness for organizational change: The systematic development of a scale. *The Journal of Applied Behavioral Science, 43*(2), 232–255.

Hsu, Y. H., & Fang, W. (2009). Intellectual capital and new product development performance: The mediating role of organizational learning capability. *Technological Forecasting and Social Change, 76*(5), 664–677.

Isaksen, S. G., & Akkermans, H. J. (2011). Creative climate: A leadership lever for innovation. *The Journal of Creative Behavior, 45*(3), 161–187.

Jaiswal, N. K., & Dhar, R. L. (2015). Transformational leadership, innovation climate, creative self-efficacy and employee creativity: A multilevel study. *International Journal of Hospitality Management, 51*, 30–41.

Kheng, Y. K., June, S., & Mahmood, R. (2013). The determinants of innovative work behavior in the knowledge intensive business services sector in Malaysia. *Asian Social Science, 9*(15), 47–59.

Kılıç, F. (2018). *Açık inovasyon kavramı ve etkileri üzerine bir uygulama.* Pamukkale Üniversitesi Sosyal Bilimler Enstitüsü Yayımlanmamış Yüksek Lisans Tezi, Denizli.

Kirrane, M., Lennon, M., O'Connor, C., & Fu, N. (2017). Linking perceived management support with employees' readiness for change: The mediating role of psychological capital. *Journal of Change Management, 17*(1), 47–66.

Klein, K. J., & Knight, A. P. (2005). Innovation implementation: Overcoming the challenge. *Current Directions in Psychological Science, 14*(5), 243–246.

Klein, K. J., & Sorra, J. S. (1996). The challenge of innovation implementation. *Academy of Management Review, 21*(4), 1055–1080.

Konyalılar, N. (2020). *Entelektüel sermaye ve inovasyonun çalışan performansına etkisi: Havacılık sektörü örneği.* İstanbul Gelişim Üniversitesi Sosyal Bilimler Enstitüsü Yayımlanmamış Doktora Tezi, İstanbul.

Kuratko, D. F. (2007). Entrepreneurial leadership in the 21st century: Guest editor's perspective. *Journal of Leadership & Organizational Studies, 13*(4), 1–11.

Lee, J. H., & Venkataraman, S. (2006). Aspirations, market offerings, and the pursuit of entrepreneurial opportunities. *Journal of Business Venturing, 21*(1), 107–123.

Leitch, C. M., McMullan, C., & Harrison, R. T. (2013). The development of entrepreneurial leadership: The role of human, social and institutional capital. *British Journal of Management, 24*(3), 347–366.

Mahendrati, H., & Mangundjaya, W. (2020). Individual readiness for change and affective commitment to change: The mediation effect of technology readiness on public sector. In *Advances in Social Science, Education and Humanities,* Research Volume 431, 52–57.

Martínez-Román, J. A., Gamero, J., & Tamayo, J. A. (2011). Analysis of innovation in SMEs using an innovative capability-based non-linear model: A study in the province of Seville (Spain). *Technovation, 31*(9), 459–475.

Meri, M. (2020). The culture of Inno-preneurs vs. human capital investment in developed countries. *European Public & Social Innovation Review, 5*(2), 27–43.

Morris, M. H., & Sexton, D. L. (1996). The concept of entrepreneurial intensity: Implications for company performance. *Journal of Business Research, 36*(1), 5–13.

Mumford, M. D., & Licuanan, B. (2004). Leading for innovation: Conclusions, issues, and directions. *The Leadership Quarterly, 15*(1), 163–171.

Myklebust, T., Motland, K., Bjørkli, C. A., & Fostervold, K. I. (2020). An empirical evaluation of the relationship between human relations climate and readiness for change. *Scandinavian Journal of Work and Organizational Psychology, 5*(1), 1–13.

Niewöhner, N., Asmar, L., Röltgen, D., Kühn, A., & Dumitrescu, R. (2020). The impact of the 4th industrial revolution on the design fields of innovation management. *Procedia CIRP, 91,* 43–48.

OECD (2005). *The Measurement of Scientific and Technological Activities: Guidelines for Collecting and Interpreting Innovation Data: Oslo Manual,* 3rd ed. OECD Publishing, Paris.

Oğuztürk, S. (2003). Yenilik kavramı ve teorik temelleri. *Süleyman Demirel Üniversitesi İktisadi ve İdari Bilimler Fakültesi Dergisi, 8*(2), 253–273.

Okan, R. Y. (2018). The influence of organizational structure and culture on innovation capability of organizations: With the mediating role of strategic decision-making process. Doctoral Thesis, Yeditepe University, İstanbul.

Oke, A. (2007). Innovation types and innovation management practices in service companies. *International Journal of Operations & Production Management, 27*(6), 564–587.

Oreg, S., Vakola, M., & Armenakis, A. A. (2011). Change recipients' reactions to organizational change: A sixty year review of quantitative studies. *Journal of Applied Behavioral Science, 47,* 461–524.

Özer, A. (2017). *Organizational Learning Culture, The Climate for Innovation, and Organizational Resilience.* Boğaziçi Universitesi Yayımlanmamış Doktora Tezi, İstanbul.

Parasuraman, A., & Colby, C. L. (2015). An updated and streamlined technology readiness index: TRI 2.0. *Journal of Service Research, 18*(1), 59–74.

Parasuraman, A. (2000). Technology readiness index (Tri): A multiple-item scale to measure readiness to embrace new technologies. *Journal of Service Research, 2*(4), 307–320.

Pieterse, A. N., Van Knippenberg, D., Schippers, M., & Stam, D. (2010). Transformational and transactional leadership and innovative behavior: The moderating role of psychological empowerment. *Journal of Organizational Behavior, 31*(4), 609–623.

Prima Lita, R., Fitriana Faisal, R., & Meuthia, M. (2020). Enhancing small and medium enterprises performance through innovation in Indonesia: A framework for creative industries supporting tourism. *Journal of Hospitality and Tourism Technology, 11*(1), 155–176.

Rafferty, A. E., & Simons, R. H. (2006). An examination of the antecedents of readiness for fine-tuning and corporate transformation changes. *Journal of Business and Psychology, 20*(3), 325–350.

Ren, F., & Zhang, J. (2015). Job stressors, organizational innovation climate, and employees' innovative behavior. *Creativity Research Journal, 27*(1), 16–23.

Roesminingsih, E., & Suyanto, T. (2019). School entrepreneurship extracurricular management. In *3rd International Conference on Education Innovation* (ICEI 2019). Atlantis Press.

Sarabi, A., Froese, F. J., Chng, D. H., & Meyer, K. E. (2020). Entrepreneurial leadership and MNE subsidiary performance: The moderating role of subsidiary context. *International Business Review, 29*(3), 101672.

Sarros, J. C., Cooper, B. K., & Santora, J. C. (2008). Building a climate for innovation through transformational leadership and organizational culture. *Journal of Leadership & Organizational Studies, 15*(2), 145–158.

Saunila, M. (2020). Innovation capability in SMEs: A systematic review of the literature. *Journal of Innovation & Knowledge, 5*(4), 260–265.

Scheepers, M. J., Hough, J., & Bloom, J. Z. (2008). Nurturing the corporate entrepreneurship capability. *Southern African Business Review, 12*(3), 50–75.

Schumpeter, J. A., & Nichol, A. J. (1934). Robinson's economics of imperfect competition. *Journal of Political Economy, 42*(2), 249–259.

Schumpeter, J. A. (1934). *The Theory of Economic Development: An Inquiry into Profits, Capital, Credit, Interest, and The Business Cycle.* Transaction Publishers, London.

Scott, S. G., & Bruce, R. A. (1994). Creating innovative behavior among R&D professionals: the moderating effect of leadership on the relationship between problem-solving style and innovation. In *Proceedings of 1994 IEEE International Engineering Management Conference* (IEMC'94).

Sharma, N., & Singh, V. K. (2016). Effect of workplace incivility on job satisfaction and turnover intentions in India. *South Asian Journal of Global Business Research, 5*(2), 234–249.

Sharma, N. (2020). Fostering positive deviance: A potential strategy to an engaged workforce. *Strategic Direction, 36*(8), 1–3. doi:10.1108/SD-10-2019-0206.

Shin, S. J., & Zhou, J. (2007). When is educational specialization heterogeneity related to creativity in research and development teams? Transformational leadership as a moderator. *Journal of Applied Psychology, 92*, 1709–1721.

Singh, S., Akbani, I., & Dhir, S. (2020). Service innovation implementation: A systematic review and research agenda. *The Service Industries Journal, 40*(7-8), 491–517.

Surie, G., & Ashley, A. (2008). Integrating pragmatism and ethics in entrepreneurial leadership for sustainable value creation. *Journal of Business Ethics, 81*(1), 235–246.

Taşgit, Y. E., & Torun, B. (2016). Yöneticilerin inovasyon algısı, inovasyon sürecini yönetme tarzı ve işletmelerin inovasyon performansı arasındaki ilişkiler: KOBİ'ler üzerinde bir araştırma. *Yönetim Bilimleri Dergisi, 14*(28), 121–156.

Tlaiss, H. A., & Kauser, S. (2019). Entrepreneurial leadership, patriarchy, gender, and identity in the Arab world: Lebanon in focus. *Journal of Small Business Management, 57*(2), 517–537.

Toivonen, M., & Tuominen, T. (2009). Emergence of innovations in services. *The Service Industries Journal, 29*(7), 887–902.

Vakola, M. (2014). What's in there for me? Individual readiness to change and the perceived impact of organizational change. *Leadership & Organization Development Journal, 35*(3), 195–209.

Wu, W. Y., Chang, M. L., & Chen, C. W. (2008). Promoting innovation through the accumulation of intellectual capital, social capital, and entrepreneurial orientation. *R&D Management, 38*(3), 265–277.

Ximenes, M., Supartha, W. G., Dewi, I. G. A. M., & Sintaasih, D. K. (2019). Entrepreneurial leadership moderating high performance work system and employee creativity on employee performance. *Cogent Business & Management, 6*(1), 1697512.

Yaman Kahyaoğlu, D. (2019). İnovasyonu destekleyen örgüt kültürünün inovasyon yeteneğine etkisinde kuşak farkının rolü: Adana ili imalat sanayii örneği. Çağ Üniversitesi Sosyal Bilimler Enstitüsü Yayımlanmamış Doktora Tezi, Adana.

Yiğit, S. (2014). Kültür, örgüt kültürü ve inovasyon ilişkisi bağlamında "İnovasyon Kültürü". *Karamanoğlu Mehmetbey Üniversitesi Sosyal ve Ekonomik Araştırmalar Dergisi, 2014*(2), 1–7.

Yiğitoğlu, V., & Şirin, M. (2020). Küçük konaklama işletmelerinde karşılaştırmalı performans analizi: Belediye belgeli konaklama işletmeleri üzerinde bir araştırma. *İşletme Araştırmaları Dergisi, 12*(3), 2297–2311.

Yorgancılar, F. N. (2011). Sürdürülebilir rekabet anlayışı olarak yenilik yeteneği. *Sosyal Ekonomik Araştırmalar Dergisi, 11*(21), 379–426.

Zainol, N. R., & Al Mamun, A. (2018). Entrepreneurial competency, competitive advantage and performance of informal women micro-entrepreneurs in Kelantan, Malaysia. *Journal of Enterprising Communities: People and Places in the Global Economy, 12*, 299–321.

Zaltman, G., Duncan, R., & Holbek, J. (1973). *Innovations and Organizations*. New York: Wiley.

© 2022 World Scientific Publishing Co. Pte. Ltd.
https://doi.org/10.1142/9789811239212_0005

Chapter 5

Boosting Human Resources Innovation in SMEs Through Crowdsourcing

Roohallah Noori* and Dariush Jahanishargh†

Management Faculty, Kharazmi University, Tehran, Iran

*rnoori@khu.ac.ir

†daryuosh.jahani@gmail.com

Abstract: One of the most prominent features that has emerged in many economies over the past decades is the role of small and medium-sized enterprises. The companies, which are the main driver of the economies in the process of industrialisation and the origin of evolution and innovation and pioneer of the emergence of new technologies, are essential for developing economies such as Iran. Nevertheless, researches and studies show that many small and medium-sized enterprises, with significant investment in research and development, have problems in human resource innovation. At the moment, there are several intelligible forces that can facilitate the process of innovation and provide a solution for SMEs. Many dynamic forces are based on open innovation and crowdsourcing. In fact, crowdsourcing is a new internet-based business model that can be used to provide innovative solutions to problems or to produce a product, and its wide range of applications in various industries are increasingly extracted and used. Therefore, the main objective of this chapter is identifying, classifying, and prioritising the applications of crowdsourcing in SMEs human resources. In this regard, this chapter has been structured in four main sections. First, small and medium-sized enterprises are generally reviewed. Second, the concept of crowdsourcing, its framework and applications are explained. Third, the role of crowdsourcing in small and medium-sized enterprises' human resource innovation and problem solving is categorised and summarised. Finally, in conclusion and further research, attempts are made to provide solutions to develop human resources innovation in small and medium-sized enterprises through crowdsourcing and providing agenda for further researches in this field.

Keywords: Crowdsourcing, Small and medium-sized enterprises (SMEs), Employees, Human resources, Crowdsourcing applications, AHP, QFD.

5.1 Introduction

Today's world is a world of virtual and internet-based infrastructures, platforms, and applications in all of the social, economic, and business areas. One of these platforms is crowdsourcing. Crowdsourcing is a platform for innovation, problem-solving, collaboration, and collective intelligence in e-commerce and social commerce (Turban *et al.*, 2018). Crowdsourcing is based on the statement: "'We' are better than 'Me' and 'We' are smarter than 'Me'" (Libert & Spector, 2007).

In the current competitive market and economy where most companies are small and medium-sized enterprises — as have been introduced as the main body of the economy — the main primary way to survive is innovation. It is in fact the factor for a distinctive and competitive advantage in comparison to other opponents. Therefore, executives in small and medium-sized enterprises ask the questions: "How to add innovation to an enterprise or facilitate the processes towards it?" and "How to use the potential abilities of employees, customers, and external population in the internet as a workforce purposefully and to develop their innovations and collaborations to improve decisions and solve their problems?" In this regard, and given the emergence of Web 2.0 and the development of social, network, and crowd-based businesses, studies on crowdsourcing and its application have drawn the attention of so many businesses and researchers, and it can be a trigger for HR innovation in small and medium-sized enterprises.

Therefore, this chapter attempts to contribute to the study by reviewing, classifying, and prioritising applications of crowdsourcing in SMEs industry and provide an effective solution for its limitations and problems. Thus, this chapter has been structured as four main sections. First, some terms and concepts especially of small and medium-sized enterprises (SMEs) are generally reviewed. Second, the concept of crowdsourcing is defined and its frameworks and applications are explained. Third, crowdsourcing in SMEs and its role in employees' innovation and problem solving are categorised and summarised. Finally, in conclusion, some solutions are provided to develop human resources innovation in SMEs through crowdsourcing and agenda for further researches in this field are presented.

5.2 Small and Medium-sized Enterprises

In the late 21st century, a new wave of change began. Small and medium-sized technology institutions were the focus of planners in developed countries. Researchers and university graduates were attracted to small specialised companies which were considered as the main part of technology development principles. Within small enterprises where researches and innovations were conducted, advanced technologies and entrepreneurs' knowledge and small institutions professionals were created; something that even huge and interconnected structure of big institutions were unable to do (Yazdani, 2011).

Improvement of living standards since the 1970s has changed consumption structures in most of the countries in the world.

Therefore, people are looking for newer products with more, various, and complicated functions. This has led to the division of markets into smaller parts. Small markets need small industries. Mass production is not profitable in these markets. Therefore, small enterprises can better meet these demands than large firms (Noori and Meshkat Zakeri, 2021).

There are many different definitions for small and medium-sized enterprises (see Table 5.1). Some of these definitions are based on quantitative criteria, such as the number of employees, the volume of transactions and assets, while others employ qualitative approaches. Some researchers state that each definition should encompass quantitative elements such as the number of employees, the volume of transactions and assets, together with financial and non-financial criteria; these definitions should also include qualitative criteria that shows how to organise a company and its operations (Akhavan *et al.*, 2008).

The EU defines small and medium-sized enterprises as companies that have less than 250 employees, annual returns of less than $50 million and annual balance sheet of less than $43 million (see Table 5.2). But in China, small and medium-sized enterprises include companies that have less than 155 employees and $30 million investment (Gilaninia *et al.*, 2012).

The Central Bank Statistics Office of Iran considers units with less than 10 employees "micro", 10 to 49 employees "small", 50 to 99 employees "average" and more than 100 employees are called "large" (Central Bank of the Islamic Republic of Iran, 2015).

Table 5.1.   Classification of SMEs by the World Bank

Categorisation of enterprises	Maximum number of employees	Maximum annual sale or turnover (thousand dollars)	Maximum asset (thousand dollars)
Micro	10	10	100
Small	50	3000	3000
Medium	300	15000	15000

Source: Gibson and Vaart (2008).

Table 5.2. Classification criteria of the EU for small and medium-sized enterprises

Categorisation of enterprises	Maximum number of employees	Maximum annual sale or turnover (thousand dollars)	Maximum asset (thousand dollars)
Micro	10	2	2
Small	50	10	10
Medium	250	50	43

Source: www.ec.europe.ed (2004).

Small and medium-sized enterprises have a great flexibility and compatibility with new technologies. They also have a great potential for innovation and export, as well as financial and human resources efficiency. In the United States, small and medium-sized enterprises form an important part of the economy and there are about 3.8 million enterprises with 5 to 99 people. Sectors dominated by small enterprises have created more than 60% of new jobs from 1994 to 2005. It should be noted that 90% of the companies in Hong Kong are in the form of small enterprises; 88% of all the companies have less than 10 employees and hold 80% of the national trade of the country. In Canada, 57% of the economic production are produced by the small and medium-sized enterprises sector which include 2.2 billion enterprises. Small and medium-sized enterprises constitute 45% of GDP, an important part of economic growth, 60% of all jobs in the economy and 75% of employment growth. They are more vulnerable due to the lack of financial and human resources, as well as information resources needed to understand and manage the organisation and the environment (Lawrence, 2011). In many EU countries, small and medium-sized enterprises make up 99% of the companies, 67% of jobs and 59% of GDP. In most of the countries, small and medium-sized enterprises have a significant contribution to GDP, a key source for new jobs, as well as a ground for fostering entrepreneurship and new business ideas. The US, the UK, Japan, Australia, New Zealand, Canada and other developed countries as well as developing countries have developed policies to facilitate the growth of small and medium-sized enterprises (Abid *et al.*, 2011).

Small entrepreneurial organisations which have always faced a lack of resources and physical limitations can provide broader network structures for sharing resources and manpower in cyberspace through communication capabilities. On the other hand, they can break geographical boundaries and expand their function in the form of electronic and e-commerce entrepreneurship while creating a global and knowledge-based platform given the added information capabilities (Kajoori, 2007).

5.3 Crowdsourcing

In this section, the theoretical framework of the concepts related to the subject of research is reviewed. First, the concept of crowdsourcing, including its definitions, backgrounds, and models, is discussed. Then, crowdsourcing in SMEs, its applications and classifications are explained.

The term crowdsourcing was first introduced by Jeff Howe and it is consisted of two words "crowd" and "outsourcing". Crowdsourcing means the outsourcing of activities to a massive population or a broad network of indeterminate individuals through a public call; while in outsourcing, an activity or a duty is assigned to a group or individual. The distinction between "crowdsourcing" and "outsourcing" is related to this issue that first is based on a public call to a massive known or unknown population (Keshtkar *et al.*, 2012). Crowdsourcing is an internet-based business model that tries to seek the help of the ability of a large number of people active on the intranet, extranet, or internet to develop innovative solutions to solve an issue or to produce a product in a creative way through a public call.

Improving employees' innovation and developing their collective intelligence for problem-solving are the main objectives of crowdsourcing strategies in SMEs (Turban *et al.*, 2018). Also, generating new products and services, improving the performance in the value chain, and focusing on qualifications are essential to survive in the competitive environment of developing companies. The rapid change of a business environment requires senior managers of organisations to apply those strategies that consider the success of the organisation and investment in activities that will bring competitive advantage to future success. In the current era, many companies are applying different strategies to solve the problems related to the costs, quality, and speed of services. Downsizing, eliminating some processes or functions, and designing strategic relationships through contracting or granting patent or leasing can be considered as examples of these types of decisions (Pourkiani & Sadeghi, 2012).

There are four definitions that can be found in the literature for crowdsourcing, which are presented by Surweiki (2004), Howe (2008), Brabham (2012), and Estellés-Arolas and González-Ladrón-de-Guevara (2012). However, there are four distinct elements in all these definitions (Pourkiani & Sadeghi, 2012): 1) public population (also called users), 2) web and online space, 3) public call, and 4) function (in the form of presenting idea or doing something by the public population).

According to Howe, crowdsourcing systems were created as a public call to the society. Different examples of crowdsourcing systems show that a public call guarantee the many respondents (SMEs human resources) who are the determining factor in finding the correct answer for small/big projects in companies or individuals who are looking for innovation and the best and fastest solutions. There are two human factors that are essential for every activity: the job/task/problem provider company and participants. On the other hand, the third factor, as a mediator, may exist to facilitate the relation between the issue/problem provider and the population. The mediator may have different forms: it can be a platform that links other factors or it can be a call center that works as a hybrid facility that provide infrastructures for the staff who do not have access to it (Howe, 2008). Generally crowdsourcing is an invitation to all people in the crowd to create, discuss, refine, and rank meaningful ideas or tasks, or contribute via the net/web through following process (see Figure 5.1):

1. Identify a problem
2. Broadcast the problem
3. The "crowd" (fans) submit solutions
4. You and the crowd vet the solutions
5. You reward winning solvers
6. Everybody profits

5.4 Framework for Crowdsourcing in SMEs

A step-by-step process as shown in Figure 5.2 has been used to design and test the appropriate crowdsourcing framework and to prioritise applications for human resource innovation and problem-solving in small and medium-sized enterprises.

5.4.1 *Theoretical Background and Literature Review*

There is not much research on crowdsourcing in general and also on crowdsourcing in small and medium enterprises. Table 5.3 summarises some of the most relevant studies in this field.

As you can see in Table 5.3, we found that although there have been numerous studies in recent years on the crowdsourcing application in various industries, all applications of crowdsourcing in a particular industry, such as SMEs, which encompass a large part of the economy, is completely new in this field and no research has been carried out in this area so far. Anyway, we will continue this section by looking at previous studies listed in Table 5.3 to identify

Figure 5.1.   The crowdsourcing steps

Source: Howe (2008); Malone *et al.* (2010); Doan *et al.* (2011); Brabham (2012).

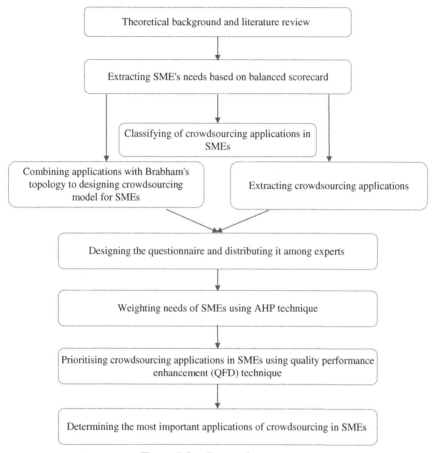

Figure 5.2. Research process

all applications of crowdsourcing that could meet the needs of SMEs.

Crowdsourcing Book: Brabham (2013a) in his book *Crowdsourcing* attempted to bring together the big, wandering conversations on crowdsourcing in an easy-to-digest form that is nuanced enough to serve as a springboard for future research and application yet simple enough to serve as an introduction for someone who has just begun to learn about crowdsourcing's promise and finally provided a four-type model for solving problems by crowdsourcing.

Table 5.3.   Study of crowdsourcing in small and medium enterprises

Researcher(s)/ Year	Subject	Results
Maiolini and Naggi (2011)	Crowdsourcing and SMEs: Opportunities and Challenges	Examining the potential benefits of crowdsourcing for SMEs, as well as exploring the challenges SMEs face in crowdsourcing activities.
Mwila (2013)	Crowdsourcing in Small and Medium Sized Enterprises	Examining the challenges and obstacles of establishing outsourcing in SMEs, which has been accompanied by providing solutions and suggestions.
Brabham *et al.* (2014)	Crowdsourcing Applications for Public Health	Provided a framework with 4 types of crowdsourcing to identify effective solutions to improve public health and reviewed the use of different outsourcing applications.
Brabham (2013b)	Using Crowdsourcing in Government	Using the Brabham typological framework, classified applications of crowdsourcing in the government sector and examined the implementation phases of these applications, which include the three phases of planning, implementation, and post-implementation.
Metellus (2017)	Crowdsourcing as a Support Mechanism for Small and Medium-sized Enterprises: A Case Study in Haiti	Investigating the concept of crowdsourcing and the possibility of using it as a supporting mechanism to improve conditions of Haitian SMEs.
Brabham (2013a)	Crowdsourcing	Examined all the concepts related to crowdsourcing and provided a four-type model for solving problems by crowdsourcing.

Table 5.3. (*Continued*)

Researcher(s)/ Year	Subject	Results
Oliveira *et al.* (2010)	Definition of Crowdsourcing Innovation Service for the European SMEs	Using crowdsourcing in European culture as a motivation factor to solve the innovation challenges of small and medium enterprises.
Mansor *et al.* (2018a)	Exploring Crowdsourcing Practices and Benefits: Validation from Small and Medium Enterprises (SMEs) Business Owners	The main purpose of this study is to investigate outsourcing projects and the benefits they have had for SMEs so far.
Afonso and Cabrita (2015)	Developing a Lean Supply Chain Performance Framework in an SME: A Perspective Based on the Balanced Scorecard	The aim of this study was to develop a conceptual framework for effective supply chain management using a balanced scorecard, which has been implemented in an SME in Portugal.
Hsu *et al.* (2017)	Identifying Key Performance Factors for Sustainability Development of SMEs: Integrating QFD and Fuzzy MADM Methods	Sustainability management of small and medium enterprises based on collecting and prioritising important factors in SME stability.
Qin *et al.* (2016)	Exploring Barriers and Opportunities in Adopting Crowdsourcing Based New Product Development in Manufacturing Smes	Identifying the needs, challenges and future development opportunities associated with adopting crowdsourcing strategies for New Product Development (NPD) in SMEs.

Definition of Crowdsourcing Innovation Service for European SMEs: This research is guiding future work on what is the adequate architecture of a web platform to support a crowdsourcing innovation intermediary service for European SMEs. In order to answer this question, it has three main conceptual focuses. First, it is necessary to deepen the understanding of the needs and specificities of European SMEs' and the expectations they hold in embracing crowdsourcing innovation. Secondly, understanding the differences between the existing intermediaries based in the USA and those based in Europe, and to understand if these intermediaries act differently when dealing with SMEs and larger companies. To do so, researchers have identified some intermediaries supporting crowdsourcing innovation in Europe that will compare with the most known intermediaries based in the North America. Thirdly, they study what motivates people to join the intermediary's network and how to best protect their intellectual property. Finally, researchers expect the prototype developed in this study to evolve into a platform for an actual intermediary supporting innovation in SMEs being defined by several projects: governance, risks, community, learning and memory, and knowledge repository (Oliveira *et al.*, 2010).

Developing a Lean Supply Chain Performance (LSCP) Framework in an SME: This empirical study provides indication of how LSCP could be assessed and improved in SMEs. It provides a wide set of metrics that can help the organisation's managers select performance measures best suited to fulfil the goals. In assessing the degree of lean company, it also aims to raise awareness among managers for lean practices, even in environments not traditionally lean. Tools such as the balanced scorecard (BSC) or analytic hierarchy process (AHP) in the evaluation of the LSCP was also successfully integrated in this study (Afonso & Cabrita, 2015).

Crowdsourcing Opportunities and Challenges in SMEs: Crowdsourcing can represent an effective way to take benefit of flexibility in cooperating with larger networks of enterprises. However, the question of how to actually organise for being a part of the network of crowdsourcing is still open and needs to be studied more (Maiolini & Naggi, 2011).

Adopting Crowdsourcing Strategies for New Product Development in SMEs: Based on the mapping of this study on the crowdsourcing services against the NPD process, there is a need for an integral crowdsourcing platform to systematically support NPD activities. To achieve this, an effective crowdsourcing system should be as follows (Qin *et al.*, 2016):

(1) User-centred (focused on the user's needs): knowing where the user (SME) is in their NPD journey across the four key business challenges (framing a problem, sourcing experts, filtering responses, managing terms of engagement) and supporting them at each stage.
(2) Based on interoperability, i.e., able to integrate with digital tools already being used, e.g., chat software, social media, etc., and make use of Application Programming Interfaces to integrate with existing organisational IT systems.
(3) Cloud based, white label system that can support iterative development in response to data about usage along with some core features, such as ID verification, contracting/IP protection, etc.
(4) Iterative and modular-based design gets the best results because its built-in flexibility allows it to respond to user needs, trends, social, economic, and technological changes.
(5) Digital tools to make crowd work more efficient (and measurable) and facilitate leadership to support culture change.
(6) Opportunities for commercial/social exploitation of a successful platform; subscriptions, brokerage fees, trading platform, opportunities to exploit aggregated data.
(7) Expand on the social media aspect. This is about several different things, from making it easy for challenges to be shared across platforms, file sharing systems, and tools that can help collate and filter responses from social media.
(8) Digital tools for crowdsourcing are still a relatively immature market. In other more mature digital markets, the marginal cost

of engagement has tended towards zero with companies (such as Google) levering their access to aggregated data. This could be an interesting model to explore in this field, e.g., offering a platform for free in order to create value from mining of aggregated data.

Crowdsourcing Practices Among Selected Malaysian SME's: Crowdsourcing practice is an effective business model to recruit a large group of undefined individuals from the community, i.e., solvers in order to complete organisational tasks. Numerous advantages and benefits can be leveraged via crowdsourcing practices, particularly in the context of Malaysian SMEs. Amongst the benefits are cost saving, reduce time product delivery, overcome peak demand, organisational innovation, brand visibility, access to specialised skills, solution diversity, and many more. Based on the qualitative data, it is proven that all SMEs business owners strongly agreed that crowdsourcing contributes positive implication to their business. The study also contributes to both theoretical and practical contributions, such as to enrich the current literature on crowdsourcing and foundation for future research particularly in the context SMEs in Malaysia. Meanwhile, the practical contributions to the policy makers could assist them in formulating and enhancing the effectiveness of current crowdsourcing programmes. To entrepreneurs the study enhances their knowledge and understanding towards crowdsourcing practices and its benefits that positively contributes to their business, eventually promoting other SMEs to embark on the crowdsourcing business model in their companies (Mansor *et al.*, 2018b).

5.4.2 *Classifying Crowdsourcing Applications in SMEs Using the Brabham Model*

Here, the applications are categorised by inspiration from the framework provided by Brabham and the three main applications of crowdsourcing in SMEs, which are financial, competitive, and learning.

Not all problems benefit from collective intelligence and can be crowdsourced. Synthesising several case studies, Brabham describes a four-type typology for understanding the nature of problems best suited for crowdsourcing (Brabham, 2012) including: the knowledge discovery and management approach, the distributed human intelligence tasking approach, the broadcast search approach, and the peer-vetted creative production approach (Table 5.4).

5.4.3 *Crowdsourcing in SMEs (Finance, Competition and Learning)*

Crowdsourcing in SMEs can generally be categorised according to these three categories. The crowdsourcing in financial aspect is considered here, as it is an important factor that has a deep impact on the development of SMEs capabilities (Green *et al.*, 2005). Competition, in addition to having a significant impact on the financial sector, has a major impact on SMEs success generally and their capacity and ability to compete, so is a suitable means for crowdsourcing (Barth *et al.*, 2008). Learning is presented as the basis on which SMEs embrace crowdsourcing as a necessary concept in their HR innovation and operational intelligence (Lloyd- Reason & Sear, 2007).

Finance: International organisations consider that small and medium-sized enterprises do not have easy access to financial resources, thus they need to be able to develop enough in this way and use only innovation to grow (European Commission, 2004). Financing offers to small and medium-sized companies by investors are generally high risk. SMEs could solve this issue through crowdsourcing. Therefore, with merging the four-type typology of crowdsourcing and financial needs in SMEs, applications of crowdsourcing in SMEs for founding can be classified as in Figure 5.3.

Competition: Competition affects SMEs in two ways. On the one hand, instant competition in the banking sector affects SMEs' access to financial resources, and on the other hand, the lack of sufficient competition between SMEs, which hinders their growth, can be solved by

Table 5.4. A typology of crowdsourcing problem types

Type	How it works	Kinds of problem	Example
Knowledge Discovery and Management	Organisation tasks crowd with finding and collecting information into a common location and format	Ideal for information management problems involving information gathering, organisation, and reporting, such as the creation of collective resources	Peer-to-patent peertopatent.org SeeClickFix seeclickfix.com
Distributed Human Intelligence Tasking	Organisation tasks crowd with analysing large amounts of information	Ideal for information management problems involving large-scale data analysis where human intelligence is more efficient or effective than computer analysis	InnoCentive innocentive.com Goldcorp Challenge Defunct
Broadcast Search	Organisation tasks crowd with solving empirical problems	Ideal for ideation problems with empirically provable solutions, such as scientific problems	Threadless threadless.com Doritos Crash the Super Bowl Contest crashthesuperbowl. com Next Stop Design nextstopdesign. com
Peer-Vetted Creative Production	Organisation tasks crowd with creating and selecting creative ideas	Ideal for ideation problems where solutions are matters of taste or market support, such as design or aesthetic problems	Amazon Mechanical Turk mturk.com Subvert and Profit Defunct

Source: Brabham (2012).

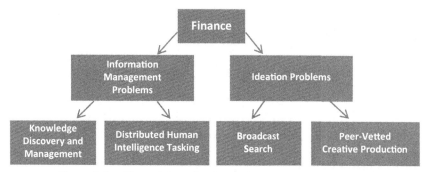

Figure 5.3.   Financial applications of crowdsourcing in SMEs

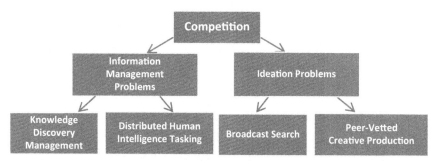

Figure 5.4.   Competitive applications of crowdsourcing in SMEs

their HR innovations and collective intelligence through crowdsourcing. Therefore, with merging the four-type typology of crowdsourcing and competitive needs in SMEs, applications of crowdsourcing in SMEs for competitiveness can be classified as in Figure 5.4.

Learning: Learning is identified as a critical input and output of crowdsourcing (Lowry & Turner, 2007). The ability and willingness to crowdsourcing depends on the level of learning of SMEs, to the extent that the level of learning of SMEs depends on their ability and willingness to crowdsourcing. However, the limited budgets for learning and development have an influence on the learning and work culture of SMEs. Also, the attitude towards learning and education in general are highly influenced by the executives. Surveys reveal that most managers of SMEs do not have a university or college education and this tends to cripple the growth of the entire SME (Mwila, 2013). Therefore, with merging the four-type typology of crowdsourcing and training and development needs in SMEs, applications of crowd-sourcing in SMEs for learning can be classified as in Figure 5.5.

5.4.4 *Extracting and Categorising the Needs of SMEs Using the Balanced Scorecard*

In this step, the main needs of SMEs are classified and listed using the balanced scorecard and divided into four main categories: finance, customer, internal processes, and growth and learning. The SME needs of each category are then identified and extracted, and their measurement metrics are all listed in Table 5.5.

The hierarchical model of SMEs needs based on a balanced scorecard is also presented in Figure 5.6.

5.4.5 *Questionnaire*

Two questionnaires are used to collect data in this research. After categorising SME needs based on balanced scorecards and determining main criteria (financial, customer, internal business, innovation and learning) and their sub-criteria, the first questionnaire is distributed among the experts for drawing weight vectors and determining the relative importance of each criterion and sub-criterion towards

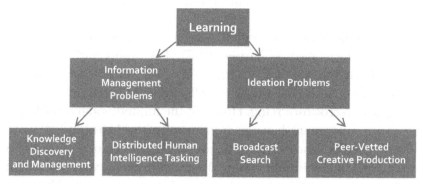

Figure 5.5. Learning applications of crowdsourcing in SMEs

Table 5.5.   SME needs based on a balanced scorecard

Balanced scorecard dimensions	SME needs	Measures
Financial (C1)	Cost reduction (S11) Return on assets (S12) Revenue growth (S13)	Value of products, value of available property, return on investment (amount of return on investment relative to investment cost), return on assets (distribution of annual profit as total company assets), return on sales, profitability, etc.
Customer (C2)	Customer satisfaction (S21) Customer value (S22) Delivery efficiency (S23)	Number of satisfied customers, market share, number of defects, amount of sales, order response time, timely delivery
Internal business (C3)	Waste reduction (S31) Supplier relationships (S32) Processes optimisation (S33)	Quality of services and processes, time of work (time from start to production of the product), number of parts and products delivered on time by suppliers, capacity utilisation, number of employees leaving work in the middle of work
Innovation and learning (C4)	Products and processes Innovation (S41) Human capital management (S42) Information flows (S43)	Number of new products and services, entry into new markets, employee satisfaction, level of trust and dissemination of information in the supply chain

the goal. Furthermore, pairwise comparisons tables associated with AHP are used to extract the opinions of decision makers. The second research questionnaire extracts the opinions of experts through the Quality Function Deployment (QFD) technique. This is done by

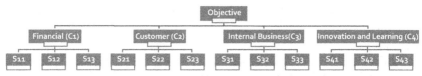

Figure 5.6.   The hierarchical model of SMEs needs

designing a relationship matrix, which is one of the main components of a QFD. In this matrix, the needs of SMEs are compared with the applications of crowdsourcing in SMEs and finally prioritised.

5.4.6 *Weighting SMEs Needs*

As explained before, by reviewing the articles and scientific texts, as well as consulting with experts, the needs are divided into four categories of main criteria (finance, customer, internal business, and innovation and learning) based on balanced scorecards, each has three sub-criteria, which are involved in the selection and ranking of options. After drawing a hierarchical structure for determining the weights of criteria, a questionnaire consisting of five questions (five pairwise comparisons matrices) is designed and presented to six experts. In this way, the viewpoint of decision makers is measured in relation to the importance of criteria and sub-criteria in the form of a pairwise comparisons questionnaire. The ranking of small and medium business needs can be seen in Table 5.6.

According to Table 5.6, the customer satisfaction (S21) with a weight of 0.245 is ranked first among 12 sub-criteria. Customer value (S22) and revenue growth (S13) ranked second and third with weights of 0.236 and 0.105, respectively. Finally, the relationship with suppliers (S32) with a weight of 0.15 is ranked last.

5.4.7 *Prioritising Crowdsourcing Applications in SMEs Using QFD Approach*

QFD, with a Japanese origin, is an organised process which is applied to define customers' qualitative wants and needs in each

Table 5.6.   Ranking SMEs needs

Weight	SMEs needs	Rank
0.245	Customer satisfaction	1
0.236	Customer value	2
0.105	Revenue growth	3
0.070	Human capital management	4
0.069	Cost reduction	5
0.066	Delivery efficiency	6
0.054	Return on investment	7
0.050	Process and product innovation	8
0.037	Waste reduction	9
0.031	Process improvement	10
0.022	Information flows	11
0.015	Relationship with suppliers	12

stage of the development of the service product, which requires the full cooperation of different parts of the organisation or institution for its proper deployment. The main reason to use QFD is that customers' qualitative wants and needs are applied in different stages with no attention to the service designers (Asadi, 2001). In this technique, quality encompasses operational, technical, manageable, and tangible actions to meet the customers' needs and expectations (Thakkar *et al.*, 2006). Tangible objectives of QFD can be summarised as designing with lower cost; eliminating regular technical changes; preliminary identifying production places that are critical; determining production processes; significantly reducing time for producing products and efficiently allocating resources; adjusting the quality of design and the planned quality; performing optimisation for competitive products; developing new products; analysing qualitative market data; identifying control points; reducing design changes; and reducing development costs and increasing market shares (Han *et al.*, 2001).

QFD Elements: Different tools and methods are used to achieve qualitative and QFD goals. The main tool to implement QFD is called Quality House which include the following (Rezaei, 2001):

(1) Customers' needs (WHAT)
(2) Planning matrix
(3) Technical requirements, the roof of the quality house (HOW)
(4) Relationship matrix
(5) Goals

Designing the Quality House Matrix and Prioritising Crowdsourcing Applications for SMEs HR: QFD has been implemented in different forms; the 4-steps and the 18-steps are among the most practical models (Zanjirchi & Torabi, 2008). This technique helps with the research of the quality house development and the information is so broad that there will be no need for taking other steps; therefore, the description of the quality house and its requirement sounds sufficient.

As mentioned before, the purpose of this study is to prioritise crowdsourcing applications for SMEs HR based on their needs; And as we have seen, the needs of SMEs are weighted with AHP and now we are going to use the QFD approach to examine these needs with crowdsourcing applications in SMEs and prioritise applications using the quality house and relationship matrix.

After extracting the crowdsourcing applications, we sought to create a relationship matrix to examine the extent to which each application is related to each of the needs. So, by forming this matrix and distributing it to the experts, we ask them to determine the intensity of each relationship in this matrix so that we could finally integrate all the answers to achieve the final prioritisation.

The important point here is that during a meeting with the experts, the applications are reviewed based on the classification presented in the research so that we can have a better understanding of the comparisons between the applications and the needs. The simplicity and fluency of the comparisons give rise to each of the applications. That is, for example, instead of bringing (finance — information management — discovery and information management), we briefly summarise it, i.e., "searching and gathering information". In general, applications in the relationship matrix are categorised and presented as Table 5.7.

In the next step, a quality house matrix is formed and experts are asked to determine the intensity of the relationship between the needs of SMEs and crowdsourcing applications based on the scale in Table 5.8.

Table 5.7. Classification of crowdsourcing applications in the relationship matrix

Dimension	Crowdsourcing applications
Finance	Searching and gathering information
	Analysing large amount of data
	Solving scientific and experimental problems
	Creating and selecting creative ideas
Competition	Searching and gathering information
	Analysing large amount of data
	Solving scientific and experimental problems
	Creating and selecting creative ideas
Learning	Searching and gathering information
	Analysing large amount of data
	Solving scientific and experimental problems
	Creating and selecting creative ideas

Table 5.8. Verbal expressions and corresponding numbers to relate needs to applications

Verbal phrase	Corresponding number
Poor Relationship	1
Medium Relationship	3
Strong Relationship	9

We then integrate the opinions of the experts using the arithmetic mean method. The results can be seen in the house of quality matrix in Table 5.9.

Finally, prioritisation of crowdsourcing applications using the human resources of small and medium-sized enterprises is described in Table 5.10.

5.5 Implications

With advancement and expansion of knowledge and technology in today's world, most innovations take place in the business environment and in the field of web-based businesses. Because new technologies and techniques are being identified and used in this field every day, all these up-to-date tools have always been created in order to make the best use of the human resources in the web space, because this way the available time and resources can be used in a more effective manner and it could be achieved in a wider range of specialisations. Many of these tools have been known and used for centuries and some years. But the arrival of new innovations and technologies has led to the development of more appropriate and successful models for the current conditions of human life and different societies.

In today's highly competitive economy and market, most of which are small and medium-sized enterprises and have been introduced as the main body of the economy, the only way to survive is innovation, which is the factor that differentiates and gains a competitive advantage over other competitors. So, the main question for many small and medium business owners is how to add innovation to the organisation or facilitate the process of achieving it? How can the potential of employees and the population in the web space be used as a shadow workforce in a targeted manner to add a competitive advantage to the organisation? Therefore, in this study, the theoretical foundations and background of crowdsourcing in small and medium companies are examined and its applications in these companies are classified according to the Brabham's model, the results of which are presented in the next section.

Table 5.9. Quality house matrix for crowdsourcing needs and applications for SMEs HR

	Crowdsourcing applications for SMEs	Needs of SMEs → Cost reduction	Return on investment	Revenue growth	Customer satisfaction	Customer value	Delivery efficiency
			Financial			**Customer**	
Finance	Searching and gathering information	9.0	5.0	7.8			
	Analysing large amount of data	9.0	5.0	7.8			
	Solving scientific and experimental problems	2.6	5.0	7.8	1.0	1.0	1.0
	Creating and selecting creative ideas	7.8	9.0	9.0	3.0	3.0	1.0
Competition	Searching and gathering information	6.6	4.6	6.2	5.0	5.0	2.0
	Analysing large amount of data	6.6	3.4	6.2	5.0	5.0	2.0
	Solving scientific and experimental problems	5.4	1.8	6.2	3.5	3.4	1.5
	Creating and selecting creative ideas	6.6	3.8	6.2	6.2	6.2	3.4
Learning	Searching and gathering information	4.0	1.5	3.8	3.7	3.7	
	Analysing large amount of data	2.0	2.0	2.6	3.7	3.7	
	Solving scientific and experimental problems	2.0	2.0	6.2	2.5	2.0	
	Creating and selecting creative ideas	4.0	2.5	5.0	4.2	3.8	1.0
	Weight of needs of SMEs	0.069	0.054	0.105	0.245	0.236	0.066

(Continued)

Table 5.9. (*Continued*)

Crowdsourcing applications for SMEs		Needs of SMEs						Relative weight of applications	Normal weight of applications
		Internal Process			Learning & Growth				
		Cost reduction	Relation with suppliers	Process improvement	Process and product innovation	Human capital management	Information flows		
Finance	Searching and gathering information	5.0		3.7	1.0	1.7	3.0	1.6	0.042
	Analysing large amount of data	9.0		5.0	1.0	1.7	3.0	1.8	0.047
	Solving scientific and experimental problems	3.0	1.5	3.0	1.7	1.0		2.1	0.054
	Creating and selecting creative ideas	3.0	1.5	3.5	2.3	2.0		3.5	0.090
Competition	Searching and gathering information	1.8	6.3	1.7	3.8	4.0	6.2	4.3	0.11
	Analysing large amount of data	1.4	6.3	1.5	4.0	3.5	5.0	4.1	0.106
	Solving scientific and experimental problems	1.0	6.3	3.0	5.5	4.6	6.2	3.4	0.09
	Creating and selecting creative ideas	1.4	4.2	3.4	9.0	5.0	4.6	5.2	0.134
Learning	Searching and gathering information	2.0	1.0	1.8	7.5	6.2	5.0	3.3	0.086
	Analysing large amount of data	2.3	1.0	1.8	6.0	5.0	5.0	3.1	0.08
	Solving scientific and experimental problems	1.0	1.0	1.5	4.6	2.2	3.4	2.4	0.062
	Creating and selecting creative ideas	1.0	1.0	1.5	9.0	7.4	6.2	3.9	0.1
Weight of needs of SMEs		0.037	0.015	0.033	0.050	0.070	0.022		

Table 5.10. Prioritisation of crowdsourcing applications in SMEs

Rank	Crowdsourcing application	Weight
1	Competitive_Ideation_Producing creative products	0.134
2	Competitive_Information management_searching and gathering information	0.110
3	Competitive_Information management_Data analysis	0.106
4	Learning_Ideation_Producing creative products	0.100
5	Finance_Ideation_Producing creative products	0.090
6	Competitive_Ideation_Solving scientific and experimental problems	0.090
7	Learning_Information management_searching and gathering information	0.086
8	Learning_Information management_Data analysis	0.080
9	Learning_Ideation_Solving scientific and experimental problems	0.062
10	Finance_Ideation_Solving scientific and experimental problems	0.054
11	Finance_Information management_Data analysis	0.047
12	Finance_Information management_searching and gathering information	0.042

5.6 Conclusion

With a developing Internet and the growth of Web 2.0, many mechanisms, tools, and technologies are designed and implemented to facilitate the achievement of innovation as well as simplify all operations and problems. One of these tools and mechanisms is crowdsourcing, a process that uses the population on the organisation's internal network and web space to access low-cost online manpower, thereby getting things done in less time, with higher quality, and at lower cost. The concept is less than 20 years old, but because of its success and positive results, it has quickly become popular among business executives.

One of the most prominent features that has emerged in many economies within the last two decades is the role and position of small and medium-sized enterprises, but many small and

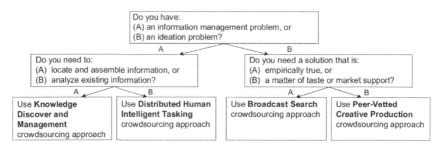

Figure 5.7. Decision tree for determining suitable crowdsourcing type based on problem (Brabham *et al.*, 2014)

medium-sized enterprises have difficulty in developing their human resources innovation and problem-solving in spite of having a noticeable capital in research and development. In order to solve this problem, crowdsourcing tools are used in this study to facilitate the access to innovation in SMEs which was done through extracting main SME needs based on balanced scorecards and then categorising the applications based on "Problem Solving Framework of Crowdsourcing" which presented by Brabham.

In other word, during this research, we attempt to answer the following 3 questions:

- What are the core needs of SMEs and what is the most important need that should be the first in their priorities?
- What are the applications of crowdsourcing that can meet the needs of SMEs and how are they classified?
- What is the best applications of crowdsourcing to meet SME needs?

Once a problem has been defined and solution parameters are known, SMEs managers or HR may pose a few simple questions to home in on the appropriate crowdsourcing approach (Figure 5.7).

The first decision is whether a problem is an information management issue or an ideation subject. Given an information management issue, one must then decide whether the information needs to be located and assembled, leading to a Knowledge Discover and Management crowdsourcing method, or whether the information that is already in hand needs to be analysed, leading to a Distributed Human Intelligent Tasking crowdsourcing method. Given an ideation subject, one must determine whether the solution will be empirically provable, leading to a Broadcast Search crowdsourcing method, or a matter of taste or market support, leading to a Peer-Vetted Creative Production crowdsourcing method.

To help managers and executives of small and medium enterprises in identifying their problems and needs, as well as selecting appropriate applications of crowdsourcing based on the above algorithm, the needs are first identified by the AHP method and crowdsourcing applications were prioritised by the QFD method, and the following results are obtained.

In the results of prioritising the dimensions related to SME needs; the customer dimension is of the highest importance, followed by finance, growth and learning, and internal processes. Thus, it is important to note that contrary to the perception of many SMEs managers who consider the availability of financial resources as the first priority and measure of success, customer satisfaction and value can be more important factors for success in small and medium enterprises. Therefore, the first priority of owners and managers of small and medium companies should be in order to maintain and develop customers, and consequently, more applications of crowdsourcing are needed and considered that can meet customer needs and create value for customers.

According to the application prioritisation table (Table 5.10), it can be seen that crowdsourcing applications that create a competitive advantage for the company are preferred because in addition to these applications being directly related to enhancing the customer demand and value, it also creates a financial advantage for them to participate and contribute to the improvement of macroeconomic conditions. On the other hand, the existence of three applications of ideation to produce a creative product among the five applications with the highest priority is not surprising and can be well understood because these applications, in addition to adding a higher level of innovation to other systems and products, have a special relationship with the demand and market share and the number of satisfied customers because the demands, plans and ideas come out of the customers' hearts and are raised, i.e. the customers themselves give ideas or choose the best among the existing ideas and products and services have been offered based on their views.

Paying attention to the table of prioritisation of applications, we will find that among the three groups of financial, competitive, and learning, producing creative products is the first priority, then applications related to search and data collection, data analysis, and finally solving scientific and experimental problems, which can be understood that one of the main concerns of SMEs is creating and innovating their human resources or facilitating access to them because it can affect all aspects of SME needs and help improve them. According to the results, the effectiveness of competitive applications on SME needs is more than learning applications which is more than financial applications.

5.7 Suggestions and Further Research

Leaders and managers of SMEs can make fundamental changes in various dimensions by using crowdsourcing applications in their companies. These changes could include improving customer experience and satisfaction, developing human resource learning and engagement, designing new products and services, enhancing their competitiveness and revenue growth, but the important point here is to providing crowdsourcing processes that lead to customer satisfaction, because customer satisfaction is the most important need for these enterprises.

Also, managers have to consider the competitive crowdsourcing platforms specially, because in addition to this type of applications and in particular the producing of the creative products can affect and cover the diverse needs of SMEs, it can also have a direct impact on improving their management and financial growth.

SMEs should be innovative in choosing applications according to the situation of the company, and especially with the help of the decision tree for determining suitable crowdsourcing type, choose an application model that has the most added value for them.

Finally, despite identifying and prioritising crowdsourcing applications in SMEs and presenting a crowdsourcing method selection model, managers should place special emphasis on motivational-training, coaching, supporting, financial and non-financial compensation, and participatory and social activities of human resources because these need to be provided to make crowdsourcing more active, creative, and at the same time much more efficient and effective.

Because a lot of research on crowdsourcing in general and in small and medium-sized companies in particular has not been done, the lack of theoretical background in this field for the research literature is an important limitation in the present study. Therefore, in order to expand scientific research in this field, this research can be repeated with greater depth and scope. Small and medium-sized companies also face many challenges and obstacles in implementing various applications of crowdsourcing that have not been addressed in this study. Therefore, identifying the challenges and barriers to using outsourcing in SMEs and then classifying and prioritising them is another issue that researchers can consider in the future.

Given that the applications of outsourcing in SMEs have been identified and categorised based on researchers' perceptions of articles and scientific texts, future researchers can list and categorise applications more accurately by interviewing SMEs managers and experts in the field of outsourcing to achieve broad and complete crowdsourcing applications in these enterprises.

References

Abid, A. A., Mahbubur, R. M. & Scheepers, H. (2011). Experienced benefits and barriers of e-business technology adoption by SME suppliers. In *Communications of the IBIMA*, 1–11. http://www.ibimapublishing. com/journals/CIBIMA/cibima.html. Vol. 2011, Article ID 791778, 11pages: DOI: 10.5171/2011.7917780.

Afonso, H. & Cabrita, M. R. (2015). Developing a lean supply chain performance framework in a SME: A perspective based on the balanced scorecard. *Procedia Engineering, 131*, 270–279.

Akhavan, P., Fathian, M., & Hoorali, M. (2008). E-readiness assessment of non-profit ICT SMEs in a developing country: The case of Iran. *Technovation, 28*(9), 578–590. [in Persian]

Asadi, A. (2001). Understanding, investigating and analyzing the needs of customers of Armelat Company, manufacturer of industrial hard flooring, using QFD quality attributes development method. Master's thesis of Industrial Engineering, Tarbiat Modares University, Tehran, Iran. [in Persian]

Barth, J. R., Caprio, G. & Levine, R. (2008). *Rethinking Banking Regulation: Till Angels Govern.* Cambridge University Press, New York, NY.

Brabham, D. C. (2012). *Crowdsourcing: A model for leveraging online communities.* In *The Participatory Cultures Handbook.* Routledge.

Brabham, D. C. (2013a). *Crowdsourcing.* The MIT Press, Boston, MA.

Brabham, D. C. (2013b). Using crowdsourcing in government. IBM Center for The Business of Government, Washington, DC.

Brabham, D. C., Ribisl, K. M., Kirchner, T. R., & Bernhardt, J. M. (2014). Crowdsourcing applications for public health. *American Journal of Preventive Medicine, 46*(2), 179–87. doi:10.1016/j.amepre.2013.10.016

Central Bank of I.R. Iran. (2015). The SME definition in Iran. Available at: https://www.cbi.ir/showitem/12096.aspx [in Persian]

Doan, A., Ramakrishnan, R., & Halevy, A. Y. (2011). Crowdsourcing systems on the world-wide web. *Communications of the ACM, 54*(4), 86–96.

Estellés-Arolas, E. & González-Ladrón-de-Guevara, F. (2012). Towards an integrated crowdsourcing definition. *Journal of Information Science, 38*(2), 189–200.

European Commission. (2004). User guide to the SME definition. Available at: https://ec.europa.eu/regional_policy/sources/conferences/state-aid/sme/smedefinitionguide_en.pdf

Gibson, T. & Vaart, H. J. van der. (2008). *Defining SMEs: A Less Imperfect Way of Defining Small and Medium Enterprises in Developing Countries.* Brookings Global Economy and Development.

Gilaninia, S., Mousavian, S. J., Omidvari, N., Bakhshalipour, A., Bakhshalipour, A., Eftekhari, F., & Zadbagher, S. (2012). The role of ICT in performance of small and medium enterprises. *Interdisciplinary Journal of Contemporary Research in Business, 32*, 833–839. [in Persian]

Green, C. J., Kirkpatrick, C. H., & Murinde, V. (2005). *Finance and Development: Surveys of Theory, Evidence and Policy.* Edward Elgar, Cheltenham, UK.

Han, S. B., Chen, S. K., Ebrahimpour, M., & Sodhi, M. S. (2001). A conceptual QFD planning model. *International Journal of Quality and Reliability Management, 18*(8), 796–812.

Hsu, C.-H., Chang, A.-Y., & Luo, W. (2017). Identifying key performance factors for sustainability development of SMEs: Integrating QFD and fuzzy MADM methods. *Journal of Cleaner Production, 161*, 629–645.

Howe, J. (2008). *Crowdsourcing: How the Power of the Crowd is driving the Future of Business.* Business Books, Great Britain.

Keshtkar, M., Pishvaei, M. S., & Mohammadi, A. (2012). *Crowdsourcing. The Impeller of Modern Business,* Vol. 1. Industrial Management Organization. [in Persian]

Kia Kajoori, K., Roudgarnezhad, F., & Nobati, A. (2007). Providing a conceptual model for investigating barriers to e-commerce in entrepreneurship in Iran (SMEs). In *The 2nd International Conference on E-commerce and World Business.* [in Persian]

Lawrence, J. E. (2011). The growth of e-commerce in developing countries: An exploratory study of opportunities and challenges for SMEs. *International Journal of ICT Research and Development in Africa, 28*(9), 5–28.

Libert, B., & Spector, J. (2007). *We Are Smarter Than Me: How to Unleash the Power of Crowds in Your Business,* 1st edition. FT Press.

Lloyd-Reason, L., & Sear, L. (2007). *Trading Places- SMEs in the Global Economy: A Critical Research Handbook.* Edward Elgar, Cheltenham, UK.

Lowry, G. R., & Turner, R. L. (2007). *Information Systems and Technology Education: From The University To The Workplac*e. doi: 10.4018/978-1-59904-114-8

Maiolini, R., & Naggi, R. (2011). Crowdsourcing and SMEs: Opportunities and challenges. In D'Atri, A., Ferrara, M., George, J., Spagnoletti, P. (Eds.), *Information Technology and Innovation Trends in Organizations.* Physica-Verlag, HD.

Malone, T. W., Laubacher, R., & Dellarocas, C. (2010). Harnessing crowds: Mapping the genome of collective intelligence. MIT Sloan School Working Paper, No. 4 732–09.

Mansor, M. F., Halim, H., & Ahmad, N. (2018a). Leveraging crowdsourcing practices in small and medium enterprises (SMEs). *Journal of Entrepreneurship Education, 21*(4), 99–111.

Mansor, M. F., Halim, H., & Ahmad, N. (2018b). Exploring crowdsourcing practices and benefits: Validation from small and medium enterprises (SMEs) business owners. In 2nd Conference on Technology &

Operations Management (2ndCTOM), February 26–27, 2018, Universiti Utara Malaysia, Kedah, Malaysia. (Unpublished)

Metellus, R. S. (2017). Crowdsourcing as a support mechanism for small and medium-sized enterprises: A case study in Haiti.

Mwila, N. K. (2013). *Small and Medium Enterprises: Concepts, Methodologies, Tools, and Applications; Crowdsourcing in Small and Medium Sized Enterprises*, pp. 1293–1307. IGI Global.

Noori, R., & Meshkat Zakeri, Z. (2021). Job security, digital skills and competencies in banking sector; are they related?. *Journal of Human Resource Management, 11*(1), 151–169. doi: 10.22034/jhrs.2021.130510.

Oliveira, F., Ramos, I., & Santos, L. (2010). Definition of crowdsourcing innovation service for the European SMEs. In *ICWE'10: Proceedings of the 10th International Conference On Current Trends In Web Engineering*, pp. 412–416.

Pourkiani, M., & Sadeghi, Z. (2012). Crowdsourcing of a modern strategy in today's trade. In *The 2nd National Conference on Modern Management Science*. Hakim Jorjani Institute of Higher Education. [in Persian]

Qin, S., Van Der Velde, D., Chatzakis, E. *et al.* (2016). Exploring barriers and opportunities in adopting crowdsourcing based new product development in manufacturing SMEs. *Chinese Journal of Mechanical Engineering, 29*, 1052–1066.

Rezaei, K. (2001). *QFD, A Customer-Oriented Approach to Design and Improve Product Quality*, Vol. 2. [in Persian]

Surowiecki, J. (2004). *The Wisdom of Crowds: Why the Many are Smarter than the Few and How Collective*. Wisdom Shapes. By. Nikki Springer.

Thakkar, J., Deshmukh, S. G, & Shastree, A. (2006). A quality function deployment (QFD) and force field analysis Approach. *Quality Assurance in Education, 14*(1), 54–74.

Turban, E., Outland, J., King, D., Lee, J. K., & Liang, T.-P. (2018). *Electronic Commerce; A Managerial and Social Networks Perspective*. Springer Texts in Business and Economics.

Yazdani Zangane, M. (2011). Effective factors of the e-commerce acceptance by SMEs in agriculture section". *Parks and Growth Centers Journal, 5*, 59–64. [in Persian]

Zanjirchi, M., & Torabi, Z. (2008). QFD in improving banking services quality. *Tadbir Journal, 193*, 44–48. [in Persian]

Chapter 6

Team Performance and the Development of Iranian Digital Start-ups: The Mediating Role of Employee Voice

Elahe Hosseini

Faculty of Management, Yazd University, Yazd, Iran

elahe.hosseini@stu.yazd.ac.ir

Mehdi Tajpour

Faculty of Entrepreneurship, University of Tehran, Iran

tajpour@ut.ac.ir

Aidin Salamzadeh*

Faculty of Management, University of Tehran, Iran

salamzadeh@ut.ac.ir

Ali Ahmadi

Smith School of Business at Queen's University, Kingston,
Ontario, Canada

21aa80@queensu.ca

* Corresponding author

Abstract: Team performance is one of the means to confront rapid change from human resource experts' point of view. So constant change in the work environment and daily work-related activities requires sharing comments and ideas as well as an increase in the need for continuous learning. Thus, inattention to employee voice can bring serious disadvantages to firms, because without regarding employees' expression of opinions, a firm cannot operate in a dynamic environment and will eventually lose its competitiveness in this contentious business environment. Therefore, this research aims to discuss the influence of team performance on the development of digital start-up companies with the mediating role of employee voice. In terms of objective, this is quantitative applied research. The statistical population of this research is the employees of 113 international Iranian digital start-up companies in the medical sector, covering 15% of the country's aggregate exports in 2019 and 2020, estimated as 423 individuals. The sample size was calculated as 201 people using the Cochran formula. In order to collect the data, a standard questionnaire with 24 questions with a five-point Likert scale was used. Finally, the data were analysed using Smart PLS 3 software. The results showed that cognitive empowerment, emotional commitment, making innovation climate, and sharing knowledge, with the mediating role of employee voice, positively influence the success and survival of a firm. In other words, team performance of firms is an attitude towards employee loyalty and a continuous process that can lead to firm development by the contribution of individuals in decision-making processes. Team performance can be considered the main factor in learning and innovation, leading to a facilitation of trust between employees and creating new ideas through conversation. Performance at the team level helps members better comprehend how they work with each other and learn ways to improve self-management to earn high levels of efficiency and effectiveness.

Keywords: Team performance, Employee voice, Innovative collaboration, Knowledge-based companies.

6.1 Introduction

Successful companies, especially digital start-up companies, are the ones that constantly create new knowledge, distribute it widely across the firm, and rapidly apply them in new technologies and products. More research and development activities are done in these firms, and growth and development in them mostly rely on developing technology and new knowledge (Salamzadeh *et al.*, 2021; Ziyae *et al.*, 2019). Digital start-up companies are the axis of development and transformation in the economy, especially in developing countries. In these companies, employees are the main capital, and they can be more valuable when the individuals' knowledge is shared with people inside and outside of the firm (Hosseini *et al.*, 2020). Due to the fact that companies are getting more team-oriented, and teams are considered as the main unit of firms, numerous studies were conducted in an effort to explore team performance. That is why effective teams play a vital role for digital start-up companies (Yang *et al.*, 2011; Salamzadeh & Dana, 2020). Furthermore, many of the employees in digital start-up companies do their cognitive and intellectual tasks as teams, making team-based performance a challenge for human resource management scholars (Vashdi *et al.*, 2007). So focusing on concepts like team performance is an important factor for team effectiveness, as it is one of the ways to confront change (Clarck, 2019). Thus, managers and employees of this era not only should be capable performers, but also fast learners (van der Lippe & Lippényi, 2020). So constant change in work environment and everyday work tasks require a continuous sharing of knowledge and ideas (Cohen & Olsen, 2015). Thus, disregard towards employees expression of opinions can bring critical outcomes and lead to a loss of competitive advantage over time (Zhang & Edgar, 2021). When uncertainty is high, employees working roles cannot get completely constructed. So in such environments, roles should reshape dynamically in response to the environment and emerging changes (Hosseini *et al.*, 2020; Tajpour, 2018). Therefore, team performance can help firm development as an essential part of gaining competitive advantage due to the permanent need for reaction in the ever-changing environment of firms and the thought of implementing the most suitable method (Wiedow & Konradt, 2011). Moreover, team performance increases employee awareness about objectives, strategies, and work environments. It can turn into a crucial tool to achieve the best way of implementation by creating a shared understanding, transparency, and a representation of differences in employee roles (Schippers *et al.*, 2007).

It is essential to note that digital start-up companies are influential in society, and they turn into the centre for the promotion of science, technology, innovation, talent nourishment, empowerment and training of thinkers, researchers, and specialists (Salamzadeh, 2018). In this regard, in order to create a relation between human resource management and development of digital start-up companies, while considering the value and importance of team performance and voice in the development and improvement of digital start-up companies, one major problem is that the connection between team performance and digital start-up companies has not been extensively developed yet. So this study helps the literature of team performance and employee voice in two ways. First, discovering the influence of team performance (namely, psychological empowerment, emotional commitment, innovation climate, and knowledge sharing) on the development of digital start-up companies. Second, explaining how team performance leads to the expression of employees' ideas and thoughts. Also, this study discusses the influence of team performance on digital start-up companies with the mediating role of employee voice because these firms are among the important factors of development and growth in society; therefore, ideas and opinions of employees are of grave importance in order to maintain competitive advantage. Moreover, yet another reason for digital start-up firms' success is the crucial role of human resources. When the manager in digital start-up companies respects the employees and encourages them to innovate and generate ideas, they feel that their leader or manager is supportive of them. In this atmosphere, they can share their experience with one another and make correct decisions in times of crisis. Finally, this study intends to assess the relationship between the two dimensions and present it to the selected digital start-up companies. In terms of research innovation, it can be stated that such research has not been conducted in the Iranian industry. So the objective of this research is to study the influence of team performance on digital start-up companies' development with the mediating role of employee voice.

6.2 Theoretical Foundations

Teams and work-teams have become rather common words in management circles, and companies are dependent on group work and teamwork. As the main factor of learning and innovation, teams facilitate trust between employees, information and knowledge sharing, and creating new ideas using discussion and conversation (Babnik *et al.*, 2014). Firm managers need to support and encourage team learning to develop service for customers (Suh & Jung, 2021). Performance management at the team level helps the members better understand how they can work with each other and improve self-management to reach higher levels of efficiency and effectiveness (Yuan & van Knippenberg, 2021). Factors such as structure design, job's social attributes, team leader behaviour, and team composition affect team effectiveness via internal team processes between members and interaction with the environment. Team performance indicators depend on teams' final objective, specific performance standards, and factors like activity-level deliverables, customer service, individual satisfaction, and financial outcomes. Synergy in teams aligns individual behaviour in order to bring up proactive effort for team issues. Thus, synergy has a positive impact on the growth and development of firms (Zoltan, 2014). Therefore, in order to advance organisational goals, managers need employees in multi-membered teams with complementary specialities. It seems team performance is a response to global economy competitions and continuous technologic innovations that had led to the complication of environmental circumstances, and thus more need for effective problem-solving in firms. In fact, it can be stated that team performance is a concept regenerated from traditional units, main characteristics of theories, and modern management approaches (Gelfand *et al.*, 2007). The significant impact of teamwork culture is so important that management science scholars believe it is necessary to acquire sustainable competitive advantage in today's vibrant environment. Team performance discusses the fact that team members, in a firm environment, act to achieve the firm's objectives by interdependent duty and multiple sources of information gained from knowledge-sharing and their individual skills (Salamzadeh & Markovic, 2018). Therefore, to achieve those objectives, they require enough flexibility to accept various roles in their teams.

H: Team performance has a positive influence on the mediating role of employee voice.

Human resource is the most important factor of efficiency in organisations and societies. The topic of empowerment, especially from a psychological approach, is among the modern viewpoints in human resource management. Empowered employees show more effective team performance and bring higher efficiency results for the organisations, making them more progressive and successful than their competitors. Capability is defined as the delegation of authority by endowing legal power to others. In this way, it helps employees to improve their self-confidence and overcome helplessness and inability (Boğan & Dedeoğlu, 2017). Still, several gaps are remaining in the literature. Therefore, empowerment requires a different kind of moral and social behaviour, and use of group work, collaborative tools, ease of access to information sources, and bilateral moral relations between employees. Put into one word: leadership based on honesty (Saeida Ardekani *et al.*, 2020; Yaghoobi *et al.*, 2018).

Empowerment is considered a communication construct that emphasises sharing firm resources and clientele contribution to decision-making processes (Ahearne *et al.*, 2005). The concept of empowerment requires individual enthusiasm at work by delegation to lower levels in which decisions can be made and executed (Thomas & Velthouse, 1990). Psychological empowerment is described as a driver or motive in teams, showing that manager's behaviour is focused on the team because competent managers share their power with the employees by being responsible and delegate to them, engaging them in the decision-making process

(Chen *et al.*, 2007). Moreover, it can be stated that managers can succeed in their organisations by empowering their employees, giving them the freedom to create new solutions for issues, and even encourage them to move towards the organisation's vision (Özaralli, 2015). Empowerment is derived originally from the theory of collaborative management (Spreitzer, 1995). Hence, many firms invest in programmes to improve their employee engagement. Employees get more engaged when they "have an action of their own" and are not treated as robots to repeat a simple and repetitive task, showing that organisations are growing and developing (Welbourne, 2011). Based on social transaction theory, when employees understand that they are receiving organisational support, they feel the urge to reciprocate this positive behaviour towards the firm (Wayne *et al.*, 1997). The critical point that can be noted in social transaction theory is that certain behaviours derived from the empowerment approach can improve employees' behaviour as well. In addition, by loudening their voice, they can express and share their ideas and thoughts with their colleagues and managers in favour of the organisation and even more than their predefined responsibility (Elsetouhi *et al.*, 2018).

H1a: Psychological empowerment has a meaningful influence on the development of digital start-up companies.
H1b: Psychological empowerment has a meaningful influence on the development of digital start-up companies with the mediating role of employee voice.

Commitment creates a feeling of collective identity between the people inside a firm, and as a result of that, it leads to social behaviours such as sharing ideas and thoughts voluntarily (Allen *et al.*, 2016). Committed human resources play an essential role in firms' success and survival (Jayabalan *et al.*, n.d.). Accordingly, organisational commitment consists of positive or negative attitudes from employees towards the whole organisation and not just the job title. In organisational commitment, the individual has a strong feeling of loyalty towards the organisation and identifies himself with that feeling (Popoola, 2009). In other words, organisational commitment is a viewpoint on employee loyalty towards an organisation in a continuous process that results in firm success by involving individuals in organisational decision making and their attention to the firm (Oyewobi *et al.*, 2019). Commitment consists of three dimensions, namely emotional, normative, and continuous. In this study, the emotional dimension is discussed (Martin-Perez & Martin-Cruz, 2015). Emotional commitment is the emotional attachment of employees towards an organisation that is determined by their happiness with the firm and their willingness to stay in the firm (Mckenna, 2005). In this type of commitment, people consider working inside the organisation as their responsibility or duty. Emotional commitment causes employees to stay in the firm because of a sense of loyalty or obligation and feel that they are doing the correct thing. This type of commitment increases by the internal pressure that arises from norms, leading to long-term commitment for the whole organisation (Petty & Hill, 2005). When managers let employees get involved with decision making by giving suggestions or ideas, employee commitment increases significantly (Anyango *et al.*, 2015).

In order to obtain employee commitment, firms should be sensitive towards employee needs in the workplace and consider their views and opinions. If the organisation cannot pay proper attention to employee voice, it can damage all organisational processes and employee commitment (Park & Nawakitphaitoon, 2018). Emotional commitment points out the emotional attachment of an individual to the organisation. In more details, emotional commitment is about employees' emotional attachment to how the organisation determines their identity (Ashkanasy, 2007). Emotional commitment refers to the degree of commitment that an individual has towards the firm, the firm's expression of individual's identity, and the amount of active involvement in organisational processes (Kim *et al.*, 2018). Therefore, emotional commitment is an outcome of employee tendency to become committed and an indicator of their mental evaluation of its probabilities at a particular time

(Gunlu *et al.*, 2010). So it can be expected that emotional commitment increases if job satisfaction increases.

H2a: Emotional commitment has a meaningful influence on the development of digital start-up companies.
H2b: Emotional commitment has a meaningful influence on the development of digital start-up companies with the mediating role of employee voice.

Climate is defined as the perception of individuals from the environment (García-Buades *et al.*, 2015). Innovation climate is defined as the general financial, economic, technological, social, and cultural environment of companies (Lawal *et al.*, 2018). Innovation climate is the common understanding of team members and organisation about methods, know-how, and behaviours that promote a new generation of knowledge in the firm (Moolenaar *et al.*, 2010). The human resource development system in every organisation should develop new ways to modify employee management, which positively impact the development of the firm and employee efficiency. Thus, it is considered among the important factors of firm survival, and its performance is dependent on human resource empowerment (Boğan & Dedeoğlu, 2017). Despite the competition in various arenas, managers intend to pay attention to creating innovation through understanding and creating a climate suitable for creating innovation in which the ability to express creativity and improvement of efficiency becomes possible (Tajpour *et al.*, 2020a). All organisations require new thoughts and novel ideas in order to survive. Creating ideas and new processes is a path through which firms can adapt to the external dynamic environment and acquire a competitive advantage (Tsai, 2011). When employees are satisfied with their job, it is more probable that they become more committed to the organisation as well (Kim *et al.*, 2018). Management should always proactively be ready to hear ideas from whoever is present in the firm, rather than inactively waiting for them to be presented. There are numerous problems and hindrances in the face of innovation that managers need to get rid of and, by supporting creative and innovative employees, create a proper context for developing innovation in their firms (Tajpour *et al.*, 2020). Based on the circumstances and the innovative climate, when team members face specific issues and problems, they get seriously involved in teamwork and interact with each other to find suitable solutions (Tsai, 2011). The main prerequisite to innovation is influencing human resources by strategic human resource actions, for it increases employees' desire and motivation for innovation, thus letting the knowledge and speciality be identified and implemented inside the organisation (Scarbrough, 2003).

H3a: Innovative climate has a positive influence on the development of digital start-up companies.
H3b: Innovative climate has a positive influence on the development of digital start-up companies with the mediating effect of employee voice.

Knowledge sharing is a complicated process with a handful of inhibitor factors and obstacles that affect its performance. Because it is one of the critical steps in a knowledge management programme, managers should identify the deterrents and provide solutions to facilitate them before developing a knowledge management strategy (Cohen & Olsen, 2015). Since sharing knowledge increases innovation and leads to organisational learning, it can be of paramount help to improve individual and organisational performance (Rahman *et al.*, 2018). Sharing knowledge is the process of identifying, distributing and exploiting the current knowledge to solve issues than the past more favourably. Sharing knowledge is about volunteer interactions between employees based on shared organisational aspects and moral norms, habits, and particular behaviours (Sabokro *et al.*, 2018). Some researchers believe that empowerment has to be noted for creating positive individual and organisational outcomes in digital start-up companies. So it can be stated that maintaining cohesion between values and behaviours of leaders is of crucial importance for employees and leaders relations (Boğan &

Dedeoğlu, 2017). The existence of a voice is desirable for employees because their opinions, worries, opportunities, and facilities in an organisation can alleviate their discontent. People that cannot express their opinions, ideas, and information and should stay silent, mostly tend to anxiety, stress, dissatisfaction, and depression, so they lose interest in their jobs, and their commitment plummets as well, leading eventually to quitting. Among the reasons for the importance of knowledge-sharing is that it reduces costs and new product development time and improves performance and customer service to develop digital start-up companies (Salamzadeh *et al.*, 2017, 2018).

H4a: Sharing knowledge has a positive influence on the development of digital start-up companies.
H4b: Sharing knowledge has a positive influence on the development of digital start-up companies with the mediating effect of employee's voice.

6.3 The Mediating Role of Employee Voice

Researchers believe that research about employee voice has exponentially increased in the past few years (Mowbray *et al.*, 2015). The issue of employee voice and research about it is of grand importance in different aspects. Firstly, presenting constructive suggestions is the first step in the innovation process. Secondly, unlike organisational silence, employee voice reflects employees' discontent about the status quo with an intent to fix the errors and mistakes, improve processes, and present new approaches to solving organisational issues. Aside from that, employee voice can identify a handful of employees' competencies (Fuller *et al.*, 2007). Many employees demand a chance for their voice to be heard, speaking about things that matter to them (Bryson *et al.*, 2006). Moreover, other researchers emphasised the value of employees as the precious source of expressing voice, suggestions, opinions for addressing and solving critical and work-related issues (Detert & Burris, 2007). Employees can share their knowledge, information, and ideas using their voice

(Nechanska *et al.*, 2020). It can be argued that employee involvement can play a central role in improving and developing digital start-up companies. Thus, understanding the voice of employees in any group at work is essential (Machokoto & Dzvimbo, 2020). Furthermore, research shows that employee voice is the most critical factor influencing management and the first essential prerequisite for advancing towards desirable objectives (Macey & Schneider, 2008).

6.4 Research Method

The type of the current study is descriptive-correlative research conducted using structural modelling (Dana & Dana, 2005). In this research, three team performance variables were considered independent variables, and the development of digital start-up companies and employee voice has been considered mediating variables by the researchers (Figure 6.1). The statistical population of this research was the employees of 113 digital start-up international Iranian companies in the medical sector, covering 15% of the country's aggregate exports in 2019 and 2020, estimated as 423 individuals. The sample size was calculated as 201 people using the Cochran formula (Dana & Dumez, 2015). In order to collect the data, a standard questionnaire with 24 questions with a five-point Likert scale (1. Strongly disagree to 5. Strongly agree) was designed and distributed online. In conclusion, the data was analysed by Smart PLS 3 software. PLS does not require normal data and has reliability for sample sizes less than 200.

6.5 Results

6.5.1 *Model Fitness (Measurement, Constructs and Overall)*

In order to evaluate the model fitness, it was analysed in three levels of measurement (reliability and validity), structural, and overall. In order to make sure about the accuracy and authenticity of the research results, technical aspects of the questionnaire were evaluated using various indexes. In order to evaluate the reliability of the questionnaire in this study, structural and content validity was used. For that purpose, firstly, a version of the questionnaire was handed to seven CEOs of digital start-up companies and university scholars to assess the reliability of the questionnaire, then their opinions and views were added to the previous version. In order to appraise the validity of the tool that measures research variables, the Cronbach alpha coefficient and combined validity of all the variables were assessed more than the acceptable limit of 0.7. So it can be claimed that the measurement tool has good validity as well.

Later on, to assess the reliability of the questionnaire, the least partial squares method was used. In this method, reliability is evaluated by two criteria of factor loads and combined reliability. Factor load was derived between 0 and 1, showing evident variable (question) power in assessing the hidden variable (main variable). The closer this number is to 1, the more powerful the question gets. The criterion for correct factor load coefficients is 0.4 (Hosseini *et al.*, 2020). The reliability and validity of the measurement model are reported in Table 6.2. In this study, as is evident in Table 6.2, all coefficients support the correctness of this criterion.

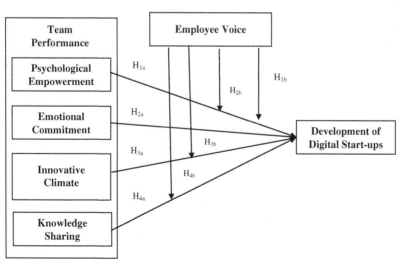

Figure 6.1. Research conceptual framework

Assessments show that the value of Cronbach alpha and combined reliability of all constructs is more than 0.7; thus, this study's constructs are desirably reliable. Furthermore, analysing average variance extracted criterion and shared reliability shows that all constructs were more than the acceptable limit of 0.5; so this study's constructs are desirably and convergently valid. According to Table 6.2, convergent validity is acceptable in all indexes because all indexes have average variance extracted more than 0.5.

In order to assess convergent validity, the average variance extracted index was used, and to evaluate divergent validity, the square root of average variance extracted squared was used. As shown in Table 6.2, the value for average variance extracted is more than the accepted minimum of 0.5; thus, research constructs are essentially convergently valid as well. Furthermore, according to the value for the square root of average variance extracted, it was more than the correlation between the aforementioned variable with other variables. Divergent validity is acceptable when the matrix's main diagonal is more than the values below their rows (Fornell & Larcker, 1981). Therefore, it can be claimed that these variables are valid, and their divergent validity is confirmed (Table 6.1).

Table 6.1.   The relations between variables and questionnaire

Variables	Statements	Cronbach's Alpha	Reference
Psychological Empowerment	1–4	0.816	Elsetouhi *et al.* (2018)
Emotional Commitment	5–8	0.820	Billingham and Sack (1987)
Innovative Climate	9–12	0.810	García-Buades *et al.* (2015)
Knowledge Sharing	13–16	0.723	Wang and Wang (2012)
Employee Voice	17–20	0.758	Van Dyne and LePine (1998)
Development of Digital Start-ups	21–24	0.738	Cirera and Muzi (2016)

Table 6.2.   Combined reliability, shared reliability, and convergent validity

Constructs	Variables	CR	rh-o	AVE	R^2	Q^2
Team Performance	Psychological Empowerment	0.881	0.854	0.654	–	–
	Emotional Commitment	0.881	0.825	0.650	–	–
	Innovative Climate	0.870	0.857	0.629	–	–
	Knowledge Sharing	0.832	0.736	0.559	–	–
Employee Voice	–	0.716	0.762	0.523	0.453	0.324
Development of Digital Start-ups	–	0.835	0.760	0.561	0.486	0.406

Based on the reported tables and output results from Smart PLS 3 software in Tables 6.2 and 6.3, measurement models have suitable validity (convergent and divergent) and reliability (factor load, combined reliability coefficient, and Cronbach alpha). In order to assess the fitness of the research structure model using the partial least squares method, various criteria are used. The first and foremost one of them is the T-value. Structural model fitness using T coefficients has to show more than 1.96 to confirm with, 95% confidence level, to be meaningful. Figure 6.2 illustrates the results of the hypotheses.

6.5.2 *Coefficient of Determination*

The second criterion to evaluate the structural model fitness in research is R^2 coefficients, related to the model's hidden endogenous variables. This criterion is used to assess the intensity of relations between constructs, yet it applies only to dependent constructs. R^2 is a criterion that shows the influence of exogeneous variables on endogenous variables. There are three amounts of 0.19, 0.33, and 0.67 for, respectively, weak, moderate, and powerful R^2 values (Hosseini *et al.*, 2020). In this study, the selected criterion for digital start-up companies (0.486), and employee voice (0.453) were calculated. So structural model has suitable fitness from this criterion. The results are illustrated in further details in Figure 6.3.

Table 6.3. Divergent validity

Variables	1	2	3	4	5	6
Innovative Climate	**0.793**					
Development of Digital Start-ups	0.583	**0.749**				
Emotional Commitment	0.279	0.377	**0.806**			
Employee Voice	0.484	0.494	0.544	**0.650**		
Knowledge Sharing	0.511	0.633	0.420	0.418	**0.747**	
Psychological Empowerment	0.241	0.200	0.606	0.474	0.330	**0.809**

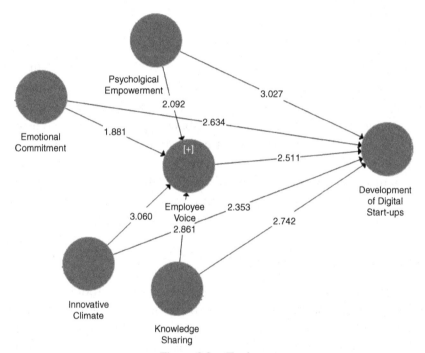

Figure 6.2. T-values

6.5.3 Q^2 *Criterion*

$Q2$ criterion is calculated for all dependent variables and shows the product of the combined values of research constructs in their coefficient of determination. Introduced by (Stone and Geisser, 1975), this criterion determines the prediction power of models in

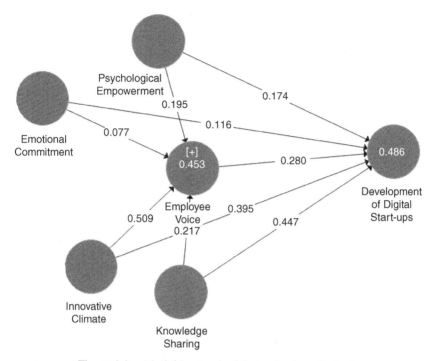

Figure 6.3. Model in standard factor load coefficients

dependent variables. In their opinion, models that have acceptable structural fitness should be able to predict indexes related to endogenous constructs of models. So if relations between constructs are defined correctly, constructs will be able to have enough impact on each other's indexes, and so hypotheses can be confirmed correctly. The value for every endogenous variable are 0.2, 0.15, and 0.35 for, respectively, low prediction power, moderate prediction power, and high prediction power (Kline, 2016). This criterion was calculated for this research and has shown for digital start-up organisations (0.406), and for employee voice (0.324); confirming high relevance and acceptable structural research model.

6.5.4 *Overall Model Fitness*

The overall model consists of both measurement and structural sides of the model, and model fitness will be completed by its confirmation. Overall model fitness is possible by GOF criterion (Goodness Of Fit). According to the calculated amount of 0.626 for GOF, overall research model fitness is assessed as very suitable and confirmed. According to the three amounts of 0.01, 0.25, and 0.36, respectively, determined as weak, moderate, and strong GOF values, 0.626 means a powerful overall research model fitness.

$$GOF = \sqrt{\text{average (commonality)} \times \text{average } (R^2)}$$

The other criterion is the standardised root mean squared residual (SRMR). According to the Table 6.4, this criterion is inside its acceptable boundaries, so it can be claimed that the overall research model has a very suitable fitting. In order to evaluate fitting, a normed fit index (NFI) can be used as well. The accepted range for this criterion is 0 to 1, and NFI has to larger than 0.9 (Kline, 2016). So as expressed in Table 6.4, this criterion was calculated as 0.915, which confirms the overall fitting of the model as well.

6.5.5 *Sobel Test and VAF*

In order to evaluate the mediating role of employee voice in the development of digital start-up organisations, the Sobel test was used.

(a) Independent and mediating variable coefficient amount = 0.324
(b) Dependent and mediating path coefficient amount = 0.280
(c) Dependent and independent variables path coefficient amount = 0.832

Table 6.4. Model fitting indexes

	SRMR	NFI
Acceptable Amount	≤0/10	≥0/9
Calculated Amount	0/012	0/915

(Sa) Standard error for independent and mediating variable paths = 0.087

(Sb) Standard error for mediating and dependent variable paths = 0.063

$$z - value = \frac{a * b}{\sqrt{(b^2 * s_a^2) + (a^2 * s_b^2) + (s_a^2 * s_b^2)}}$$

6.5.6 *Sobel Test for Mediating Variable*

The amount of 2.813 was calculated in this test, which is more than the critical value of 1.96, showing a mediating role for employee voice. VAF value shows that the intensity of mediating role of employee voice is equal to 0.098, meaning that the intensity is small. Based on these results, model fitness is confirmed in two sections of measurement and structure.

$$VAF = (a \times b) / (a \times b) + c$$

6.5.7 *Testing Hypotheses*

In this step, in order to assess the hypothesised relations between variables, T-variable was used. There have been eight sub-hypotheses used to test the main hypothesis and based on Table 6.5, T coefficients for seven of the relations were confirmed. In order to determine the degree of impact for predictive variables on dependent variables, standardised factor load coefficients of each hypothesis path is explored. These coefficients state that how much (how many per cents) the changes in dependent variables can be determined by independent variables.

6.6 Discussion

In this turbulent and highly competitive era, paying attention to human resources to acquire competitive advantage has been considered by organisations. Thus, this research aims to study the

Table 6.5.   T-values and research influence coefficient

Path	t-test	Influence coefficient	Result
Psychological empowerment — Developing digital start-up companies	3.027	0.174	Supported
Psychological empowerment — Employee voice — developing digital start-up companies	2.092	0.195	Supported
Emotional commitment — Developing digital start-up companies	2.634	0.116	Supported
Emotional commitment — Developing digital start-up companies — Employee voice	1.881	0.077	Not supported
Innovative climate — Developing digital start-up companies	2.353	0.395	Supported
Developing digital start-up companies — Innovation climate — Employee voice	3.060	0.509	Supported
Sharing knowledge — Developing digital start-up companies	2.742	0.447	Supported
Sharing knowledge — Developing digital start-up companies — Employee voice	2.861	0.217	Supported

influence of team performance on the development of digital start-up companies with the mediating effect of employee voice. The structural equations analysis results, using Smart PLS 3, showed that seven out of eight prior hypotheses were confirmed.

Hypothesis 1 states that there will be an influence of psychological empowerment on the development of digital start-up companies. While its sub hypothesis suggests that the "psychological empowerment has a meaningful influence on the development of digital start-up companies under the mediating role of employee voice". Since the calculated T-value for these two relations is higher than the critical value of (1.96) in the confidence level of 95%, it can be concluded that the gathered data approves this hypothesis. Results from this hypothesis is aligned with Özaralli (2015), Boğan and Dedeoğlu (2017), Saeida Ardekani *et al.* (2020), and Yuan and van Knippenberg (2021). When the leader behaves honestly and lets the employees get involved in decision making, he or she helps them learn new and updated skills from the industry and improve their efficiency, boosting their courage and self-confidence to speak about their opinions and thoughts with colleagues or members of the team without hesitation or intimidation about doing so. It is also suggested that managers promote employees' choices for personal gain through monthly meetings for decision-making involvement or providing an opportunity for personal growth. Regarding the fact that empowerment is an internal concept and as long as the employees' do not have the desire to do something, one cannot empower them; we urge respected managers to use managerial decentralisation strategies, shrinking absenteeism rules, increasing employees' decision-making involvement, providing the requirements for independent working styles, and by paying attention to employee trust, make the firm ready for psychological empowerment. Managers can focus on the competency dimension of psychological empowerment, foster a feeling in the employees that suggests that they can perform the activities they are responsible for, or set clear and fair job conditions from the beginnings so that the appropriateness between employees and job positions are kept, leading to the development of digital start-up companies.

Hypothesis 2 states that emotional commitment has a meaningful influence on the development of digital start-up companies. With its sub hypothesis being emotional commitment has a meaningful influence on the development of digital start-up companies with the mediating role of employee voice. Since the calculated T-value for the straight path hypothesis is higher than the critical value of (1.96) in the confidence level of 95%, being (2.634), it can be concluded that the gathered data approves this hypothesis. But for the sub-hypothesis, due to the T-value of (1.881), which is less than the critical value of (1.96) in the confidence level of 95%, this hypothesis is then hereby rejected. The results from this sub-hypothesis is maligned with Mckenna (2005), Anyango *et al.* (2015), Kim *et al.* (2018), and Oyewobi *et al.* (2019). Therefore, in order to increase the emotional commitment of employees, managers need to determine firm values and objectives clearly and truthfully.

Furthermore, managers should get to know their employees' objectives and values by using beneficial and effective communication with them and helps the two sets of objectives and values get aligned. It is then possible that employees feel responsible for the firm, effectively improve responsibilities and firm roles by volunteer and intrinsic behaviour. This will even reshape hiring, as people will join the company with an attitude to stay and an emotional attachment to the company. It is prescribed that decision-making teams be used, rather than making personal decisions in setting goals or strategic programmes because team's responsibility is always more than individuals.

According to Hypothesis 3, an innovative climate positively influences the development of digital start-up companies. With its sub hypothesis being innovative climate has a positive influence on the development of digital start-up companies with the mediating effect of employee voice. Since the calculated T-value for these two relations is higher than the critical value of (1.96) in the confidence level of 95%, it can be concluded that the gathered data approves this hypothesis. Results from this hypothesis is aligned with Moolenaar *et al.* (2010), Boğan and Dedeoğlu (2017), and Tajpour *et al.* (2020). It can be stated that inappropriate culture can create tension and clashes, making more obstacles for innovation and creativity. In order to set sails for the development of digital start-up companies, one should focus on their organisational culture and emphasise the alignment of employees' values and norms because innovative companies have rather similar cultures. They promote experiencing, cherish new experiences, they reward or punish success and failure by considering the context, gain experience from mistakes, and respond to environmental challenges in the fastest and most suitable way. Thus, shaping an innovative climate in digital start-up companies helps people use their ideas, knowledge, and experience in alignment with firm development. In this essence, it is suggested to managers to pay enough attention to organisational culture and specifications such as respect, friendly behaviour, appropriate social relations, and creating conditions in which people can express their ideas, which all in all can lead to improved innovative climate. It is also recommended to managers, in order to promote an innovative climate, to consider approaches such as innovative learning in problem-solving, preparation for change, self-sufficiency, and development of creativity. By creating a calm, unofficial environment for employees, giving relevant scores and rewards to innovators, preparing people for change, and supporting workplace enthusiasm, managers are able to improve innovative climate in firms. Innovative climate can also be escalated by holding seminars, scientific conferences, personal development courses for employees, and laying the foundations for involvement and engagement of more scientific employees. By caring about entrepreneurial skills and providing perquisites for learning them to employees, managers can further push innovation climate, and using employees' capabilities and innovative ideas, help develop the digital start-up company. Organisations should also be able to have an estimate of employees' innovative results, so that when they do their tasks correctly, they are appropriately and relevantly awarded.

According to Hypothesis 4, sharing knowledge has a positive influence on the development of digital start-up companies. While its sub hypothesis suggests that "sharing knowledge has a positive influence on the development of digital start-up companies under the mediating effect of employee's voice". Since the calculated T-value for these two relations is higher than the critical value of (1.96) in the confidence level of 95%, it can be concluded that the gathered data approves this hypothesis. Results from this hypothesis is aligned with Babnik *et al.* (2014), Rahman *et al.* (2018) and Kim *et al.* (2018). It can be stated that a lack of reasonable relationship between managers and digital start-up companies' employees in the development of rules and executive regulations is the main source to reduce individuals' motivation for performance. That is the reason why communicating with employees by the extensive release of information can turn them into productive ideas that may solve issues in digital start-up companies. Along with that, team spirit, self-sufficiency, and self-confidence improve through honest behaviour in sharing information. Collaborative decision making in digital start-up companies can improve subordinate efficiency by offering opportunities to learn new skills, learning from each other, and distributing knowledge elsewhere; because people retell their personal experience as opinions and ideas without fear. Such behaviour results in quick sensing of challenges, and employees can show high performance from themselves. Top managers should also support research and development teams since they are among the first who should respond to environmental changes.

6.7 Conclusion

The effort to improve employee voice should be practised and evaluated. Employee voice in digital start-up companies is of paramount importance in Iran because the country is confronting numerous challenges such as sanctions and economic problems. Thus, managers should focus their attention on employee voice. If employees genuinely perceive that the managers are being honest and try to empower them by coaching, collaborative decision making, and communication, these employees will reciprocate their voice as constructive suggestions. Accordingly, empowered employees can create new and exclusive ideas to help digital start-up companies survive in a competitive environment, provide support for colleagues, and bring fundamental and quick suggestions for their leaders to fight back with the problems they are encountering within the industry. Managers can take part in collaboration and conversation with team members, then they will be able to determine shared objectives, satisfy social and group needs, develop bilateral communication, grow skills and specialities of employees, and make the whole group more dynamic than before. By involvement and more accountability of employees' for their high responsibilities and experiences, managers can bring creativity, innovation, and entrepreneurship. In fact, managers should listen to employees' needs and demands and cooperate with them more proactively. After removing communicative obstacles inside a firm, managers can develop digital start-up companies in their own specific industry sector. On the one hand, managers can hold continuous or friendly meetings with employees to lay the ground for hearing out their ideas, opinions, and thoughts, and on the other hand, clear out job descriptions and objectives for teams and the whole organisation. This strategy will increase employee satisfaction and bring the firm closer to the realisation of firm objectives. Furthermore, finally, it can be stated that managers can take collaborative methods in general, methods in which employees are involved in making decisions, which makes employees feel that the organisation values their existence. This can ideally increase the development of digital start-up companies. Due to limitations in the unavailability of demographic data analysis as a mediator variable and the presence of another mediator in this study, it is suggested that other researchers take demographic variable inside the equation or use other variables such as workplace attitudes.

References

Ahearne, M., Mathieu, J., & Rapp, A. (2005). To empower or not to empower your sales force? An empirical examination of the influence of leadership empowerment behavior on customer satisfaction and performance. *Journal of Applied Psychology*, *90*(5), 945–955. https://doi.org/10.1037/0021-9010.90.5.945

Allen, T. J., Gloor, P. A., Fronzetti Colladon, A., Woerner, S. L., & Raz, O. (2016). The power of reciprocal knowledge sharing relationships for startup success. *Journal of Small Business and Enterprise Development*, *23*(3), 636–651. https://doi.org/10.1108/JSBED-08-2015-0110

Anyango, C., Ojera, P., & Ochieng, I. (2015). Meaning and application of employee voice. *International Journal of Scientific Research and Innovative Technology*, *2*(5), 1–12.

Ashkanasy, N. M. (2007). Emotion research in work and service settings. *XVIth Conference of the International Society for Research on Emotions ISRE 2007*, *1*, 16–16.

Babnik, K., Širca, N. T., & Dermol, V. (2014). Individuals learning in work teams: Support to knowledge management initiatives and an important source of organizational learning. *Procedia — Social and Behavioral Sciences*, *124*, 178–185. https://doi.org/10.1016/j.sbspro.2014.02.475

Billingham, R. E., & Sack, A. R. (1987). Conflict tactics and the level of emotional commitment among unmarrieds. *Human Relations*, *40*(1), 59–74.

Boğan, E., & Dedeoğlu, B. B. (2017). The effects of perceived behavioral integrity of supervisors on employee outcomes: Moderating effects of tenure. *Journal of Hospitality Marketing and Management, 26*(5), 511–531. https://doi.org/10.1080/19368623.2017.1269711

Bryson, A., Charlwood, A., & Forth, J. (2006). Worker voice, managerial response and labour productivity: An empirical investigation. *Industrial Relations Journal, 37*(5), 438–455. https://doi.org/10.1111/j.1468-2338.2006.00414.x

Chen, G., Kirkman, B. L., Kanfer, R., Allen, D., & Rosen, B. (2007). A multilevel study of leadership, empowerment, and performance in teams. *Journal of Applied Psychology, 92*(2), 331–346. https://doi.org/10.1037/0021-9010.92.2.331

Cirera, X., & Muzi, S. (2020). Measuring innovation using firm-level surveys: Evidence from developing countries. *Research Policy, 49*(3), 103912.

Clarck, J. (2019). The role of shared leadership in enhancing the quantity and quality of team performance: The influence of perceived task complexity. *Human Resource Management International Digest, 27*(5), 30–32.

Cohen, J. F., & Olsen, K. (2015). Knowledge management capabilities and firm performance: A test of universalistic, contingency and complementarity perspectives. *Expert Systems with Applications, 42*(3), 1178–1188. https://doi.org/10.1016/j.eswa.2014.09.002

Dana, L. P., & Dana, T. E. (2005). Expanding the scope of methodologies used in entrepreneurship research. *International Journal of Entrepreneurship and Small Business, 2*(1), 79–88. https://doi.org/10.1504/IJESB.2005.006071

Dana, L. P., & Dumez, H. (2015). Qualitative research revisited: Epistemology of a comprehensive approach. *International Journal of Entrepreneurship and Small Business, 26*(2), 154–170. https://doi.org/10.1504/IJESB.2015.071822

Detert, J. R., & Burris, E. R. (2007). Leadership behavior and employee voice: Is the door really open? *Academy of Management Journal, 50*(4), 869–884. https://doi.org/10.5465/AMJ.2007.26279183

Elsetouhi, A. M., Hammad, A. A., Nagm, A. E. A., & Elbaz, A. M. (2018). Perceived leader behavioral integrity and employee voice in SMEs travel agents: The mediating role of empowering leader behaviors. *Tourism Management, 65*, 100–115. https://doi.org/10.1016/j.tourman.2017.09.022

Fornell, C., & Larcker, D. F. (1981). Structural equation models with unobservable variables and measurement error: Algebra and statistics. *Journal of Marketing Research*, *18*(3), 382–388. https://doi.org/10.1177/002224378101800313

Fuller, J. B., Barnett, T., Hester, K., Relyea, C., & Frey, L. (2007). An exploratory examination of voice behavior from an impression management perspective. *Journal of Managerial Issues*, *19*(1), 134–151. http://www.jstor.org/stable/40601197

García-Buades, M. E., Ramis-Palmer, C., & Manassero-Mas, M. A. (2015). Climate for innovation, performance, and job satisfaction of local police in Spain. *Policing*, *38*(4), 722–737. https://doi.org/10.1108/PIJPSM-02-2015-0019

Gelfand, M. J., Erez, M., & Aycan, Z. (2007). Cross-cultural organizational behavior. In *Annual Review of Psychology* (Vol. 58, pp. 479–514). Annual Reviews. https://doi.org/10.1146/annurev.psych.58.110405.085559

Gunlu, E., Aksarayli, M., & Perçin, N. Ş. (2010). Job satisfaction and organizational commitment of hotel managers in Turkey. *International Journal of Contemporary Hospitality Management*, *22*(5), 693–717. https://doi.org/10.1108/09596111011053819

Hosseini, E., Tajpour, M., & Lashkarbooluki, M. (2020). The impact of entrepreneurial skills on manager's job performance. *International Journal of Human Capital in Urban Management*, *5*(4), 361–372. https://doi.org/10.22034/IJHCUM.2020.04.08

Jayabalan, J., Appannan, J. S., Low, M. P., & Ming, K. S. (n.d.). Perception of employee on the relationship between internal corporate social responsibility (CSR) and organizational affective commitment. *Journal of Progressive Research in Social Sciences*, *3*(2), 168–175. http://www.scitecresearch.com/journals/index.php/jprss/article/view/595

Kim, M. R., Choi, L., Borchgrevink, C. P., Knutson, B., & Cha, J. M. (2018). Effects of Gen Y hotel employee's voice and team-member exchange on satisfaction and affective commitment between the U.S. and China. *International Journal of Contemporary Hospitality Management*, *30*(5), 2230–2248. https://doi.org/10.1108/IJCHM-12-2016-0653

Kline, R. B. (2016). Principles and practice of structural equation modeling, 4th ed. In *Principles and Practice of Structural Equation Modeling*, Guilford Press.

Lawal, F. A., Iyiola, O. O., Adegbuyi, O. A., Ogunnaike, O. O., & Taiwo, A. A. (2018). Modelling the relationship between entrepreneurial climate and venture performance: The moderating role of entrepreneurial competencies. *Academy of Entrepreneurship Journal, 24*(1), 1–16.

Macey, W. H., & Schneider, B. (2008). The meaning of employee engagement. *Industrial and Organizational Psychology, 1*(1), 3–30. https://doi.org/10.1111/j.1754-9434.2007.0002.x

Machokoto, W., & A. Dzvimbo, M. (2020). The employee voice behaviours in African context: The case of Zimbabwe. *Asian Journal of Interdisciplinary Research, 3*(1), 125–135. https://doi.org/10.34256/ajir2019

Martin-Perez, V., & Martin-Cruz, N. (2015). The mediating role of affective commitment in the rewards–knowledge transfer relation. *Journal of Knowledge Management, 19*(6), 1167–1185. https://doi.org/10.1108/JKM-03-2015-0114

Mckenna, S. (2005). Organisational commitment in the small entrepreneurial business in Singapore. *Cross Cultural Management: An International Journal, 12*(2), 16–37. https://doi.org/10.1108/13527600510797999

Moolenaar, N. M., Daly, A. J., & Sleegers, P. J. C. (2010). Occupying the principal position: Examining relationships between transformational leadership, social network position, and schools' innovative climate. *Educational Administration Quarterly, 46*(5), 623–670. https://doi.org/10.1177/0013161X10378689

Mowbray, P. K., Wilkinson, A., & Tse, H. H. M. (2015). An integrative review of employee voice: Identifying a common conceptualization and research agenda. *International Journal of Management Reviews, 17*(3), 382–400. https://doi.org/10.1111/ijmr.12045

Nechanska, E., Hughes, E., & Dundon, T. (2020). Towards an integration of employee voice and silence. *Human Resource Management Review, 30*(1), 100674. https://doi.org/10.1016/j.hrmr.2018.11.002

Oyewobi, L. O., Oke, A. E., Adeneye, T. D., & Jimoh, R. A. (2019). Influence of organizational commitment on work–life balance and organizational performance of female construction professionals. *Engineering, Construction and Architectural Management, 26*(10), 2243–2263. https://doi.org/10.1108/ECAM-07-2018-0277

Özaralli, N. (2015). Linking Empowering leader to creativity: The moderating role of psychological (felt) empowerment. *Procedia — Social and Behavioral Sciences, 181*, 366–376. https://doi.org/10.1016/j.sbspro.2015.04.899

Park, J. Y., & Nawakitphaitoon, K. (2018). The cross-cultural study of LMX and individual employee voice: The moderating role of conflict avoidance. *Human Resource Management Journal, 28*(1), 14–30. https://doi.org/10.1111/1748-8583.12158

Petty, G. C., & Hill, R. B. (2005). Work ethic characteristics: Perceived work ethics of supervisors and workers. *Journal of STEm Teacher Education, 42*(2), 5–20. https://eric.ed.gov/?id=EJ753122

Popoola, S. O. (2009). Organizational commitment of records management personnel in Nigerian private universities. *Records Management Journal, 19*(3), 204–217. https://doi.org/10.1108/09565690910999193

Rahman, M. S., Mannan, M., Hossain, M. A., Zaman, M. H., & Hassan, H. (2018). Tacit knowledge-sharing behavior among the academic staff: Trust, self-efficacy, motivation and Big Five personality traits embedded model. *International Journal of Educational Management, 32*(5), 761–782. https://doi.org/10.1108/IJEM-08-2017-0193

Sabokro, M., Tajpour, M., & Hosseini, E. (2018). Investigating the knowledge management effect on managers' skills improvement. *International Journal of Human Capital in Urban Management, 3*(2), 125–132. https://doi.org/10.22034/IJHCUM.2018.02.05

Saeida Ardekani, S., Tajpour, M., & Hosseini, E. (2020). The investigation of the impact of employee empowerment on knowledge sharing in post and telecommunication company (PTC) of Shiraz city. *Management Tomorrow, 18*(60), 47–60.

Salamzadeh, A. (2018). Start-up boom in an emerging market: A niche market approach. In *Competitiveness in Emerging Markets*, pp. 233–243. Springer, Cham. https://doi.org/10.1007/978-3-319-71722-7_13

Salamzadeh, A., & Markovic, M. R. (2018). Shortening the learning curve of media start-ups in accelerators: Case of a developing country. In *Evaluating Media Richness In Organizational Learning*, pp. 36–48. IGI Global. https://doi.org/10.4018/978-1-5225-2956-9.ch003

Salamzadeh, A., & Dana, L. P. (2021). The coronavirus (COVID-19) pandemic: Challenges among Iranian startups. *Journal of Small Business & Entrepreneurship, 33*(5), 489–512.

Salamzadeh, A., Arasti, Z., & Elyasi, G. M. (2017). Creation of ICT-based social start-ups in Iran: A multiple case study. *Journal of Enterprising Culture, 25*(1), 97–122. https://doi.org/10.1142/S0218495817500042

Salamzadeh, A., Arasti, Z., & Elyasi, G. M. (2018). Proposing a supportive framework for creation of social startups in accelerators. *Social Capital Management, 5*(3), 365–384. https://dx.doi.org/10.22059/jscm.2018.252206.1550

Salamzadeh, A., Tajpour, M., Hosseini, E., & Salembrahmi, M. (2021). Human capital and the performance of Iranian digital Startups: The moderating role of knowledge sharing behaviour. *International Journal of Public Sector Performance Management.* https://scholar.google.com/scholar?cluster=2640487719560857717&hl=en&oi=scholarr

Scarbrough, H. (2003). Knowledge management, HRM and the innovation process. *International Journal of Manpower, 24*(5), 501–516, 615. https://doi.org/10.1108/01437720310491053

Schippers, M. C., Den Hartog, D. N., & Koopman, P. L. (2007). Reflexivity in teams: A measure and correlates. *Applied Psychology, 56*(2), 189–211. https://doi.org/10.1111/j.1464-0597.2006.00250.x

Spreitzer, G. M. (1995). Psychological empowerment in the workplace: Dimensions, measurement, and validation. *Academy of Management Journal, 38*(5), 1442–1465. https://doi.org/10.5465/256865

Suh, K., & Jung, S. (2021). The effect of leader's self-deception behavior on team learning: Mediating effect of psychological safety and silent climate. *The Journal of the Korea Contents Association, 21*(3), 478–489. https://doi.org/10.5392/JKCA.2021.21.03.478

Tajpour, M. (2018). investigate the effect of organizational mobbing behaviors on job and organizational attitude. *Quarterly Journal of Public Organzations Management, 6*(2), 117–136.

Tajpour, M., Hosseini, E., & Salamzadeh, A. (2020). The effect of innovation components on organisational performance: Case of the governorate of Golestan Province. *International Journal of Public Sector Performance Management, 6*(6), 817–830. https://doi.org/10.1504/IJPSPM.2020.110987

Tajpour, M., Kawamorita, H., & Demiryurek, K. (2020). Towards the third generation of universities with an entrepreneurial approach. *International Journal of Technoentrepreneurship, 4*(2), 122–133. https://doi.org/10.1504/IJTE.2020.113927

Thomas, K. W., & Velthouse, B. A. (1990). Cognitive elements of empowerment: An "interpretive" model of intrinsic task motivation. *Academy of Management Review, 15*(4), 666–681. https://doi.org/10.5465/amr.1990.4310926

Tsai, C. (2011). Innovative behaviors between employment modes in knowledge intensive organizations. *International Journal of Humanities and Social Science, 1*(6), 153–162.

van der Lippe, T., & Lippényi, Z. (2020). Co-workers working from home and individual and team performance. *New Technology, Work and Employment, 35*(1), 60–79. https://doi.org/10.1111/ntwe.12153

Van Dyne, L., & LePine, J. A. (1998). Helping and voice extra-role behaviors: Evidence of construct and predictive validity. *Academy of Management Journal, 41*(1), 108–119.

Vashdi, D. R., Bamberger, P. A., Erez, M., & Weiss-Meilik, A. (2007). Briefing-debriefing: Using a reflexive organizational learning model from the military to enhance the performance of surgical teams. *Human Resource Management, 46*(1), 115–142. https://doi.org/10.1002/hrm.20148

Wang, Z., & Wang, N. (2012). Knowledge sharing, innovation and firm performance. *Expert Systems with Applications, 39*(10), 8899–8908.

Wayne, S. J., Shore, L. M., & Liden, R. C. (1997). Perceived organizational support and leader-member exchange: A social exchange perspective. *Academy of Management Journal, 40*(1), 82–111. https://doi.org/10.5465/257021

Welbourne, T. M. (2011). 50 years of voice in HRM. *Human Resource Management, 50*(1), 1–2.

Wiedow, A., & Konradt, U. (2011). Two-dimensional structure of team process improvement: Team reflection and team adaptation. *Small Group Research, 42*(1), 32–54. https://doi.org/10.1177/1046496410377358

Yaghoobi, N. M., Koohi-khor, M., Kamalian, A. R., & Tajpour, M. (2018). Investigate the effect of organizational mobbing behaviors on job and organizational attitude. *Quarterly Journal of Public Organizations Management, 6*(2), 117–136.

Yang, L. R., Huang, C. F., & Wu, K. S. (2011). The association among project manager's leadership style, teamwork and project success. *International Journal of Project Management, 29*(3), 258–267. https://doi.org/10.1016/j.ijproman.2010.03.006

Yuan, Y., & van Knippenberg, D. (2021). Leader network centrality and team performance: team size as moderator and collaboration as mediator. *Journal of Business and Psychology, 36*(6), 1–14. https://doi.org/10.1007/s10869-021-09745-4

Zhang, J. A., & Edgar, F. (2021). HRM systems, employee proactivity and capability in the SME context. *International Journal of Human Resource Management.* https://doi.org/10.1080/09585192.2021.1905682

Ziyae, B., Rezvani, M., Mobarki, M. H., & Tajpour, M. (2019). The impact of academic spinoffs components in development of internationalization of universities. *Iranian Higher Education, 11*(3), 27–48.

Zoltan, R. C. (2014). Synergy effects in work teams. *Network Intelligence Studies, 3,* 122–129.

https://doi.org/10.1142/9789811239212_0007

Chapter 7

Key Variables in Team Dynamics in Small Businesses and Start-ups

Kumar Shalender

Chitkara Business School, Chitkara University, Punjab, India

kumar.shalender@chitkara.edu.in

Abstract: The study identifies key variables that can affect team dynamics in small organisations and start-ups. The top management of the organisation has to keep these variables in mind so as to manage the teams and its dynamics successfully. The management of team dynamics is also prominent because the net output and performance of a team is heavily dependent on its dynamics. In addition to identifying key variables, the research also recommends measures that can prove effective in taking all team members along. Effective team management can prove extremely helpful in addressing a changing business environment by equipping it with ability to constantly respond/adjust to both external and internal pressures. This flexibility, in turn, makes sure that businesses continue to remain agile and meet the demands of all stakeholders in a desirable manner.

Keywords: Team dynamics, Team performance, Challenges, Small businesses, Start-ups.

7.1 Introduction

The concept of team dynamics has become more complex over the years. The evolutionary nature of the business environment coupled with diversified, dispersed, and digitally connected teams have made the management of teams extremely challenging. Further, the research conducted by Antoncic *et al.* (2015), Darnihamedani (2016), and Jawabri (2020) showed that managing team dynamics is particularly challenging in the context of small businesses and start-ups. So, the key question that this study aims to answer is to identify the key variables that can help businesses effectively manage team dynamics. Teams today face a different set of challenges than organisations used to face earlier. Team members today belong to diverse background, spatially dispersed, heavily rely on digital technologies, and feature a varied level of experience. Despite these new challenges, the fundamental set of principles for successful collaboration and delivery outcomes continues to remain the same.

As demonstrated by J. Richard Hackman, an eminent researcher in the field of organisational behaviour with more than 40 years of research experience in exploring facets of team management, the most important element for team success is not the behaviour, attitude, or personality of team members. Instead, what a successful team requires the most is "empowering conditions" that help them to thrive and succeed in achieving desired objectives. These conditions are further divided into various variables that this study looks in greater detail in the following sections. In addition to exploring key variables, the chapter also recommends strategies that will help small businesses and start-ups to not only manage their teams effectively but also help them to improve the culture of the organisation for improved resilience and better output.

7.2 Variables in Team Dynamics

The impact of team dynamics on its performance outcomes is well established in the literature. Researches in the past have studied a wide range of variables that can have a significant impact on its performance. For example, the effect of the top leadership and chief executive officer on team dynamics have been studied by Chiu *et al.* (2021), Creasy and Carnes (2017), and Peterson *et al.* (2003). Similarly, studies were carried out to determine the impact of other important variables such as attitude and monitoring (Bono, 2004; Barrick *et al.*, 2005), openness and flexibility (Shepherd & Rudd, 2014; Dhir & Sushil, 2017), and networking capabilities (Sharma *et al.*, 2010; Xiu *et al.*, 2017). In the specific context of small businesses and start-ups, the variables discussed below can prove extremely helpful in managing team dynamics.

7.2.1 *Compelling Vision*

Creating a "compelling vision" is at the heart of successful team management. Specifically, in the context of small businesses and start-ups, this variable is a prerequisite for attaining the desired goals. The foundation of an empowered team is based on a compelling vision. The vision statement energises the whole team and provides them with a compelling reason to achieve what they set out to achieve. It not only orients and energises the team's efforts but also help members to channelise their efforts in a single direction. The team leader should carefully craft the vision statement in consultation with the top leadership as it will help both vision statements to provide a "consistent and coherent" message to members. When Hindustan Unilever acquired the Indulekha Brand in 2015 for Rs 330 crore, the then chairman and managing director of the company, Sanjiv Mehta, specifically directed the team tasked with acquisition of the brand to create a "vision" for successful acquisition and implementation of the project. He specifically emphasised that the team must work in line with the "HUL's values" so that the task can be completed in conformation with the "working culture" of the organisation.

In order to make sure the vision statement is well-understood by team members, it must be communicated to all members in a "written form". It must be concise, clear, and free of any unambiguity, thereby stating in concrete terms "what the team has to achieve" and the "time frame within which desired objectives need to be accomplished". One of the critical mistakes that teams commit is not putting it into written form and rather just communicating it verbally. This could potentially lead to "distortion" of the statement and thereby, leading to "disorientation" among team members. Also, sometimes verbal communication might not prove good enough, especially in the case of geographically dispersed teams. In such situations, supplying team members with a "written vision" statement is the best way to make sure the message reaches each and every member of the team unambiguously.

Recommendation: Top management and team leader must ensure that team members get thoroughly acquainted with the "vision statement" of both organisation and team's task. This will help them to work in a unified manner and accomplish desired objectives within stipulated time frame.

7.2.2 Connecting Team Members

United by a compelling vision, the next variable in creating an empowering environment is "connecting" them with each other. It might sound simple and plain but in reality, most organisations and start-ups fail to connect the aspirations of team members. Especially in the case of spatially dispersed teams, connecting the needs, dreams, hopes, and aspirations of teams are significantly challenging. The rationale behind making members know and understand each other thoroughly is to develop a "spirit of cooperation" between them. This will help them to work effectively as a team and collectively work towards the attainment of goals. The teams at Tata Motors working on different projects have a "regular get-together" and the thing that makes unions special is their "informal agenda" for these meetings. These meetings are proving especially relevant in "energising teams" and helping the organisation to achieve "excellent results" on all its team works.

To help team members connect, top management should aim for "informal interactions" as these assemblies help teams to get thoroughly acquainted with each other. As well-noted by Tata

Motors, good team dynamics not only requires "professional commitment" but also mandates team members to build "strong rapport" among each other. This will facilitate members to work more closely on issues and challenges they find relevant for the optimum performance of the team. Full freedom must be given to the team leader to organise such "informal meetings" where discussions should be held "outside the domain" of the professional commitment. Also owing to personality difference, it may happen that some of the team members are not comfortable talking outside the professional domain — it is absolutely all right as even listening to the others' views can help tremendously to transform the team dynamics for the better.

Recommendation: Organise "informal meetings" so that team members get to know each other well beyond their professional roles and responsibilities.

7.2.3 *Diversity in Team Structure*

A well-balanced team structure is essential for its success, besides managing it for higher task efficiency and work effectiveness. To decide the structure, the team leader should carefully decide on a) the number of team members and b) their level of experience. It has been observed that teams that set new performance benchmarks include balanced numbers with varied skills. For typical project work, try to limit the numbers anywhere between 8–12, as often used by the consumer electronics behemoth LG. The company is well-known for the successful planning and execution of inter-functional projects. It tries to limit the team size to a "manageable number" (up to 12) as it helps the team to remain "agile and competitive" while aiding in "quick decision making". The company has successfully implemented many of its projects and made a successful "transition from an electronic-goods manufacturer to a diversified conglomerate" owing to small team characteristic.

The diversity in experience level is also desirable and in fact, contrary to the popular belief, it's not mandatory for teams to have all members with "superlative skills and knowledge". Instead, a well-balanced team should have an optimum mix consisting of both experienced and fresh members as a part of the initiative. This will bring "novelty and fresh approach" to the table and keep the "perspective fresh" while dealing with a constantly changing business environment. Diversity in terms of knowledge, skills, and views, as well as in age, race, gender, and culture, can really prove effective in avoiding the "trap of groupthink". However, the biggest benefit of having a diversified team is to have a "high creativity" in the working of the team. This aspect is particularly relevant in the case of smaller organisations and start-ups where the business realities keep on changing continuously. This "ever-evolving competitive scenario" also warrants the teams to have "manageable numbers" and a "diversified background" so that optimum results can be achieved in a stipulated period of time.

Recommendation: An "optimum team structure" should have a "manageable number" as well as diversity in age, skills, and knowledge to encourage "creativity" in the working culture of the team.

7.2.4 *Define Deadlines Clearly*

Often team members have to work within "tight deadlines" and this is exactly where the importance of "clearly communicating time limits" comes into prominence. Team leaders should make sure that no ambiguity should surround the "objectives and timelines" within which these goals need to be achieved by the team. There might be some apprehensions initially when deadlines are being pronounced to the team members, but it's better to clear everything upfront that to let things be shrouded in vagaries. One of the most-admired organisations in the world, Apple is ruthlessly straightforward when it comes to communicating deadlines to its product developments teams. Team leaders are well-informed in advance the "work and time frame" within which they have to deliver the desirable results. This clear communication leaves little space for "obfuscation" and motivate teams to channelise their collective energy to complete tasks within the given finish date.

This aspect is particularly relevant for small organisations and start-ups as they have to work within severe time and money constraints. By clearly communicating time limits, teams get on with the task right from "day one". The members have a clear idea in their minds about the project and its completion time which help them to remain steady in their pursuits. Also, team members when working under strict time limits get a chance to develop strong connections among themselves. This, in turn, further helps to foster strong "team spirit" wherein members start rallying around the joy and happiness of helping each other. Once such a "team spirit" and "rapport" develop, no challenge will be able to contain the team and its performance. Consider a situation where the client has "comprehensively reconfigured" the requirements of the products or one of primary "design software system" has failed just in the nick of the time. In such situations, if team members are not ready to help each other, the situation could slip out of hand very easily. Therefore, it's essential for the top management to help team members connect in such a manner that they get habituated to help each other and, in the process, feel happy and empowered.

Recommendation: Team leader must define tasks and their achievement deadlines in the "clearest and most unambiguous" terms.

7.2.5 *Open Feedback*

The importance of creating a culture of "open feedback" in managing team dynamics couldn't be overemphasised. Successful teams the world over value the culture of "honest and unbiased feedback". Regardless of the "tenure and position" of team members, open feedback can help the team to perform optimally. To build such a culture, team leaders can start by asking members feedback on their behaviour. This will instil confidence and assure team members that their suggestions are truly valued by the leadership. Toyota Motors Corporation is revered for its implementation of a "360-degree feedback" system. The system not only involves its employees in the feedback process but also take inputs from various stakeholders, including partners, customers, regulators, suppliers, etc. Such comprehensive feedback has helped the organisation tremendously in reviving process and procedural mechanisms for better output and efficiency. Toyota's top leadership encourages teams to put forth their honest views and its "active involvement" reassures employees to give their suggestions without any apprehensions. In the case of new projects on which inter-departmental teams are working, Toyota not only asks the employees for feedback but also integrate the feasible and customer-oriented feedback it receives from its suppliers as well as partners including dealerships, service centres, etc.

The integration of the feedback is just as much as important as taking it from stakeholders. While it may not be practical to incorporate all suggestions at times, the team leader, in consultation with the top management, should strive to implement changes that don't require substantial resources or rework. In fact, even the integration of small suggestions from members can help them to become more candid in their future suggestions, thereby creating an environment of trust and assurance within the team. This will further have a positive impact on the "performance" and "realisation" of the goals by teams.

Recommendation: The creation of an "open feedback" culture entails a two-step procedure: a) gathering the honest feedback and b) quick analysis and integration of feedback to upgrade the functional processes and working mechanisms.

7.2.6 *Building Integrity*

The integrity of team members is crucial for their proper management and performance. Everybody in the team must "trust each other" and "do the right thing" irrespective of whether someone is watching or not. Without integrity, it's hard to imagine the success of the team. Integrity leads to the faith that everyone is working towards the same purpose and they must align efforts to achieve the predetermined goal in a manner that is right. In the case of start-ups, everybody from investors to customers and from stakeholders to partners is working in close coordination with each other. In such situations, all the stakeholders must have faith that the team they are working with won't compromise on integrity. This faith is necessary for stakeholders and team members to "stick around" for long and create a "win-win situation" for all.

In order to bring a high level of integrity into the teams' working culture, team members must follow a "robust value system". The values have to be derived from the "vision statement" and should be decided by the team leader in consultation with both top management and team members. It goes without saying that the values of the team must align with the values of the organisation, or else the team might face a conflict at a later stage. Sometimes there is "undue pressure" from clients or partners which can force teams to adopt a "compromised approach". In such circumstances, having a robust "value system" will help teams to stay firm on the path of integrity.

Recommendation: Decide the "value system" and align the values of team members with the value of the team and the organisation. Any divergence in the "value system" could derail teams, causing a decline in their performance.

7.2.7 *Keeping Promises*

For actively managing team dynamics, it is crucial that team members must keep their promises — not only the ones they have made to each other but also to other external stakeholders involved in the business. One of the effective ways to help teams deliver on their promises is to bring them to the "debate table" and give them a chance to have "healthy arguments". This might feel counterintuitive but in the long term, debates can be helpful in providing a platform where team members can disagree and handle queries in a "respectable manner". These debates can prove very useful in finding the "novel solutions" to issues and problems that keep on plaguing the companies indefinitely. It has been closely observed that teams that don't perform optimally are ones that "stick to their views" and largely remain indifferent to "innovation" and "unconventional approach".

By offering a platform for debate, arguments, consultation, and collaboration, it becomes easy for the team leaders to manage their "dynamics and performance" effectively. It is also recommended that "ground rules" must be set before any such discussion so that team members must have clarity on the procedure of the debate. By actively involving teams in such activities, top management can easily ensure that teams develop a healthy "culture of argumentation" and become a "conducive element for change" in the working methodology of the entire company. Creating such a platform is not only relevant for managing the "team dynamics" but also for integrating the aspects of "healthy debates and deliberations" in the work culture of the company. These exchanges are helpful in "instilling creativity" and building an "innovation culture" among team members. This, in turn, will have a positive impact on the output of the organisation.

Recommendation: Create a platform where employees and team members can participate in healthy "debates and discussions" to foster an environment of "creativity and innovation".

7.2.8 *Shared Mindset*

Creating a shared mindset can help teams perform optimally. A shared mindset can also effectively reduce "conflicts" by providing team members with a "common identity" to achieve their objectives. Creating a shared mindset is a "challenging task" with teams today being increasingly becoming "spatially dispersed". Sometimes differences emerge among teams on account of the "information gap" with only a few team members having access to "critical information" related to the project. Such imbalance can hurt the working of teams and make management of their dynamics difficult for team leaders. Similarly, the differences among the team members could emerge on account of difference in their perceptions and expectations. Although it's natural to have differences within teams, these must be addressed in a "constructive manner".

The aspect of a shared mindset will also boost the performance of the team by propelling the efforts in a single, unified direction. The mindset will also be helpful in achieving coherence in efforts so that the efficiency and effectiveness of the team can be enhanced successfully. In the case of dispersed teams, this aspect is very important and can help the team to stay united in the face of emerging challenges, rising difficulties, and strict deadlines. Again, the responsibility of creating a shared mindset lies on the shoulders of top management and the team leader. Instructions about having a common mission and objectives must flow from the "position of authority". Once the value of "shared mindset" is inculcated in the working culture of the team, then following up with this incredible quality is not a difficult task. Team members will realise the incredible benefits of the shared mindset and in due course, everyone will acknowledge that it's in their own best interest that they adopt the shared mindset.

Recommendation: Top management and team leaders must encourage teams to imbibe the idea of a "shared mindset". This will be helpful in not only managing the team dynamics but also prove successful in taking the performance levels of teams notches higher than before.

7.3 *Pulling It Together*

Managing team dynamics is a difficult task. Especially in the case of small businesses and start-ups, top management has to make sure that the efforts of the team members are aligned in the same direction so as to achieve desirable results on various performance indicators. The relevance of managing team dynamics have become even more important in contemporary settings where businesses are facing emerging challenges from stakeholders across the value chain. Customers' interests are flickering, government regulations are altering, expectations of partners are shifting, and resources are becoming scarcer by the day. In such a competitive environment, organisations cannot afford teams that are not able to deliver optimum results. The variables mentioned above in the chapter can prove extremely helpful in making sure that teams not only "perform optimally" but also become a "conducive instrument" for creating a culture of "shared mindset" and "collaboration" in the organisation.

References

Antoncic, B., Bratkovic Kregar, T., Singh, G., & Denoble, A. F. (2015). The big five personality-entrepreneurship relationship: Evidence from Slovenia. *Journal of Small Business Management, 53*(3), 819–841.

Barrick, M. R., Parks, L., & Mount, M. K. (2005). Self-monitoring as a moderator of the relationships between personality traits and performance. *Personnel Psychology, 58*(3), 745–767.

Bono, J. E., & Judge, T. A. (2004). Personality and transformational and transactional leadership: A meta-analysis. *Journal of Applied Psychology, 89*(5), 901–910.

Chiu, C.-Y. (C.), Lin, H.-C., & Ostroff, C. (2021). Fostering team learning orientation magnitude and strength: Roles of transformational leadership, team personality heterogeneity, and behavioural integration. *Journal of Occupational and Organizational Psychology, 94*(1), 187–216.

Creasy, T., & Carnes, A. (2017). The effects of workplace bullying on team learning, innovation and project success as mediated through virtual and traditional team dynamics. *International Journal of Project Management, 35*, 964–977.

Darnihamedani, P. (2016). Individual characteristics, contextual factors and entrepreneurial behavior. Doctoral thesis, Erasmus University Rotterdam.

Dhir, S., & Sushil. (2017). Flexibility in modification and termination of cross-border joint ventures. *Global Journal of Flexible Systems Management, 18*(2), 139–151.

Jawabri, A. (2020). The impact of big-5 model leadership traits on team entrepreneurship: An empirical study of small businesses in the UAE. *Management Science Letters, 10*(3), 497–506.

Peterson, R. S., Smith, D. B., Martorana, P. V., & Owens, P. D., (2003). The impact of chief executive officer personality on top management team dynamics: One mechanism by which leadership affects organizational performance. *Journal of Applied Psychology, 88*(8), 795–808.

Sharma, M. K., Sushil, & Jain, P. K. (2010). Revisiting flexibility in organizations: Exploring its impact on performance. *Global Journal of Flexible Systems Management, 11*(3), 51–68.

Shepherd, N. G., & Rudd, J. M. (2014). The influence of context on the strategic decision-making process: A review of the literature. *International Journal of Management Reviews, 16*(3), 340–363.

Xiu, L., Liang, X., Chen, Z., & Xu, W. (2017). Strategic flexibility, innovative HR practices, and firm performance: A moderated mediation model. *Personnel Review, 46*(7), 1335–1357.

Chapter 8

The COVID-19 Pandemic Overlaps Entrepreneurial Activities and Triggered New Challenges: A Review Study

Erum Shaikh*

The University of Modern Sciences, Tando Muhammad Khan,
Sindh, Pakistan University of Sindh, Jamshoro, Pakistan

erum.shaikh@ums.edu.pk

Muhammad Nawaz Tunio

Greenwich University, Karachi, Pakistan Alpen Adria
University of Klagenfurt, Austria

drnawaz@greenwich.edu.pk

Wali Muhammad Khoso

Nanjing University of Aeronautics and Astronautics, Nanjing, China

wali_muhammad27@hotmail.com

Mohsen Brahmi

FEMS Faculty, University of Sfax, Sfax, Tunisia

brahmi.mohsen@gmail.com

---

*Corresponding author

Shahid Rasool

School of Management sciences, Ghulam Ishaq Khan
Institute of Engineering Sciences and Technology,
Khyber Pakhtunkhwa, Pakistan

shahid.rasool24@gmail.com

Abstract: The aim of the study is to explore how the COVID-19 pandemic has taken entrepreneurship in its fold across different situations and from different geographic locations. This is a review study in which an extensive review is conducted from extant and relevant literature. The searching of the articles is based on the major research constructs of the study, which are entrepreneurship, small business, SMEs, entrepreneurs, and employees with relation to the COVID-19. As COVID-19 is a burning issue, therefore, the time frame of the search was from January 2020 to January 2021. Based on the review, a conceptual model was developed in which hypotheses are proposed. The finding of the study indicates that small business is always vulnerable in disasters as compared to any other forms of the economic mechanism. Entrepreneurial activities are at the front to receive warnings and threats from the pandemic situation where survival becomes very challenging without the support and relief of the respective countries' government and their policies. This study provides implications for international organisations, non-government organisations, government agencies, and policymakers to design strategies and approaches to support small businesses through different relief and packages. This study contributes to the literature and enhances understanding about the COVID-19, and its influence on the entrepreneurial activities. However, to the best of the author's knowledge, this is a novel study that incorporates more emphasis on entrepreneurs, employees, and SMEs into the research on COVID-19.

Keywords: Entrepreneurship, COVID-19 pandemic, Challenges, Small and medium business.

8.1 Introduction

Economic activities in the form of entrepreneurship are growing and existing as a nexus of opportunities. This nexus characterises the opportunities associated with entrepreneurial activities, entrepreneurial actions, entrepreneurs, and supporting actors (Maritz *et al.*, 2020). However, the actual level of entrepreneurship is ambiguous. Entrepreneurial activities are, sometimes, undertaken and dominated by the solo self-employed, while the dynamics of entrepreneurship are closely concerned with age, qualification, and gender of the entrepreneur (Dvoulety, 2019).

Due to the flexible nature of entrepreneurship, a variety of components influence entrepreneurial activities which sometimes cause rise and sometimes decline (Bögenhold, 2019). Entrepreneurial activities have not only to face challenges due to competition in the market, but also uncertain threats to the survival of the business (Audretsch *et al.*, 2019).

There are different threats that can cause economic shrinkage, which will directly and indirectly influence entrepreneurial activities; in the existing situation of the COVID-19 crisis, businesses in all forms are surviving at high risk (Katper *et al.*, 2020). The advent of the COVID-19 crisis has worsened the economy, and it has raised concerns about the future of the local, national, and international business and enterprises of all sizes and kinds (Secundo *et al.*, 2021). There are concerns about how businesses will survive after COVID-19 and how the business world will look. In this context, this study attempts to ascertain the spillover of the COVID-19 crisis on entrepreneurship (Zahra, 2021). Several studies conducted previously offer insights into how enterprises managed to survive after such adverse events and thus, they provide lessons to deal with the COVID-19 pandemic who has affected people and businesses globally.

COVID-19 has touched all segments of the society and has spread to all corners of the world. However, different from previous catastrophes, COVID-19 has caused chronic health crises in multiple dimensions (Nadia *et al.*, 2021). The adverse effects of COVID-19 are beyond estimates and have very wide effects on the world's businesses (World Health Organization, 2020c). Moreover, according to the International Labour Organization (2020), most labourers lost their jobs due to the uncertainties triggered by COVID-19. With a greater informal economy ratio, people have experienced massive harm with regards to their income and earnings.

The nexus of entrepreneurship is a backbone of economic development at regional and global levels (Papadopoulos *et al.*, 2020). However, this nexus is hit very hard by COVID-19 and the pandemic wave has caused unexpected fluctuations (Castro & Zermeño, 2020). Preventive measures like lockdown, social distancing, and self-isolation have also adversely affected entrepreneurs socially, economically, psychologically, and physically. This crisis of the COVID-19 has created disruptions on the downstream and upstream of businesses worldwide.

These disruptions are in the form of closure of businesses and employment and self-employment opportunities taken away from many people, which have been converted into economic burden (Ratten, 2020c). Lockdowns forcefully applied by government(s) paused all social activities, commuting, and made all people stay at home and eat at home. This situation caused severe business loss to the food sector and suppliers (Korsgaard *et al.*, 2020). Lockdowns and sometimes curfews applied in different countries stopped human movement (Brahmi & Adaala, 2014), and travel and transport mechanisms are slowed down to a fundamental level. This condition reduced tourism — a substantial income source and revenue (Syriopoulos, 2020). Thus, this pandemic has caused an economic recession, not only in the food and tourism sector, but also in all forms of the entrepreneurial activities. Therefore, this study aims to explore how COVID-19 has taken entrepreneurship in its fold across different situations and from different geographic locations.

In this regard, an evaluation of the relevant and latest research articles is conducted. Articles are sorted out with keywords "entrepreneurship, COVID-19 and entrepreneurship, effects of COVID-19 on small business, challenges, future threats to the business". As for the time range, articles are sorted from two aspects: coverage of entrepreneurship is sorted within the recent five years, and regarding the pandemic, articles are sorted by the year January 2020. The findings of the study are presented under relevant headings as mentioned below.

8.2 Methodology

This is a conceptual paper where extant and relevant literature is analysed. The articles were searched through Web of Science, Elsevier, and Google Scholar research engines. The selection criteria of articles were using keywords: entrepreneurship, self-employment, and small business in relation with COVID-19. The research articles were searched using the keywords related to the COVID-19 crisis. However, the search was limited to the specific time period of last one year due to the nature of the issue. Furthermore, based on the review (Crick *et al.*, 2021), a conceptual framework is developed, and hypotheses are proposed for future direction.

8.2.1 *Dynamics of Entrepreneurship*

According to Haynie *et al.* (2010), the definition of entrepreneurship is "the ability to be flexible, dynamic, and self-regulating in one's given dynamic and uncertain task environments". Entrepreneurial skills enable individuals to recognise and understand how to create opportunities for new businesses. This information can be very helpful and beneficial for the wellbeing of individuals in society. The aim of entrepreneurship is to improve businesses' competitiveness through risk taking and innovation. Entrepreneurship offers different places and status quo for businesses to reestablish and make changes that emphasise more on innovation. Reinvigoration, value creation, and integration are three important motivations in the field of entrepreneurship (Ratten, 2017).

There are three components of an individual's attitude to entrepreneurship i.e., affective, cognitive, and behavioural components.

Affective components are concerned with the emotions and feeling of the individual towards entrepreneurship, cognitive refers to the knowledge, beliefs, and thoughts which an individual processes, whereas behavioural is concerned with the response of the individual towards entrepreneurship activities, meaning they will act differently according to the given situations. Entrepreneurs can be divided into two types according to the level of risk — one is sinking the boat and the other is missing the boat. Sinking the boat means a business failure which stops the business and creates barriers in future possibilities. In contrast, missing the boat means they are not benefitting from the available or given opportunity (Ratten & Jones, 2020). Consequently, entrepreneurs sometimes face massive risk in every kind of decision they ever made, ranging from high to low depending on the given situations.

Entrepreneurship is considered a competitive model of the 20th century, which introduces innovative thinking, how to reestablish, reorganize, and recraft a broad range of spaces and settings, and goals which help in transformation and social change which is far beyond simple economic initiatives and commerce (Steyaert & Katz, 2004). Some individuals have more entrepreneurial abilities than many others; some people can figure out acceptable behaviours in a more entrepreneurial way. So, there is a typical understanding among makers of policies that the intentions of entrepreneurship can make a positive impact on society. Entrepreneurship helps and contributes equally to the welfare of the society and an ecologically sustainable economy (Dean & McMullen, 2007). Entrepreneurship opens door of new opportunities and paves way for the self-employment for those people who attend higher education and remain worried secure the employment (Hattab, 2014).

Entrepreneurship has a significant impact on the welfare of the economy. Empirical results in the literature show that there is a positive effect of entrepreneurship in the formation and development of regions/areas which increases the performance of the economy. On the other side, entrepreneurship has a significant impact on the GDP and employment level of the country; furthermore, entrepreneurship is positively effective on social welfare. Poverty can be removed with self-employment in short-term, and inequality in income can be decreased with the help of self-employment in the medium duration (Neumann, 2020).

8.2.2 *The COVID-19 Puzzle*

An infectious virus with an unpredictable nature — later named COVID-19 — started spreading from Wuhan, China (Toresdahl & Asif, 2020). It was officially declared a Public Health Emergency on January 30 and a pandemic on March 11, 2020 by the World Health Organization (World Health Organization, 2020a, 2020b; Cucinotta & Vanelli, 2020). To date, a report from John Hopkins University shows that 51.2 million cases have been reported worldwide. Yet, it is just a small glimpse of what happened back in 1918, when a chaotic situation created by a deadly influenza pandemic affected about 500 million people globally (Nicola *et al.*, 2020). It is just not possible to stop COVID-19 from spreading as top infection disease experts believe this virus is not going anywhere anytime soon, and infected cases are surging at a rapid pace every single day.

Various efforts and strategies have been proposed and implemented by different countries to control the mysterious behaviour of COVID-19, which have been proved to be partially effective, so that the world can get back to normalisation (Chaudhry *et al.*, 2020). However, the world is not in favour of being locked down until the virus completely disappears (Gupta *et al.*, 2020). If such policies and strategies are imposed for an extended period, unimaginable loss of economy will take years to recover. In the beginning, when countries decided to lock down their countries and limit the access of their networks with other countries, all kinds of businesses, whether large or small, came under serious threat.

COVID-19 has not just affected public health; a significant part of the world's economy has also been severely affected (Nicola *et al.*, 2020). COVID-19 has caused stress in psychological as well as social ways of life at individual, however, at large, it has created stress in overall business activities around the world (Ratten, 2020a, 2020b).

Currently, every single business sector has been seriously affected, which has caused a slowdown of the global economy (Hasanat *et al.*, 2020). Tourist and hospitality industries, which rely on close communication between individuals, have been most affected by restrictions, suggesting that the world should get ready for the most significant recession (Ratten, 2020a) after the global financial crisis of 2008. It is safe to say that the world economy is on the verge of recovering from 2008, but the COVID-19 effect on the global economy has not been fully discovered yet; therefore, the recovery of the global economy post-COVID-19 would be either a myth or mystery.

When it comes to giant/multinational companies coping with the disastrous situation, they may take some time. Still, ultimately, they will find some rhythm in their business activities once they go past such periods. The nature of the entrepreneurship business model varies in the global economy and is more vulnerable to sustain in the market if their flow stops for some reason (Morgan *et al.*, 2020). Therefore, COVID-19 has put a serious challenge for entrepreneurs to cope with the uncertain situation.

8.2.3 *COVID-19 Overlap*

While entrepreneurship activity is one of the essential components of the global economy, COVID-19 has had a significant influence on its ability to remain profitable (Parnell *et al.*, 2020). In today's business-oriented society, entrepreneurship has widely been regarded as an essential and most promising force for the socio-economic, competitiveness, and business sectors (Jones *et al.*, 2018). Following the perception that all business industries (Mohsen & Sonia, 2014) have a creative nature, the COVID-19 downturn has given rise to uncertainty and discontent over what should be done (Kraus *et al.*, 2020; Liguori & Winkler., 2020; Alon *et al.*, 2020).

The current COVID-19 pandemic has given rise to predictions of economic recession and crisis triggered by a high degree of instability (Nicola *et al.*, 2020). Some facets of culture have been influenced by COVID-19, such as the introduction of new social measures, for instance, self-isolation and social distancing (Briscese *et al.*, 2020). Primarily, the coronavirus was based in China but then expanded to other regions of Asia, including Japan and South Korea (Sohrabi *et al.*, 2020). After that, Italy was the epicenter of the novel virus for a while.

Then, COVID-19 started spreading to Spain, Germany, France, and other European countries and sustained a high level of cases (Pullano *et al.*, 2020; Stoecklin *et al.*, 2020; Rothe *et al.*, 2020; Haltiwanger, 2021). After only a month, the United States and Brazil were the two new epicenters of COVID-19 (Pereira *et al.*, 2020; Neiva *et al.*, 2020). It just took a few months for almost every country to find the symptoms of the COVID-19 virus.

The way COVID-19 spread was detrimental not just for people's survival, entrepreneurship practices/activities around the world were also affected severely (Facebook/OECD/World Bank, 2020). The global economy soon started to shiver under the COVID-19 threat. Industries' structure began to tremble, and the global economy was significantly affected at a fast pace (Szostak & Sulkowski, 2021). It was an appalling situation for many businesses, especially small and medium enterprises (SMEs) which have been considered as the most threatened group as they have limited resources and are financially constraint. To evaluate the whole COVID-19 situation, part of this research will analyse the countrywide effect of the pandemic.

The COVID-19 pandemic and the economic shutdowns have a massive effect on small and medium-sized businesses worldwide (Haltiwanger, 2021). Most countries have implemented lockdown policies, which have directly compelled much business to stop in-person operations. While small and medium-sized firms can always be resilient in responding to economic circumstances, the pandemic severity has amplified many of the difficulties they face even during regular cycles, including access to capital, restrictions on cash flow, and disturbances to supply chains (Shepherd, 2020).

A survey conducted by the OCED reports that during the period of January to May 2020, 26% or more than one-quarter of businesses had closed their businesses, although significant variations were found at the regional and country-level (Bartik *et al.*, 2020). In the OCED survey, it was found that 46% of SMEs were closed in South Asian countries, which includes Bangladesh and India, where about 50% and 47% were affected respectively. The Pacific region and East Asian countries contributed to 18% of surveyed countries. Europe was about 21%; countries like Germany had lesser closure rate at 8%.

It was discovered through another survey that more than half of the businesses were closed due to government and health authority concerns. In the Pacific region and East Asia, the closure rates of SMEs was reported as 4% in Taiwan, 10% in Japan, and 10% in South Korea. The closure rates of these countries are compared with Singapore having 31%, where the most stringent lockdown measures were taken (Oxford COVID-19 Government Response Tracker, 2020).

Several possible causes have been reported for this heterogeneity because of time variations, outbreak severity of COVID-19, differing responses through policies, and economic features throughout the regions, for instance, sectoral structure. Related differences have been found in European countries. SMEs in the Netherlands, Sweden, Czech Republic, and Germany registered closure rate at less than 10%, as the countries introduced comparatively restricted locking controls.

On the other hand, Ireland (58%) and the United Kingdom (43%) had the highest closure rate in the region. Closing rates were also increased, though less volatile, throughout sub-Saharan Africa (SSA), the Middle East and North Africa (MENA), and Latin American countries. These regions were severely affected as SMEs' closure rates were between 35–45%, as reported by the Organisation for Economic Cooperation and Development (OECD) survey (Ratten, 2020c; Brown *et al.*, 2020).

As countries prepared to implement lockdowns, the highest number of SMEs closed their businesses by the directives of the government and health authorities. Nigeria and Ghana were exceptional, where approximately 50% of closed SMEs registered financial constraints. Given the lockout steps, this trend puts some shade on the capacity of SMEs to continue working. Indeed, as per the Oxford COVID-19 Government Response Tracker calculation, the association between the stringency of government lockdown measures and SMEs closure rate was found distinct in these regions (Zahra, 2021).

The COVID-19 pandemic timing and the subsequent constraints imposed on non-essential business were both linked to SME closures. About 53% of SMEs that were reported to be closed were active in the business until March 2020. It was the month when governments in many countries implemented stringent lockout and social distancing restrictions. Take for example Peru, where 63% of businesses closed in March, correlating with the lockdown measures implemented around March 16. Consumer-focused business (Chaudhry *et al.*, 2021) and micro-businesses have been significantly impacted by tourism and associated businesses. The lists of industries that were shut down, as reported in the OECD survey, are listed below (Maritz *et al.*, 2020).

(1) Tourism and travel agencies, 55%
(2) Event services and hospitality, 47%
(3) Childcare services and education, 45%
(4) Entertainment and performing arts, 36%
(5) Restaurants, cafes, and hotels, 32%

Smaller firms have lower capacities to survive a protracted economic crisis with restricted access to capital and cash reserves (JPMCI, 2020). Moreover, about 19% of SMEs with greater than 50 employees were listed as being closed. Micro-enterprises, identified here as small and medium-sized enterprises owned and run by one person, were the most vulnerable. At the time of the study, micro-businesses reported a 30% closure rate because of the current scenario (Verma & Gustafsson, 2020).

It can be noticed that the overall effect of the pandemic on businesses has been a devastating influence on their survival. G20 leaders projected a V-shaped curve with a sharp and short-lived dip, accompanied by a fast acceleration in economic activities to rebound from the financial crisis. Secretary General of the OECD, Angel Gurría, strongly disagreed with these statements. He concluded that the road to sustainable prosperity is more likely to resemble a U curve, with coming years of prolonged economic stagnation (Szu, 2020).

8.2.4 *Trajectory Path of Entrepreneurship in the Future*

The emergence of the COVID-19 pandemic has created an unprecedented disturbance in economic, social, and cultural systems worldwide. Almost every sector of the economy is effective by this global pandemic, whether it is related to social distancing, public health care system, production, education, etc. The ongoing issues and challenges fuel us to think about post-COVID-19 precautions, so policymakers should take initiative measures to protect the social and economic systems of their country. Entrepreneurship is a great contributor in the social welfare of the economy and entrepreneurs are playing a very vital role in reorganising the economic system, although it is expectedly affected by COVID-19. This global pandemic has transformed and changed human life today and for years to come. COVID-19 is the burning issue and therefore, numerous research scholars are putting their contribution in this topic. This research addresses how entrepreneurs can survive in this global pandemic situation now and in the coming future.

Today and for many coming years, COVID-19 has changed the living standard of humans in many aspects globally and transforms everything towards digitalisation. COVID-19 has pushed many organisations (SMEs) and industries to continue their work remotely on online platforms such as Zoom, Microsoft Teams, Webinar, Skype and so on. The majority of organisations and employees have embarked on such type of work practices for the very first time. In certain situation, it is very challenging for some organisations to maintain their organisational culture in remote environments (Barnes, 2020).

Some organisations and industries like finance, information and communication, entrepreneurship, businesses, and education have the ability to adopt and access new technologies like home-working by using the above-mentioned services and available skills. A central point of contention is the degree to which new innovation-empowered work practices will get implanted or will keep on changing after the pandemic (Filipe Bela *et al.*, 2020; Shaikh *et al.*, 2021b).

Due to the pandemic, online shopping is growing massively, consumers prefer to buy goods and services through online. In the situation of lockdown, online sales have increased significantly, many countries experiencing extremely large increase in online customers and consumers. In the meantime, various businesses have pivoted towards online/digital business to generate revenue and save themselves from losses, whereas prevailing online businesses like online supermarkets, hardware stores have prospered. Entrepreneurs are adopting innovations in technologies in COVID-19 situations because these technologies can provide the virtual platform to create and improve the engagement and interaction of consumers (Carter, 2020).

Zahra (2021) stated that COVID-19 has affected almost $90 trillion of the economy globally, which was not experienced before by any country in previous pandemics. COVID-19 has altered the environment of the businesses by initiating challenging barriers in the expansion of international ventures. It has also divested many SMEs in many ways (Brahmi & Sonia, 2013). The world is offering many opportunities for these kinds of SMEs in this pandemic. In reality, many organisations and entrepreneurs found different ways for their survival and are experiencing growth in their business since this pandemic begins by turning their business into a new shape, e.g., home entertainment, telemedicine, enterprise technology services, robotics, suppliers of medical equipment's, e-learning, e-commerce retailers, delivery services, sanitary manufactured products (Bögenhold, 2021), and courier pickups are some among them.

Besides this, entrepreneurs need to speed up to take advantages from their re-orientation of entrepreneurial activities by analysing the risk and innovations and making different strategic planning proactively. These SMEs should maintain their entrepreneurialism by getting support from human capital, reducing the cost through outsourcing workers, and replenishing their most skilled, dedicated, and knowledgeable workers who preserve and create the knowledgeable base of the organisations with their core competencies and skills.

Brown and Rocha (2020) state that during the pandemic, investors and entrepreneurs were unable to interact or meet with their clients, affecting their different networks and functions and also their underlying processes of investments were ceased. Entrepreneurs should take quick strategic decisions in response to tackle such crises along with governmental policies, e.g., officials of many countries offered incentives of time bound investments to help entrepreneurs deflect the decrease in finance, especially those who were significantly affected by the pandemic (Hasani & O'Reilly, 2021).

Furthermore, policymakers also facilitate entrepreneurs and investors with online platforms so that they can carry out their private engagement of equity crowd-funding between them. These online brokerages firms can help to ease the informational issues related to financial distancing throughout the COVID-19 crisis. Moreover, authors suggest that the theory of entrepreneurial behaviour (Mihir & Mohsen, 2021) seems to be a potential for entrepreneurs to response towards the parsimony of resources brought by the pandemic, specifically in starting up financial innovations and different experimental approaches.

It is suggested by Giones *et al.* (2020) that entrepreneurs should shape resilience by embracing innovative opportunities and promote social support during social distancing and in the future. Based on recent literature on the crisis caused by the pandemic, and regarding what should be the planning of entrepreneurs for their survival, emotional support, and frugality and for start-up of their businesses (Dana *et al.*, 2021), entrepreneurs and other stakeholders are advised to adopt a frugal culture in their organisations to prioritise and protect the resources which are meaningful for the venture in a long period of time, try to adjust in more frequent and less formal planning or business activities, and manage to exchange the internal and external emotional support to run their businesses smoothly.

Ratten (2020) suggests that entrepreneurs and stakeholders should design innovative solutions which have the component of value addition which can integrate strategically with the entrepreneurial orientation explicitly. They can also increase their capitalisation with the use of innovative planning of technology in augmented reality. Kuckertz *et al.* (2020) stated in their study that entrepreneurs should initiate creative ideas to get opportunities and to solve problems; to operate businesses during the pandemic, some adjustments are required which should be specific to certain situations.

These adjustments can incorporate lifestyle, social, and cultural changes to integrate with hygiene and social distancing, so as to continue the perspective of entrepreneurial lifestyle which balance the work and lifestyle of the entrepreneurs during the pandemic. Additionally, SMEs should take advantage by gaining opportunities to increase total productively and efficiency, c.g., work remotely, which will help them to improve ideas related to the progress of the business, community, social entrepreneurship, and non-profit activities (Aifuwa *et al.*, 2020).

8.3 Conceptual Framework

8.3.1 *COVID-19 and Entrepreneurs*

The aim of entrepreneurship is to improve businesses' competitiveness through risk taking and innovation. Entrepreneurship offers different places and status quo for the business to reestablish and make changes that emphasis more on the innovation (Ratten, 2017). The way COVID-19 spread was unfavourable not just for people's survival, entrepreneurship practices and activities were also affected severely around the world (Facebook/OECD/World Bank, 2020).

Entrepreneurship is a great contributor to the social welfare of the economy. Entrepreneurs are playing a very vital role in reorganising the economic system, although they are expectedly greatly affected by the COVID-19 crisis (Ratten, 2020c, 2021). COVID-19 has created great disruption for the entrepreneurs and has negative effect because of the financial loss, and it is very challenging for businesses and entrepreneurs as in how they will respond towards this crisis (Alon *et al.*, 2020; Shaikh *et al.*, 2021a).

Different solutions or approaches are needed to manage the COVID-19 crisis which are more powerful than all previous pandemics. Entrepreneurs are much more active in terms of socio-economic activities which give an approach to society to recuperate from the novel coronavirus crisis (Ratten, 2020c, 2021). In this context, the study tries to ascertain the spillover of the COVID on entrepreneurship (Zahra, 2021). On the basis of above-mentioned emerging perspective of literature on how COVID-19 affects entrepreneurs and as mentioned in the Figure 8.1, the following research hypothesis is formulated:

H1: The COVID-19 crisis significantly affects entrepreneurs.

8.3.2 *COVID-19 and Employees*

Hamouche (2020) stated that the novel coronavirus outbreak has a negative effect on the mental and physical health of employees, especially depression and psychological distress because of loss of job and financial crisis. According to the International Labour Organization (2020), most labourers lost their jobs due to the uncertainties triggered by COVID-19. With a greater informal economy ratio, people have experienced massive harm regarding their income and earnings.

These disruptions are in the form of the closure of business and snatched employment and self-employment opportunities from many people, which were converted into an economic burden (Ratten, 2020c). Following the perception that all business industries have a creative nature, the COVID-19 downturn has given rise to uncertainty and discontent over what should be done (Kraus *et al.*, 2020; Liguori & Winkler, 2020; Alon *et al.*, 2020).

The global economy started shivering under the COVID-19 threat. Bajrami *et al.* (2020) tested the different effects of the novel coronavirus on employees with respect to mental health because of isolation, work from home, job insecurity, and

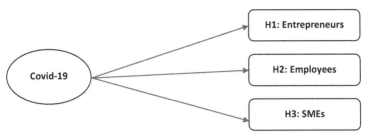

Figure 8.1.   Conceptual model

different changes in the atmosphere of the organisation (Mohsen & Luigi, 2021).

The results show that there is a negative effect of COVID-19 on employees and intentions of the turnover of employees. On the basis of the above emerging perspective of literature on how COVID-19 affects employees and as mentioned in the Figure 8.1, the following research hypothesis is formulated:

H2: The COVID-19 crisis significantly affects the employees.

8.3.3 *COVID-19 and SMEs*

The COVID-19 pandemic and subsequent economic shutdowns have had a massive effect on small and medium-sized businesses worldwide (Nadia *et al.*, 2021). Most countries have implemented lockdown policies, which have directly compelled many businesses to stop in-person operations (Ratten, 2020c). While small and medium-sized firms can always be resilient in responding to economic circumstances (Mohsen *et al.*, 2014), the pandemic's severity has amplified many of the difficulties they face even during regular cycles, including access to capital, restrictions on cash flow, and disturbances to supply chains (Shepherd, 2020). Industries' structure began to tremble, and the global economy was significantly affected at a fast pace.

It was a deplorable situation for many businesses, especially SMEs. In this regard, there are concerns about how businesses will survive after COVID-19 and how the business world will look like. A survey conducted by OCED reports that during the period of January to May 2020, 26%, or more than one-quarter of businesses, had closed their businesses (Mohsen, 2013). However, significant variations were found at the regional and country-level (Bartik *et al.*, 2020).

This crisis of the COVID-19 pandemic has created disruptions in the downstream and upstream of businesses worldwide. Smaller firms have less capacity to survive a protracted economic crisis, as they have restricted access to capital and cash reserves (JPMCI, 2020). Moreover, about 19% of SMEs with greater than 50 employees were listed as being closed (Zahra, 2021). On the basis of the above emerging perspective of literature on COVID-19 crises affects employees and as mentioned in the Figure 8.1, the following research hypothesis is formulated:

H3: The COVID-19 crisis significantly affects SMEs.

8.4 Conceptual Framework

We proposed the conceptual model to be tested that suggests three hypotheses. The model proposes that COVID-19 has significant impact on three entities i.e. entrepreneurs, their employees as well as SMEs as a whole.

8.5 Policy Implications

The COVID-19 pandemic has produced social and economic shocks, considering such drastic conditions. The study provides the following implications. Through this study, stakeholders of the COVID-19 affected countries worldwide will know how to encourage entrepreneurial activities to survive after the COVID-19 pandemic. Additionally, entrepreneurs will gain insights from this study, in that they will know from the suggestions made, how to navigate the tough times in their businesses through shifting to the digital market to import or supply products.

Furthermore, on the basis of the literature, this research study proposes the conceptual model on the effects of COVID-19 on entrepreneurs, employees, and SMEs (Brahmi & Laadjal, 2015) which is a very important and significant contribution of this research study. This conceptual model tries to focus on the effects of the COVID-19 pandemic and how entrepreneurs, employees, and SMEs can survive from such crises. Much research has been done on the effects of COVID-19, but less attention is paid to this research area. This study has proposed the model for empirical analysis only, which creates a gap for future researchers to analyse this conceptual model statistically and fill this research gap. This is also the limitation of this current study.

8.5.1 *Future Recommendations*

(a) Countries around the globe need to provide different business incentives to small businesses in tax rebates, suspended loan repayment, interest-free loans, and stimulus schemes to keep them afloat while the COVID-19 crisis persists.

(b) Entrepreneurship and entrepreneurs on their part should work hard to automate their operational processes to reduce cost, time, and physical contact with people, and communicate and coordinate online.

8.5.2 *Future Research Direction*

The transformations brought by the COVID-19 pandemic have changed the environment for entrepreneurship activities, which are very intensive, and lasting. Such transformations present a multitude of challenges and opportunities for enterprises and entrepreneurs. Based on the new normal, entrepreneurs are likely to establish new approaches to reframe the issues in order to carry on entrepreneurial activities and to embark on innovation.

This study was conducted after the first wave of COVID-19 and the second wave was on its way, amid this situation, mutated strands of COVID-19 were found in the UK and South Africa, which were predicted to be more severe and rapidly contagious. This was a new warning to the world and might pose new and uncertain threats all walks of life and business activities.

8.6 Conclusion

The questions and issues outlined in the preceding paragraphs do not fully capture all potentially interesting questions to be studied in future research. They simply illustrate the rich variety of topics that researchers are likely to encounter as they analyse entrepreneurial activities during the pandemic era. What is clear is that a new and powerful wave of creative destruction has occurred, leading to a great transformation of the global business environment that the COVID-19 crisis has caused.

Thus, research on entrepreneurship entails that entrepreneur are the driving force of disruption (Chaves-Maza & Martel, 2020). The existing situation caused by the COVID-19 pandemic caused the disruption in the entire system and the world order. With respect to the conceptual model as mentioned in the Figure 8.1, such disruption has triggered a new normal. In this new normal, the role of the entrepreneur is very challenging to play. This situation can be compared to the role of local entrepreneurs who had shown interest to build back better in response to the 2010 Haiti earthquake (Williams & Shepherd, 2016). By the way, it is uncertain to say that the liquidity of everything can affect entrepreneurial intentions and actions to build back a new normal and bring back to the equilibrium (Kuckertz *et al.*, 2020).

However, prior studies believe that emerging technologies and dynamic markets have extended the duration of the stability that is penetrated by the disruptions. The outbreak of the virus may be translated as the magnitude and frequency of the adverse events and activities as disruptions are emerging. Resultantly, there will be a new normal in every walk of life. Entrepreneurship scholars are well-positioned to explore how people, organisations, and nations effectively respond to these adverse events, and in doing so, contribute to the knowledge of resilience at and across multiple levels of analysis.

The COVID-19 pandemic has caused creative destruction to the world of business and transformed all traditional methods and approaches to novel and innovative approaches. Restrictions to mobility of people and lockdowns have caused total shutdown to major economic activities and have adversely affected the overall growth of businesses and the world economy.

Tucker (2020) suggested the outbreak of COVID-19 escalated bankruptcy. Simultaneously, Naveen and Anders (2020) indicated a disruption in countries' business frequency due to COVID-19. That is very true for entrepreneurial activities, and their survival received a significant threat at native, national, and international levels. However, shifting to online could be a possible survival solution, although depending on the nature of the business activities. The analysis of the study exposes a reality about entrepreneurship, in that entrepreneurial activities of all nature and kinds are hanging in the balance and all may not come out of the pandemic unscathed.

References

Aifuwa, H. O., Saidu, M., & Aifuwa, S. A. (2020). Coronavirus pandemic outbreak and firm's performance in Nigeria. *Management and Human Resources Research, 12*(3), 287–302.

Alon, I., Farrell, M., & Li, S. (2020). Regime type and COVID-19 response. *FIIB Business Review, 9*(3), 152–160.

Audretsch, D. B., Cunningham, J. A., Kuratko, D. F., Lehmann, E. E., & Menter, M. (2019). Entrepreneurial ecosystems: economic, technological, and societal impacts. *The Journal of Technology Transfer, 44*(2), 313–325.

Bajrami, D. D., Terzić, A., Petrović, M. D., Radovanović, M., Tretiakova, T. N., & Hadoud, A. (2020). Will we have the same employees in hospitality after all? The impact of COVID-19 on employees' work attitudes and turnover intentions. *International Journal of Hospitality Management,* 102754.

Barnes, S. J. (2020). Information management research and practice in the post-COVID-19 world. *International Journal of Information Management, 55*, 102175.

Bartik, A. W., Bertrand, M., Cullen, Z., Glaeser, E. L., Luca, M., & Stanton, C. (2020). The impact of COVID-19 on small business outcomes and expectations. *Proceedings of the National Academy of Sciences, 117*(30), 17656–17666.

Bögenhold, D. (2019). From hybrid entrepreneurs to entrepreneurial billionaires: Observations on the socioeconomic heterogeneity of self-employment. *American Behavioral Scientist, 63*(2), 129–146.

Bögenhold, D. (2020). History of Economic Thought as an Analytic Tool: why Past Intellectual Ideas Must Be Acknowledged as Lighthouses for the Future. International Advances in Economic Research, *26*(1).

Brahmi, M., & Adaala, A. (2014), Main indicators of the Tunisian banking system, inflation and financial context: possibility of inflation targets as a remedy. *International Journal of Economics, Business and Finance, 2*(6), 1–22.

Brahmi, M., & Laadjal, A. (2015), The strategic choices of small medium-sized enterprises integration: Evidence from specific economic territory. *Acta Universitatis Danubius. Economica, 11*(2), 254–271.

Brahmi, M., & Sonia, Z. (2013). Transformations de l'économie mondiale, dernière crise financière et récessions économiques mondiales: mesures et précautions. *Strategy and Development Review, 4*(7), 23–71. http://193.194.91.150:8080/en/article/7908

Briscese, G., Lacetera, N., Macis, M., & Tonin, M. (2020). Compliance with Covid-19 social-distancing measures in Italy: The role of expectations and duration (No. w26916). National Bureau of Economic Research.

Brown, R., & Rocha, A. (2020). Entrepreneurial uncertainty during the Covid-19 crisis: Mapping the temporal dynamics of entrepreneurial finance. *Journal of Business Venturing Insights, 14*, e00174.

Brown, R., Rocha, A., & Cowling, M. (2020). Financing entrepreneurship in times of crisis: Exploring the impact of COVID-19 on the market for entrepreneurial finance in the United Kingdom. *International Small Business Journal, 38*(5), 380–390.

Carter, S. (2020). UX and e-commerce: Comparing the best practices in Europe, Asia, North America, South America, and Africa. In *Handbook of Research on User Experience in Web 2.0 Technologies and Its Impact on Universities and Businesses*, pp. 316–352. IGI Global.

Castro, M. P., & Zermeño, M. G. G. (2020). Being an entrepreneur post-COVID-19–resilience in times of crisis: a systematic literature review. *Journal of Entrepreneurship in Emerging Economies*, 2053–4604. doi:10.1108/JEEE-07-2020-0246

Chaudhry, I. S., Paquibut, R. Y., & Tunio, M. N. (2021). Do workforce diversity, inclusion practices, & organizational characteristics contribute to organizational innovation? Evidence from the UAE. *Cogent Business & Management, 8*(1), 1947549.

Chaudhry, R., Dranitsaris, G., Mubashir, T., Bartoszko, J., & Riazi, S. (2020). A country level analysis measuring the impact of government actions, country preparedness and socioeconomic factors on COVID-19 mortality and related health outcomes. *EClinicalMedicine, 25*, 100464.

Chaves-Maza, M., & Martel, E. M. F. (2020). Entrepreneurship support ways after the COVID-19 crisis. *Entrepreneurship and Sustainability Issues, 8*(2), 662.

Crick, J. M. (2021). Qualitative research in marketing: What can academics do better? *Journal of Strategic Marketing, 29*(5), 390–429.

Cucinotta, D., & Vanelli, M. (2020). WHO declares COVID-19 a pandemic? *Acta Bio Medica: Atenei Parmensis, 91*(1), 157.

Dana, L. P., Tajpour, M., Salamzadeh, A., Hosseini, E., & Zolfaghari, M. (2021). The impact of entrepreneurial education on technology-based enterprises development: The mediating role of motivation. *Administrative Sciences, 11*(4), 105.

Dean, T. J., & McMullen, J. S. (2007). Toward a theory of sustainable entrepreneurship: Reducing environmental degradation through entrepreneurial action. *Journal of Business Venturing, 22*(1), 50–76.

Dvouletý, O. (2019). Development of entrepreneurial activity in the Czech Republic over the years 2005–2017. *Journal of Open Innovation: Technology, Market, and Complexity, 5*(3), 38.

Facebook/OECD/World Bank (2020), The future of business survey. Available at: dataforgood.fb.com/global-state-of-smb

Filipe Bela, A., Wilkinson, D., & Monahan, E. (2020). Technology intensity and homeworking in the UK. Available at: https://www.ons.gov.uk/employmentandlabourmarket/peopleinwork/employmentandemployeetypes/articles/technologyintensityandhomeworkingintheuk/2020-05-01

Giones, F., Brem, A., Pollack, J. M., Michaelis, T. L., Klyver, K., & Brinckmann, J. (2020). Revising entrepreneurial action in response to exogenous shocks: Considering the COVID-19 pandemic. *Journal of Business Venturing Insights, 14*, e00186.

Govindarajo, N. S., Kumar, D., Shaikh, E., Kumar, M., & Kumar, P. (2021). Industry 4.0 and Business Policy Development: Strategic Imperatives for SME Performance. *ETIKONOMI, 20*(2), 239–258.

Gupta, S., Nguyen, T. D., Rojas, F. L., Raman, S., Lee, B., Bento, A., ... & Wing, C. (2020). Tracking public and private responses to the COVID-19 epidemic: evidence from state and local government actions (No. w27027). National Bureau of Economic Research.

Haltiwanger, J. (2021). Entrepreneurship during the COVID-19 pandemic: Evidence from the business formation statistics. NBER Chapters.

Hamouche, S. (2020). COVID-19 and employees' mental health: stressors, moderators, and agenda for organizational actions. *Emerald Open Research, 2.*

Hasanat, M. W., Hoque A., Shikha, F. A., Anwar, M., Hamid, A. B. A., & Tat, H. H. (2020). The impact of coronavirus (COVID-19) on e-business in Malaysia. *Asian Journal of Multidisciplinary Studies, 3*(1), 85–90.

Hasani, T., & O'Reilly, N. (2021). Analyzing antecedents affecting the organizational performance of start-up businesses. *Journal of Entrepreneurship in Emerging Economies, 13*(1), 107–130.

Hattab, H. (2014). Impact of entrepreneurship education on entrepreneurial intentions of university students in Egypt. *The Journal of Entrepreneurship, 23*(1), 1–18.

Haynie, J., Shepherd, D., Mosakowski, E., & Earley, P. (2010). A situated metacognitive model for the entrepreneurial mindset. *Journal of Business Venturing, 25*(2), 217–229.

International Labour Organization (2020). As job losses escalate, nearly half of global workforce at risk of losing livelihoods. Available at: https://www.ilo.org/global/about-the-ilo/newsroom/news/WCMS_743036/lang–en/index.htm

Jones, P., Klapper, R., Ratten, V., & Fayolle, A. (2018). Emerging themes in entrepreneurial behaviours, identities, and contexts. *The International Journal of Entrepreneurship and Innovation, 19*(4), 233–236.

Katper, N. K., Tunio, M. N., Hussain, N., Junejo, A., & Gilal, F. G. (2020). COVID-19 Crises: Global Economic Shocks vs Pakistan Economic Shocks. *Advances in Science, Technology and Engineering Systems Journal, 5*(4), 645–654.

Korsgaard, S., Hunt, R. A., Townsend, D. M., & Ingstrup, M. B. (2020). COVID-19 and the importance of space in entrepreneurship research and policy. *International Small Business Journal,* 0266242620963942.

Kraus, S., Clauss, T., Breier, M., Gast, J., Zardini, A., & Tiberius, V. (2020). The economics of COVID-19: Initial empirical evidence on how family firms in five European countries cope with the corona crisis. *International Journal of Entrepreneurial Behavior & Research, 26*(5), 1067–1092.

Kuckertz, A., Brändle, L., Gaudig, A., Hinderer, S., Reyes, C. A. M., Prochotta, A., Steinbrink, K. M., & Berger, E. S. (2020). Start-ups in times of crisis — A rapid response to the COVID-19 pandemic. *Journal of Business Venturing Insights*, e00169.

Liguori, E., & Winkler, C. (2020). From offline to online: Challenges and opportunities for entrepreneurship education following the COVID-19 pandemic. *Entrepreneurship Education and Pedagogy, 3*(4), 346–351.

Maritz, A., Perenyi, A., de Waal, G., & Buck, C. (2020). Entrepreneurship as the unsung hero during the current COVID-19 economic crisis: Australian perspectives. *Sustainability, 12*(11), 4612.

Mohsen, B., (2013). Indicateurs statistiques de performance économique et du positionnement mondial de l'industrie minière en Tunisie (1990–2010): Regard avant la révolution 2011. Book of Acts, Informal economy and development: employment, financing and regulation in a context of crisis, the University Paris-Est-Créteil, 6, 7 and 8 June 2013 Paris, France.

Mohsen, B., Sonia, Z., & Bensalem, K. (2014). TIC, innovation et impacts sur l'analyse concurrentielle: Leader Firme du Bassin Minier Tunisien. *International Journal of Innovation and Applied Studies, 10*(1), 195–217. Available at: http://citeseerx.ist.psu.edu/viewdoc/download?doi=10.1.1.679.6710&rep=rep1&type=pdf

Mohsen, B., & Sonia, Z., (2014). The employment policy in the mining industry: A critical study on gender discrimination. *Journal of Asian Business Strategy, 4*(8), 98–107. Available at: http://www.aessweb.com/pdf-files/1-142-4(8)2014-JABS-98-107.pdf

Morgan, T., Anokhin, S., Ofstein, L., & Friske, W. (2020). SME response to major exogenous shocks: The bright and dark sides of business model pivoting. *International Small Business Journal, 38*(5), 369–379.

Neiva, M. B., Carvalho, I., Costa Filho, E. D. S., Barbosa-Junior, F., Bernardi, F. A., Sanches, T. Neu L. M., & Alves, D. (2020). Brazil: The emerging epicenter of COVID-19 pandemic. *Revista da Sociedade Brasileira de Medicina Tropical, 53.*

Neumann, T. (2020). The impact of entrepreneurship on economic, social, and environmental welfare and its determinants: A systematic review. *Management Review Quarterly, 71*(3), 1–32.

Nicola, M., Alsafi, Z., Sohrabi, C., Kerwan, A., Al-Jabir, A., Iosifidis, C., Agha, M., & Agha, R. (2020). The socio-economic implications of the coronavirus and COVID-19 pandemic: A review. *International Journal of Surgery, 78*, 185–193.

Oxford COVID-19 Government Response Tracker (2020). Relationship between several COVID-19 cases and government response. Available at: https://COVIDtracker.bsg.ox.ac.uk/stringency-scatter

Papadopoulos, T., Baltas, K. N., & Balta, M. E. (2020). The use of digital technologies by small and medium enterprises during COVID-19: Implications for theory and practice. *International Journal of Information Management, 55*, 102192.

Parnell, D., Widdop, P., Bond, A., & Wilson, R. (2020). COVID-19, networks, and sport. *Managing Sport and Leisure*, 1–7.

Pereira, M. R., Mohan, S., Cohen, D. J., Husain, S. A., Dube, G. K., Ratner, L. E., ... & Verna, E. C. (2020). COVID-19 in solid organ transplant recipients: initial report from the US epicenter. *American Journal of Transplantation, 20*(7), 1800–1808.

Pullano, G., Pinotti, F., Valdano, E., Boëlle, P. Y., Poletto, C., & Colizza, V. (2020). Novel coronavirus (2019-nCoV) early-stage importation risk to Europe, January 2020. *Eurosurveillance, 25*(4), 2000057.

Ratten, V. (2017). Entrepreneurial universities: The role of communities, people, and places. *Journal of Enterprising Communities: People and Places in the Global Economy, 11*(3), 310–315.

Ratten, V. (2020a). Coronavirus (COVID-19) and entrepreneurship: Changing life and work landscape. *Journal of Small Business & Entrepreneurship, 32*(5), 503–516.

Ratten, V. (2020b). Coronavirus disease (COVID-19) and sport entrepreneurship. *International Journal of Entrepreneurial Behavior & Research, 26*(6), 1379–1388.

Ratten, V. (2020c). Coronavirus (COVID-19) and entrepreneurship: Cultural, lifestyle and societal changes. *Journal of Entrepreneurship in Emerging Economies, 13*(4), 747–761.

Ratten, V. (2021). COVID-19 and entrepreneurship: Future research directions. *Strategic Change, 30*(2), 91–98.

Ratten, V., & Jones, P. (2020). Entrepreneurship and management education: Exploring trends and gaps. *The International Journal of Management Education*, 100431.

Rothe, C., Schunk, M., Sothmann, P., Bretzel, G., Froeschl, G., Wallrauch, C., ... & Hoelscher, M. (2020). Transmission of 2019-nCoV infection from an asymptomatic contact in Germany. *New England Journal of Medicine, 382*(10), 970–971.

Secundo, G., Gioconda, M. E. L. E., Del Vecchio, P., Gianluca, E. L. I. A., Margherita, A., & Valentina, N. D. O. U. (2021). Threat or opportunity? A case study of digital-enabled redesign of entrepreneurship education in the COVID-19 emergency. *Technological forecasting and social change, 166*, 120565.

Shaikh, E., Mishra, V., Ahmed, F., Krishnan, D., & Dagar, V. (2021a). Exchange Rate, Stock Price and Trade Volume in US-China Trade War during COVID-19: An Empirical Study. *Studies of Applied Economics, 39*(8).

Shaikh, E., Tunio, M. N., & Qureshi, F. (2021b). Finance and women's entrepreneurship in DETEs: A literature review. *Entrepreneurial Finance, Innovation and Development*, 191–209.

Shepherd, D. A. (2020). COVID 19 and entrepreneurship: Time to pivot? *Journal of Management Studies, 57*(8), 1750–1753.

Sohrabi, C., Alsafi, Z., O'Neill, N., Khan, M., Kerwan, A., Al-Jabir, A., Iosifidis, C., & Agha, R. (2020). World Health Organization declares global emergency: A review of the 2019 novel coronavirus (COVID-19). *International Journal of Surgery, 76*, 71–76.

Steyaert, C., & Katz, J. (2004). Reclaiming the space of entrepreneurship in society: geographical, discursive, and social dimensions. *Entrepreneurship & Regional Development, 16*(3), 179–196.

Stoecklin, S. B., Rolland, P., Silue, Y., Mailles, A., Campese, C., Simondon, A., ... & Levy-Bruhl, D. (2020). First cases of coronavirus disease 2019 (COVID-19) in France: surveillance, investigations and control measures, January 2020. *Eurosurveillance, 25*(6), 2000094.

Syriopoulos, K. (2020). The impact of COVID-19 on entrepreneurship and SMES. *Journal of the International Academy for Case Studies, 26*(2), 1–2.

Szostak, M., & Sułkowski, Ł. (2021). Identity crisis of artists during the COVID-19 pandemic and shift towards entrepreneurship. *Entrepreneurial Business and Economics Review, 9*(3).

Szu, P. C. (2020, March 23), Global economy will suffer for "years to Come". BBC News. Available at: https://www.bbc.com/ news/business-52000219

Toresdahl, B. G., & Asif, I. M. (2020). Coronavirus disease 2019 (COVID-19): considerations for the competitive athlete. *Sports Health, 12*(3), 221–224.

Tucker, H. (2020). *Coronavirus bankruptcy tracker: These major companies are failing amid the shutdown.* Forbes.

Verma, S., & Gustafsson, A. (2020). Investigating the emerging COVID-19 research trends in the field of business and management: A bibliometric analysis approach. *Journal of Business Research, 118*, 253–261.

Williams, T. A., & Shepherd, D. A. (2016). Building resilience or providing sustenance: Different paths of emergent ventures in the aftermath of the Haiti earthquake. *Academy of Management Journal, 59*(6), 2069–2102.

World Health Organization (2020a). COVID-19 as a Public Health Emergency of International Concern (PHEIC) under the IHR. Available at: https://extranet.who.int/sph/COVID-19-public-health-emergency-international-concern-pheic-under-ihr

World Health Organization (2020b). WHO Director-General's opening remarks at the media briefing on COVID-19 - 11 March 2020. Available at: https://www.who.int/dg/speeches/detail/who-director-general-s-opening-remarks-at-the-media-briefing-on-COVID-19---11-march-2020

World Health Organization (2020c). WHO coronavirus disease (COVID-19) dashboard. Available at: https://COVID19.who.int/?gclid=EAIaIQobCh MIzJ235bzK6gIVDvDACh1fIADVEAAYASAAEgJ6zfD_BwE

Zahra, S. A. (2021). International entrepreneurship in the post COVID world. *Journal of World Business, 56*(1), 101143.

https://doi.org/10.1142/9789811239212_0009

Chapter 9

Relationship Between Personality, Leadership Styles, and Work Environment: A Study of Micro, Small and Medium Enterprises (MSMEs)

Priyanka Sharma

Department of Commerce, Punjabi University, Patiala,
Punjab, India

pspriyanka827@gmail.com

Sandeep Singh

Punjabi University Regional Centre for IT and Management,
Mohali, Punjab, India

banger.singh36@gmail.com

Rajni Bala

Chitkara Business School, Chitkara University, Punjab, India

bala.rajni@chitkara.edu.in

Abstract: Personality, leadership style, and work environment affect the performance of an individual in an organisation. The objective of the study is to examine the relationship between personality, leadership styles, and work environment. The sample of 285 managers working at Micro, Small and Medium Enterprises (MSMEs) in Punjab, India is taken. A quantitative method is used in the study and the data is collected by using standardised questionnaire. The result of the study shows that majority of personality traits were found associated with transactional leadership style and work environment, while various non-significant correlation results were found between personality and transformational leadership subscales, the transformational leadership style failed to establish a significant relationship with any of the personality subscales, and the personality traits correlated positively, while others negatively with some of the subscales of transactional and transformational leadership and work environment. The study also finds that transactional leadership styles were significantly but negatively correlated with work environment and transformational leadership styles were not significantly correlated with work environment, thus aggregate work environment was significantly correlated with transactional leadership styles.

Keywords: Personality, Work environment, Leadership styles, MSME, Punjab.

9.1 Introduction

Human resource is the most significant and valuable resource in organisations of any size and nature, regardless of where they are located on the planet. According to Qureshi *et al.* (2010), over the past 25 years, the impact of human resource management (HRM) on organisation performance has become hugely significant, showing a powerful association between human resource practices and organisational performance. Many past studies have demonstrated that good service likely appears from workers with great leadership skills and personality. In the performance of the employee, both the developing effect of personality traits and the method of managing employees are important. A high level of personality can perform the required work and easily adapt to the organisational environment. Therefore, to evaluate the performance of the employee based on personality is a fundamental prerequisite as it impacts the decision of the profession, as per Hogan and Holland (2003). As a result, personality traits are the primary elements influencing the performance of an employee in the organisation. Moreover, the management has stringent rules for appraising the personality of the likely employee for the organisation. As indicated by Shalley and Gilson (2004), leadership plays a major role in the performance of employees, while Grant (2012) stated that to build followers performance, transformational leadership is important in inspiring them to rise above personal circumstance. Additionally, transformational leadership can improve employee's performance (Liaw *et al.*, 2010). The work environment is perhaps the fundamental factor for keeping an employee fulfilled in today's business world, as per the latest literature on HRM, while keeping other factors constant. Many studies confirmed a positive and significant impact of work environment on employee performance (Chandrasekar, 2011; Gunaseelan & Ollukkaran, 2012; Leblebici, 2012).

In today's era of globalisation where there is a lot of competition, the performance of any organisation determines its prosperity and survival. There are different specialised and behavioural factors that would influence the performance of an organisation. The applicable commitment of behavioural factors is as significant as specialised variables (Singh, 2017; Singh & Bala, 2020). Behavioural science has remained a focal zone and has led to different investigations into behavioural approaches which has been set up legitimately or in a roundabout way to maximise profits and authorise practices. A hierarchical process is a set of commitment made by a large number of workers working in an organisation. The management staff is relied upon to create and maximise profits. Different behavioural factors decide the quality of the management staff. Identity is a mix of different attributes that impact the behaviour of a person. As indicated by Pervin *et al.* (2005), personality alludes to those qualities of the individual that represent steady examples of thinking, behaving, and feelings. Ruch (1963) underlined that personality ought to incorporate outside appearance and conduct, the inward attention to self as a lasting sorting out power, and a specific example of quantifiable characteristics both internal and external.

Personality is related to the mental development and improvement of a person as it reflects the process of progress. Different variables decide personality. It is sorted into biological components, family elements, social elements, and situational factors. Extensive research conducted on personality and its connection between leadership styles have demonstrated a relationship between personality and leadership behaviour (Larsen & Buss, 2011). Leadership is the ability to motivate others to enthusiastically pursue a stated goal. It is the human factor that integrates a social phenomenon and propels it towards the destination. The management, for instance, would be stressed with masterminding, dealing with leadership issues unless the leader or the boss activates his motivation power on the people and connects them to the goal. Leadership changes potential into reality. It is a conclusive showing which seeks to advance the recognised outcomes in affiliations and family (Strauss, 1966). According to Bennis (1959), a leader is a bit of an administrator, yet only one out of many aspects. He combines the needs of his admirers with the greater needs of the entire population in which it exists. The work environment is a play area in which each of these factors comes into play in real life. If any event in the work environment is negative, it influences the inclusion, activity, and confidence of the workers. The work environment has an important role in group building and relationship among the workers. Moos (1994) highlighted the importance of considering the work environment because assessing the work environment is exceptionally important for leaders and directors. The fundamental goal of evaluating the workplace is to acquire a change in the organisation. These evaluations would help leaders learn how the adjustment in leadership would affect the work environment (Singh & Dhaliwal, 2015, 2018; Neemta & Singh, 2020).

With a worldwide presence, skill management is a key administrative task in multinational companies and different companies, however, its importance in start-ups and small organisations can't be underestimated. Managing individuals in start-ups and small organisations requires consistency with the appropriate work laws, creating a channel for managing employee issues at any level in an organisation. In a small organisation, the cost of not having the right employees with the right skills can be amazingly high. Although the majority of entrepreneurs initially only think about clients, advertising, production, and finance, this implies that they sometimes neglect to deal with the HR function. Previous studies explained the relationship between personality, leadership style, and work environment in how they affect the performance of an employee in an organisation. As per the best of my knowledge, there is a lack of studies showing an in-depth relationship between the selected variables. Hence, this study will be useful to determine the links between these variables in future.

According to Dana (2000) and Pio and Dana (2014), in order to change the social approach concerning entrepreneurship, endeavours have been made to empower entrepreneurs by giving youths the confidence to be successful people as entrepreneurial skills are considered to be very important with Indians. An entrepreneur is someone who has an inquisitive character and helps to improve the way of life in a society (Dana, 1993; Dana & Dana, 2005). According to Sharma and Singh (2021), the last decade has seen a growing number of start-ups in Punjab. As of August 2018, the Department of Industrial Policy and Promotion (DIPP) has enrolled more than 140 start-ups, and the number is increasing each day. Many people have started to understand the business and educational passion of start-ups. In the last few years, they have shown capability and ability, which has attracted world monetary experts to investigate Punjab's start-up ecosystem. The industry of Punjab is dominated by small and medium enterprises (SMEs) and has a rich, current base of Micro, Small and Medium Enterprises (MSMEs), numbering about 160,000 units, which is significant for industry development. Various promotional steps for industry development have been launched by the Punjab government and monetary sponsorship has been upheld by the Government of India, opening the way for the setting up of MSME ventures that increase the complexity in the state.

9.2 Personality

Personality has been characterised as a trademark example of a person's reasoning, emotion, and practice, as well as the mental systems that drive them. It is a powerful term that is used to refer to the whole psychological, emotional, and intellectual components of human behaviour. Personality is the whole mental union of human character: insightfulness, temperament, ability, profound quality, and every frame of mind that has been developed over a mind-blowing span (Warren & Carmichael, 1930). It isn't dictated by or gained from organic quickness. Personality is the dynamic association inside the person of those psychophysical frameworks that decide his remarkable acclimations to this condition (Allport, 1937) as it is formed by a social and social milieu (Socrokin, 1947). It is the most sufficient conceptualisation of an individual's behaviour in the entirety of its detail (McClelland, 1951). Personality is something which allows a forecast of what an individual will do in a given circumstance (Cattell, 1966). As indicated by Guilford (1959), personality is an individual's exceptional example of characteristics as it is the totality of individual to clairvoyant characteristics, which incorporates personality, one's method of response and character, to object of one's response (Leatt, 1980). Personality grasps all the one-of-a-kind attributes and examples of modification of a person in his relationship with others and his condition (Kalasa, 1970).

9.3 Leadership

Leadership is both a field of research and a practical skill that involves an individual's ability to "lead" or guide different people, groups, or organisations as a whole. It is characterised as a procedure of social impact wherein an individual can enrol the guide and bolster others in the achievement of a typical errand (Chemers, 1997; Chin, 2015). Individuals are our most valuable piece of the organisation and their improvement is a significant obligation through powerful leadership. Newstrom and Davis

(1993) clarified that leadership styles incorporate the complete example of express and verifiable activities performed by their leader. Without leadership, an organisation is nevertheless a jumble of men and machines (Zalaik, 1966). The transformational leadership style was first presented by James M. Burns, who is one of the main researchers that recognised the transformational leadership hypothesis in 1978. The transformational leader directs the devotees to take care of the organisation's issues and improve their organisations by changing how they take a gander at the issue. Yukl (1999) reports that transformational leadership centres around a leader's comprehension of their impact on how adherents feel trust, appreciation, steadfastness, and regard toward the leader and how supporters are propelled to accomplish more than anticipated. Transactional leadership centres on control, not adjustment (Tracey & Hinkin, 1994). Burns (1978) characterises transactional leaders as methodologies supporters with the end goal of trading one thing for another. The idea of transactional leadership is tight in that it doesn't take the whole circumstance, worker, or fate of the organisation as a top priority when offering rewards (Crosby, 1996).

9.4 Work Environment

Yusuf and Metiboba (2012, p. 37) characterise the work environment as three important sub environments, namely the human environment, the organisational environment, and the technical environment (Singh *et al.*, 2021; Bala & Singh, 2021). Accordingly, the technical environment alludes to instruments, gear, innovative foundation, and other physical or technical components of the work environment. The human environment incorporates the colleagues, others with whom workers relate to, group and work gatherings, interactional issues, the leaders, and the executives. An ideal work environment makes the workforce likes going to work, and this is responsible as the inspiration in supporting them as the day progresses. As indicated by Awan and Tahir (2015), environment generally refers to everything that affects individuals for the duration of their life expectancy. A work environment is an environment where people on the whole work on accomplishing hierarchical objectives. It outlines the frameworks, procedures, structures, and devices and each one of these works together with workers and have an encouraging effect on employee performance in positive or negative ways. The work environment can likewise be characterised as one where a task is completed. When the focus is on the working environment, the work environment involves a physical topographical area, for example, a building site or office structure (Singh *et al.*, 2017). It usually comprises different components related to the working environment, for example, air quality commotion and additional business benefits, for example, free childcare or unlimited espresso or sufficient parking space. According to Yusuf and Metiboba (2012), the organisational environment incorporates frameworks, methods, practices, qualities, and rationalities which work under the control of the board.

9.5 Review of Literature

Gibb (1969) infers that few personality attributes can't be secluded to decide leadership positions. Gibb's outline demonstrates that: (1) it is beyond the realm of imagination to expect to discover one explicit personality quality that describes leaders and (2) it is unimaginable to expect to seclude various attributes, which joined, clarify leadership. The research has neglected to locate a reasonable relationship between personality and leadership. Gibb (1969, p. 227) believes that examination has emerged as a logical reason for a relationship between attributes and driving positions. In any case, he points out that personality traits can't be ruled out in leadership as they are probably not without consequences (Gibb, 1969). Stogdill (1974) states that personality has restricted esteem while anticipating a person's leadership potential. In any case, there are signs that qualities work with different factors in the leadership position. Westerman and Simmons (2007) inspected the impact of the work environment on the relationship between personality and execution. Objective direction was an interceding factor influencing personality and work environment because parts of personality and work environment were intertwined. Extraversion, awareness, and enthusiastic dependability were seen as indications of inclination towards the goal. At long last, research had uncovered that objective direction was in charge of the relationship between personality and work environment. Abdul and Ojonimi (2014) inspected personality, work environment, and learning exchange. The outcome inferred that each working individual had two kinds of personality. The principal kind of personality was one's personality and another sort of personality was created by the work environment. It was reasoned that a viable attribute of personality was the claim personality which couldn't be influenced by the work environment. Ivansevich (2008) states that leadership is the capacity of an individual to utilise the impact of the environment or the circumstances of the organisation to create the impact of importance and effect on the accomplishment of objectives. Politis (2004) uncovered the relationship between of some elements of leadership and work environment that determined innovativeness. Particularly, stimulant and obstacle determinants of the work environment were connected with leadership styles (transformational and transactional) for inventiveness. The obstacle determinants of the work environment were observed to be adversely related to transactional and transformational leadership styles. Further, it was found that transformational leadership had a strong relationship with the stimulant determinants of the work environment for inventiveness. At last, it was presumed that transformational leadership was a capable factor to create a work environment and corporate culture that spurred employees towards development and innovativeness.

9.6 The Objective of the Study

To examine the relationship between personality, leadership styles, and work environment.

9.7 Research Methodology

The study was limited to the state of Punjab in India. The sample of the study was 285 managers. Micro, Small and Medium Enterprises (MSME) were considered for the study. The sample was selected based on the judgment sampling technique. Finally, it was estimated based on the sample calculation formula that sample size was appropriate to explain the population. The study was descriptive in nature. To collect the information from the respondents, three standardised questionnaires were used which are the Big Five Inventory (John & Srivastava, 1999), Multifactor Leadership Questionnaire (5 X-Short) (Avolio and Bass, 2004) and Work Environment Scale (Moos, 1994). The personality inventory and leadership inventory were measured on a 5 point Likert scale. The reliability of scales was tested by Cronbach alpha. According to Malhotra (2007), the value of Cronbach alpha must be more than 0.6 and present study has met this criterion. The reliability of the work environment was tested by the test-retest technique & the coefficient of correlation was found to be 0.70 which was an imperial proof of reliability. The validity of constructs has been ensured with expert advice further, the inter-dimension coefficient of correlation was calculated and the results showed that the majority of the values were non-significant. Dimensions of personality inventory as explained by John and Srivastava (1999) are Extraversion, Agreeableness, Conscientiousness, Neuroticism, and Openness; dimensions of transformational leadership are Idealised Influence Attributed, Idealised Influence Behaviour, Inspirational Motivation, Intellectual Stimulation, and Intellectual Consideration; dimensions of transactional leadership by Avolio and Bass (2004) are Contingent Reward, Management by Exception (active), Management by Exception (passive), and Laissez-faire; dimensions of work environment by Moos (1994) are Involvement, Coworker Cohesion, Supervisory Support, Autonomy, Task Orientation, Work Pressure, Clarity, Managerial Control, Innovation, and Physical Comfort.

9.8 Analysis and Interpretation

Table 9.1 shows the correlation coefficients between personality and the multifactor leadership questionnaire (MLQ). The extraversion score was correlated with the overall index of transactional leadership styles ($r = 0.133$, $p < 0.05$). Out of the four components of transactional leadership only laissez-faire ($r = 0.250$, $p < 0.01$) had shown a significant link with extraversion. The remaining components of transactional leadership failed to establish any significant relationship with extraversion. The agreeableness personality score did not achieve any significant relationship with any sub-scale of the transactional leadership styles. The conscientiousness score of the subjects was negatively correlated with the transactional leadership styles ($r = -0.360$, $p < 0.01$). Further the respective values of $r = -0.616$, $p < 0.01$ and -0.121, $p < 0.05$ against the two sub-scales of transactional leadership style, i.e., management by exception (active) and (passive) reflected that these were adversely correlated with conscientiousness. The neuroticism score was significantly linked with the

Table 9.1. Correlation of personality with transactional leadership style and transformational leadership style

	EX	AG	CO	NR	OP
CR	−0.046	−0.041	0.018	−0.077	−0.081
MBEA	0.050	0.043	−0.616**	−0.166**	0.446**
MBEP	−0.009	0.069	−0.121*	−0.137*	−0.024
LF	0.250**	−0.090	−0.073	0.086	−0.086
TSLS (total)	0.133*	−0.023	−0.360**	−0.122*	0.105
IIA	0.008	0.016	−0.051	0.010	0.049
IIB	0.176**	−0.108	−0.031	0.047	−0.021
IM	−0.015	−0.152**	−0.102	0.091	0.054
IS	−0.107	0.046	−0.009	0.061	0.048
IC	0.006	0.083	0.080	−0.141*	0.101
TMLS (total)	0.019	−0.031	−0.036	0.017	0.0101

$p^{**} < 0.01$, $p^* < 0.05$, $N = 285$.

management by exception (active and passive) as indicated by the values of $r = -0.166$, $p < 0.01$ and $r = -0.137$, $p < 0.05$ respectively. The overall index of transactional leadership was also correlated with the neuroticism score of the subjects ($r = -0.122$, $p < 0.05$). Openness was only correlated with the management by exception (active) ($r = 0.446$, $p < 0.01$).

The overall index of transformational leadership styles failed to attain a significant relationship with any personality sub-scales. But various significant correlations were found between the sub-scales of personality and transformational leadership style. Extraversion was positively correlated with idealised influence (behaviour) ($r = 0.176$, $p < 0.01$). The rest of the subscale scores were not significantly correlated with the extraversion score. Agreeableness had correlated adversely with inspirational motivation only ($r = -0.152$, $p < 0.05$). Neuroticism established an indirect relationship with individual consideration ($r = -0.141$, $p < 0.05$). The rest of the subscales of transformational leadership were not correlated with neuroticism. Openness personality trait did not attain a significant correlation with any sub-scale of transformational leadership styles.

In sum, the findings of the current study have some similarity with those of previous research works. Avolio and Bass (2004) revealed that the entire personality trait would predict the rating of transformational leadership. However, the result was reversed by Yahaya *et al.* (2011) who found that agreeableness, openness to experience, and conscientiousness had a direct and significant relationship with the transformational leadership style. Garcia *et al.* (2014) revealed that open and emotionally stable traits can be seen in transactional leaders. The relationship between transactional leadership and personality can be moderated by the other variables. De Hoogh *et al.* (2005) found that perceived work environment moderated the relationship of personality with charismatic and transactional leadership. Thus, based on overall results, it can be concluded that some of the personality traits correlated positively, while others negatively with some of the sub-scales of transactional and transformation leadership.

The relationship between personality and work environment showed that only the conscientiousness score was positively correlated with the overall index of the work environment ($r = 0.226$, $p < 0.01$). Hence, various significant relationships were found between the subscales of personality and work environment (Table 9.2). Extraversion had an indirect relationship with managerial control ($r = -0.156$, $p < 0.01$). All other subscales of the work environment were not significantly correlated with extraversion. Agreeableness was positively correlated with supervisor support ($r = 0.117$, $p < 0.01$). Conscientiousness was correlated with task orientation, work pressure, and physical comfort with the respective "r" values of 0.219, $p < 0.01$ & 0.115, 0.114, $p < 0.05$. Neuroticism was adversely correlated with involvement ($r = -0.114$, $p < 0.05$) and positively correlated with the work pressure ($r = 0.116$, $p < 0.05$). Openness failed to establish a significant link with any of the subscales of the work environment.

Regarding the relationship of personality and work environment, Westerman and Simmons (2007) revealed that goal

Table 9.2. Correlation between personality and work environment

	EX	AG	CO	NR	OP
IN	0.072	0.079	0.032	−0.114*	0.054
CC	0.012	0.000	0.093	−0.050	−0.092
SS	−0.077	0.117*	0.096	−0.056	0.063
AU	−0.028	0.004	0.092	−0.100	−0.005
TO	0.030	0.049	0.219**	−0.027	−0.090
WP	−0.021	0.045	0.115*	0.116*	−0.037
CL	−0.066	0.038	0.079	0.061	−0.112
MC	−0.156**	−0.025	0.091	0.076	−0.068
INN	0.079	0.003	0.102	0.050	−0.093
PC	−0.029	−0.016	0.114*	0.067	−0.096
WE (total)	−0.043	0.007	0.226**	0.061	−0.106

$p^{**} < 0.01$, $p^{*} < 0.05$, $N = 285$.

orientation was the mediating factor that established the relationship between personality and work environment. Abdul and Ojonimi (2014) concluded that every working person had two types of personality. The first type of personality was one's personality, while the other was the personality developed by the work environment. Previous research had also established a direct or indirect relationship between personality and work environment.

The relationship between the overall index of the transactional leadership style and work environment showed a highly significant negative relationship ($r = -0.134$, $p < 0.05$). Contingent reward was adversely correlated with managerial control ($r = -0.155$, $p < 0.01$). Management by exception (active) was only correlated with task orientation ($r = -0.123$, $p < 0.05$). Management by exception (passive) and laissez-faire scores failed to establish a significant relationship with all the subscales of the work environment.

Table 9.3 shows that the overall score of transformational leadership styles was not significantly correlated with work environment ($r = -0.051$, $p > 0.05$). Idealised influence (attributed) was adversely correlated with involvement ($r = -0.128$, $p < 0.05$). Idealised influence (behaviour) was found to be correlated with supervisor support ($r = -0.123$, $p < 0.05$). Inspirational motivation and individual consideration failed to establish a significant relationship with any subscale of work environment. Intellectual stimulation was positively related to managerial control ($r = 0.117$, $p < 0.05$).

9.9 Conclusion & Discussion

The majority of personality traits were found associated with the transactional leadership style and work environment, while various non-significant correlation results were found between personality and transformational leadership subscales. Extraversion was positively correlated with the transactional leadership style. Out of the four components of transactional leadership, only laissez-faire had shown a significant relation with extraversion. The remaining transactional leadership components failed to establish a significant relationship with extraversion. The agreeableness personality score

Table 9.3. Correlations of transactional leadership style and transformational leadership style with work environment

	IN	CC	SS	AU	TO	WP	CL	MC	INN	PC	WE (total)
CR	0.023	-0.053	-0.063	-0.018	-0.002	-0.016	-0.065	-0.155**	0.003	0.001	-0.078
MBEA	0.031	0.002	-0.019	0.017	-0.123*	-0.051	-0.064	-0.049	-0.113	-0.040	-0.090
MBEP	0.010	0.002	0.027	-0.011	-0.051	-0.006	0.017	-0.092	-0.047	-0.013	-0.038
LF	0.028	-0.032	-0.094	0.015	-0.071	-0.069	-0.073	-0.072	0.047	0.001	-0.071
TSLS (total)	0.045	-0.042	-0.081	0.002	-0.117*	-0.072	-0.095	-0.176**	-0.043	-0.022	-0.134*
IIA	-0.128*	-0.110	-0.033	-0.034	-0.116*	-0.061	-0.027	-0.031	-0.076	-0.032	-0.141*
IIB	-0.063	-0.081	-0.123*	0.012	0.006	-0.032	-0.029	-0.040	0.011	-0.029	-0.079
IM	-0.035	-0.022	-0.048	-0.047	0.084	-0.031	0.095	0.091	-0.062	-0.025	0.005
IS	0.081	-0.020	0.041	-0.041	0.027	-0.008	0.089	0.117*	0.048	0.014	0.077
IC	0.013	-0.104	0.005	0.019	0.078	0.004	-0.057	0.041	-0.056	0.014	-0.007
TMLS (total)	-0.044	-0.140*	-0.057	-0.036	0.038	-0.049	0.028	0.079	-0.054	-0.019	-0.051

$p^{**} < 0.01$, $p^* < 0.05$, $N = 285$.

failed to establish a significant relationship with any subscale of transactional leadership styles. The conscientiousness score of the subjects was negatively correlated with transactional leadership style. Further, two subscales of transactional leadership style, i.e., management by exception (active and passive) were adversely correlated with conscientiousness. Neuroticism score was significantly associated with management by exception (active and passive). The overall index of transactional leadership style also showed a correlation with neuroticism. Openness was only correlated with management by exception (active). The transformational leadership style failed to establish a significant relationship with any of the personality subscales. But various significant correlations were found between the subscales of personality and transformational leadership style. Extraversion was positively correlated with idealised influence (behaviour). The rest of the subscales were not significantly correlated with extraversion. Agreeableness had correlated adversely with inspirational motivation only. Neuroticism established an indirect relationship with individual consideration. The remaining subscales of transformational leadership were not correlated with neuroticism. The personality trait of openness failed to establish a significant correlation with any subscale of transformational leadership styles. Finally, the correlation results about personality and work environment depicted that only conscientiousness was positively correlated with the overall index of the work environment. Some other significant relationships were also observed between the subscales of personality and the work environment. Extraversion had an indirect relationship with managerial control. All other subscales of the work environment were not significantly correlated with extraversion. Agreeableness was positively correlated with supervisor support. Conscientiousness was correlated with task orientation, work pressure, and physical comfort. Neuroticism was adversely correlated with involvement and positively correlated with work pressure. Openness failed to establish a significant connection with any of the subscales of the work environment. On the whole, it can be concluded that some of the personality traits correlated positively, while others negatively with some of the subscales of transactional and transformational leadership and work environment.

The correlation analysis of this segment showed that transactional leadership styles were significantly but negatively correlated with the work environment. The contingent reward was adversely correlated with managerial control. Management by exception (active) was only negatively correlated with task orientation. Management by exception (passive) and laissez-faire scores failed to register a significant relationship with all the subscales of the work environment. On the other hand, transformational leadership styles were not significantly correlated with the work environment. But some significant results emerged between the subscales. Idealised influence (attributed) was adversely correlated with involvement and task orientation. Idealised influence (behaviour) was negatively correlated with supervisor support. Inspirational motivation and individual consideration failed to record a significant relationship with any of the sub-scales of the work environment. Intellectual stimulation showed a positive correlation with managerial control. Thus, the aggregate work environment was significantly correlated with transactional leadership styles.

9.10 Recommendations

Managing individuals in start-ups and small organisations calls for consistency with the appropriate work laws, creating a channel for managing worker issues at any level in an organisation. In a small organisation, the cost of not having the right employees with the right skills can be amazingly high. Although the majority of entrepreneurs initially only think about clients, advertising, production, and finance, this implies that they sometimes neglect to deal with the HR function. Previous studies have explained the relationship between personality, leadership styles, and work environment on how they affect the performance of an employee in an organisation. Therefore, by using the scales, the organisation can collect information about the psychological aspects of human behaviour like personality, attitude, leadership, motivation, etc. Such information should be conveyed to the employees. Apart from organisational efforts, individuals can themselves adopt the various techniques and attend counselling programmes arranged for them by the organisation. It is likely to affect the performance of an individual in the organisation. The relationship between personality, leadership styles, and work environment will lead to identifying the relevant training needs. Thus, organisations can quickly identify the core training areas. The relationship between personality, leadership styles, and work environment will provide information which will help in hiring employees, creating training modules, and appraising performance. By using the model, organisations can identify the core areas where improvement is required.

9.11 Future Scope and Limitations of Study

The relationship between personality, leadership styles, and work environment can be studied in large scale units of the industry. Some other variables, such as stress, motivation, and performance can be taken up for the study of personality in the future. The study can be replicated in other industries also. The study can be conducted at the national, state, and district level in other industrial sectors. Various relationships between the dimensions of scales were studied, hence the present study provides a major scope of mediation and moderation studies in this regard. The study is restricted to the state of Punjab only. Not all potential respondents were willing to become the respondents in this study, because of their busyness, time limitation, and fear as to how the answers will affect them. Due to the limited availability of supporting data, this research is limited to discussion of the three variables, which should be expanded by adding an intervening variable.

References

Abdul, H. & Ojonimi, F. (2014). Acquired personality from changing work environment and obstacles to learning transfer. *Journal of Good Governance and Sustainable Development in Africa, 2*(2), 13–24.

Allport, G. W. (1937). *Personality: A Psychological Interpretation.* Henry Holt, New York.

Avolio, B. J., & Bass, B. M. (2004). *Multifactor Leadership Questionnaire.* Mind Garden, California.

Awan A. G., & Tahir, M. T. (2015). Impact of working environment on employee's productivity: A case study of banks and insurance companies in Pakistan. *European Journal of Business and Management, 7*(1), 329–347.

Bala, R., & Singh, S. (2021). Role of government in sustainable growth and eco-development of economy. *World Review of Entrepreneurship, Management and Sustainable Development, 17*(2-3), 264–275.

Bennis, W. G. (1959). Leadership theory and administrative behaviour: The problem of authority. *Administrative Science Quarterly, 4*(3), 259–301.

Burns, J. M. (1978). *Leadership.* HarperCollins, New York, NY.

Cattell, R. B. (1966). *The Scientific Analysis of Personality.* Aldine Pub. Co., Chicago.

Chandrasekar, K. (2011). Workplace environment and its impact on organisational performance in public sector organisations. *International Journal of Enterprise Computing and Business System, 1*(1), 1–19.

Chemers, M. (1997). An Integrative Theory of Leadership. *Lawrence Erlbaum Associates.*

Chin, R. (2015). Examining teamwork and leadership in the fields of public administration, leadership, and management. *Team Performance Management, 21*(3/4), 199–216. doi:10.1108/TPM-07-2014-0037

Crosby, P. B. (1996). The leadership and quality nexus. *Journal for Quality and Participation, 19*(3), 18.

Dana, L. P. (1993). Environment for entrepreneurship: A model of public policy and economic development. *Journal of Entrepreneurship, 2*(1), 73–86. https://doi.org/10.1177%2F097135579300200105

Dana, L. P. (2000). Creating entrepreneurs in India. *Journal of Small Business Management, 38*(1), 86–91.

Dana, L. P., & Dana, T. E. (2005). Expanding the scope of methodologies used in entrepreneurship research. *International Journal of Entrepreneurship and Small Business, 2*(1), 79–88. https://doi.org/10.1504/IJESB.2005.006071

De Hoogh, A. H., Den Hartog, D. N., & Koopman, P. L. (2005). Linking the big five-factors of personality to charismatic and transactional leadership; Perceived dynamic work environment as a moderator. *Journal of Organisational Behaviour, 26*(7), 839–865.

Garcia, M., Duncan, P., Carmody-Bubb, M., & Ree, M. J. (2014). You have what? Personality traits that predict leadership styles for elementary principals. *Psychology*, 5, 204–212.

Gibb, C. A. (1969). Leadership. In Gardner, L., & Aronson, E. (Eds.), *The Handbook of Social Psychology*, Vol. IV, pp. 205–281. Addison-Wesley, Cambridge, MA.

Grant, A. M. (2012). Leading with meaning: Beneficiary contact, prosocial impact, and the performance effects of transformational leadership. *Academy of Management Journal*, 55(2), 458–476.

Guilford, J. P (1959): *Personality*. McGraw Hill Book company, Inc. New York.

Gunaseelan, R., & Ollukkaran, B. A. (2012). A study on the impact of work environment on employee performance. *International Journal of Management Research*, 71(2), 1–16.

Hogan, J., & Holland, B. (2003). Using theory to evaluate personality and job-performance relations: A socioanalytic perspective. *Journal of Applied Psychology*, 88(1), 100.

Ivancevich, J., Konopaske, R., & Matteson, M. (2008). *Organisational Behavior and Management*. Eason, Jakarta.

John, O. P., & Srivastava, S. (1999). The big five trait taxonomy: History, measurement, and theoretical perspectives. *Handbook of Personality: Theory and Research*, 2, 102–138.

Kalasa, B. J. (1970). *Introduction To Behavioural Science for Business*. Wiley Eastern, New Delhi.

Larsen, R. J., & Buss, D. M. (2011). *Personality Psychology*. McGraw-Hill, New York.

Leatt, P., & Schneck, R. (1980). Differences in stress perceived by head nurses across nursing specialties in hospitals. *Journal of Advanced Nursing*, 2, 31–46.

Leblebici, D. (2012). Impact of workplace quality on employee's productivity: Case study of a bank in Turkey. *Journal of Business Economic & Finance*, 1(1), 38–49.

Liaw, Y. J., Chi, N. W., & Chuang, A. (2010). Examining the mechanisms linking transformational leadership, employee customer orientation, and service performance: The mediating roles of perceived supervisor and coworker support. *Journal of Business and Psychology*, 25(3), 477–492.

Malhotra, N. K. (2007). *Marketing Research. An Applied Orientation*, 5th ed. Prentice Hall, New Jersey.

McClelland, D. C. (1951): *Personality*. Holt, Rinehart and Winston, New York.

Moos, R. H. (1994). *Work Environment Scale Manual*, 3nd ed. Consulting Psychologists Press, California.

Neemta, G., & Singh, S. (2020). Procrastination pattern of working individuals. *International Bilingual Peer Reviewed Refereed Research Journal, 10*(40), 67–74.

Newstrom, J. W., & Davis, K. (1993). *Organisational Behavior: Human Behavior at Work*. McGraw-Hill, New York.

Pervin, L. A., Cervone, D., & John, O. P. (2005). *Personality: Theory and Research*, 9th ed. John Wiley & Sons, Hoboken, NJ.

Pio, E., & Dana, L.-P. (2014). An exploratory empirical study of Indian entrepreneurs in Christchurch, New Zealand. *International Journal of Entrepreneurship and Small Business, 22*(1), 17–35. https://doi.org/10.1504/IJESB.2014.062128

Politis, J. D. (2004). Transformational and transactional leadership predictors of the "stimulant" determinants to creativity in organisational work environments. *Electronic Journal of Knowledge Management, 2*(2), 23–34.

Qureshi, T. M., Akbar, A. Khan, M. A., Sheikh, R. A., & Hijazi, S. T. (2010). Do human resource management practices have an impact on financial performance of banks? *African Journal of Business Management, 4*(7), 1281–1288.

Ruch, F. L. (1963). *Personality and Life*. Scott Foresman, Chicago.

Shalley, C. E., & Gilson, L. L. (2004). What leaders need to know: A review of social and contextual factors that can foster or hinder creativity? *The Leadership Quarterly, 15*(1), 33–53.

Sharma, P., & Singh, S. (2021). Entrepreneurship in Punjab. In Dana, L. P., Sharma, N., & Acharya, S. R. (Eds.), *Organising Entrepreneurship and MSMEs Across India*, Vol. 11, pp. 63-86. World Scientific, Singapore.

Singh, P. (2013). An exploratory study on internet banking usage in semi-urban areas in India. *International Journal of Scientific and Research Publications, 3*(8), 1–5.

Singh, S. (2017). Linking procrastination behaviour with perceived psychological performance. *Gyan Joyti e-Journal, 7*(3), 20–26.

Singh, S., & Bala, R. (2020). Mediating role of self-efficacy on the relationship between conscientiousness and procrastination. *International Journal of Work Organisation and Emotion, 11*(1), 41–61.

Singh, S., & Dhaliwal, R. (2015). Procrastination patterns of transactional and transformational leaders. *Pacific Business Review International*, *8*(1), 33–40.

Singh, S., & Dhaliwal, R. S. (2018). Perceived performance and procrastination in hospitality industry: Examining the mediator role of work environment. *Journal of Hospitality Application and Research*, *13*(2), 44–62.

Singh, S., Dhaliwal, R., & Bala, R. (2017). Analysis of procrastination behaviour among teachers: A non-parametric approach. *Singaporean Journal of Business Economics, And Management Studies*, *5*(7), 26–34.

Singh, S., Sharma, P., Garg, N., & Bala, R. (2021). Groping environmental sensitivity as an antecedent of environmental behavioural intentions through perceived environmental responsibility. *Journal of Enterprising Communities: People and Places in the Global Economy*, Vol. ahead-of-print No. ahead-of-print. https://doi.org/10.1108/JEC-09-2020-0169

Socrokin, P. A. (1947). *Culture and Personality*. Harper and Brose, New York.

Stogdill, R. M. (1974). *Handbook of Leadership: A Survey of Theory and Research*. Free Press, New York.

Strauss, G. (1966). Discussion. In Geralt, G. S. (Ed.), *Proceedings of the Eighteenth Annual Winter Meeting*, p. 84. Wish Industrial Relations Research Association, Madison.

Tracey, J. B., & Hinkin, T. R. (1994). Transformational leaders in the hospitality industry. *Cornell Hotel and Restaurant Administration Quarterly*, *35*(2), 18–24.

Warren, H. C., & Carmichael, L. (1930). *Elements of Human Psychology*. Houghton Mifflin, Boston.

Westerman, J. W., & Simmons, B. L. (2007). The effects of work environment on the personality-performance relationship: An exploratory study. *Journal of Managerial Issues*, *19*(2), 288–305.

Yahaya, A., Boon, Y., & Hashim, S. (2011). Relationship between leadership personality types and source of power and leadership styles among managers. *African Journal of Business Management*, *5*, 9635–9648.

Yukl, G. A. (1999). An evaluation of conceptual weakness in transformational and charismatic leadership theories. *Leadership Quarterly*, *10*(2), 285–305.

Yusuf, N., & Metiboba, S. (2012) Work environment and job attitude among employees in a Nigerian work organisation. *Journal of Sustainable Society*, *1*(2), 36–43.

Zalaik, A. (1966). *Human Dilemmas of Leadership*. Harper and Row, New York.

Chapter 10

Social Capital as a Tool for Managing Human Resources in Agile Entrepreneurial Organisations

Yamini Chandra

School of Commerce, Narsee Monjee Institute of Management Studies, Mumbai, India

yaminichandra23@gmail.com

Abstract: Careful investment of social and human capital within the organisation structure has been believed to improve the performance of the workforce and firms and is also observed to have a constructive impact on the firm and employee performance. A superior human capital and social capital is the accelerator of a firm's growth. While entrepreneurial firms are agile in themselves, they need to have strong ties with their customers, clients, teams/employees, investors, ecosystem and industry experts, debtors, vendors, subcontractors, etc. and here the need and benefits of social skills not only among owners/founders but also in their teams and employees are always in high demand. A young enterprise faces many challenges, the same as any giant corporate firm. Founders often experience that they are working against the clock in managing both business and human resource challenges, even though they do agree that the entrepreneurial-agile and high-performance-driven culture should not be a substitute for an ethical-courageous-people-friendly culture. This chapter discusses various challenges and issues faced by small and medium businesses and employees of small business firms at their level, and how both parties collectively are trying to support and overcome these challenges, so as to make the work as effective as possible. The chapter is prepared through a comprehensive literature review and data/information has been derived from various secondary sources with a discussion with some start-up founders and small business owners. The chapter also focused on other challenges such as related to human resource development practices, innovation, decision making, and the negative impact of the COVID-19 pandemic on some small businesses are also discussed. The chapter also shares recommended solutions to alter current practices, policies, and processes which can help in addressing operative challenges and can help in developing sustainable practices.

Keywords: Entrepreneurial firms, Human capital, Human resource practices, Social capital.

10.1 Introduction

Careful investment of social and human capital within the organisation structure has been found to improve the performance of the workforce and firms. Scholars have advocated that investing in social capital will enhance entrepreneurial performance, leading to the fact that ideas do have "potential value" in them, but it needs to be aligned with not only the market knowledge but also how these ideas converted into newer products/or services (here the business ideas are the potential solutions to the problems faced by potential customers) will be developed, but also how the founders' vision and values will be integrated into the system and to the work teams/ employees, as most practitioners say — ideas are easy to build but difficult to pursue. For decades, scholars have worked extensively in analysing "what factors lead to investment in human and social capital besides the impact of talent in entrepreneurial performance" (Bishop, 1994; Arthur, 1994; MacDuffie, 1995; Blanchflower & Oswald, 1998; Audretsch & Thurik, 2001;

Bosma *et al.*, 2004). A very interesting study in this area by Bosma *et al.* (2004, pp. 227–228) was conducted using a survey on 1000 new business founders in the Netherlands during the years 1994–1997. They discovered that there requires three ways of investment at the social and human capital level by these young enterprises to address specific business challenges. These investments are focused at the overall general level in the firms, the investments at industry-specific, and entrepreneurship-specific investment. This study highlights that for a young firm to survive and move ahead, the investment should be not only on both industry, and entrepreneurship specific but more emphasis should be given to human and social capital which significantly enhances the cross-sectional variance of small firms and contributes in productivity of firms and its employees.

10.1.1 *Social and Human Capital as a Tool to Strategise Human Resource Practices*

Social and human capital in young entrepreneurial firms does not only belong to the employees or work teams, rather this term also refers to the owners' human capital. Since the 1970s, scholars have promoted the constructive impact of these on firm and employee performance (Mincer, 1974). Small businesses are agile in themselves. They need to have strong ties with their customers, clients, work teams/employees, investors, ecosystem and industry experts, debtors, vendors, subcontractors, etc. and here the need and benefits of social skills are always in high demand (Blanchflower, 2000). The perception these parties will have on these firms is directly correlated with the type/quality of the firm and its founder. Most of the investors have directly/indirectly been communicating that a major proportion of investment decisions are made on the team's or founders' personality and then the product/service they are offering. Hence for small and medium businesses, the investment in social and human capital can be a signal to grab high investment in their choice of talented and skilled teams (Spence, 1974; Milgrom & Roberts, 1992).

Social capital is the extent of people's interaction with each other whether in a personal or professional environment. The term social capital refers to the aggregate of actual or potential resources which are linked to a group of people who do not only share common properties but also are linked by permanent and useful ties (Bourdieu, 1985, p. 02). Social capital in organisations is a result of the cross-fertilisation of various phenomena. In organisational theory it ascertains the purposeful interactions of human capital with business capital, treating work and individual workers as an instrument to enhance market commodity, developing social relationship, investing in relations to other individuals leading to a win-win situation for organisations and employees (Gummer, 1998; Nahapiet & Ghoshal, 1998; Burt, 2000).

In this book chapter, the usage of terms such as "the social and human capital of promotors of small and medium-sized businesses (SMBs)" refers to various factors such as their education, knowledge, skills, abilities, aptitude, temperament, and the determinant choice of selecting the journey of entrepreneurship which in itself is full of challenges. Further, their experiences in business ownership, experience in leadership, networking, and emotional support from founders' family/spouse, are also referred to collectively in the social capital (Acharya & Chandra, 2019, p. 186). Most of the practitioners have affirmed that the owners/founders of start-ups are often in search of only those people to be included in their team (or are recruited as employees), who share the same personality characteristics of owners/founders, such as being risk-taking, good and fast decision making, critical and analytical reasoning, entrepreneurial leadership, and vision which is instrumental in the overall entrepreneurial performance.

10.1.2 *Need for a Robust Human Resource Practice at Entrepreneurial-Agile and High-Performance-Driven Culture*

A young enterprise faces many challenges same as any giant corporate firm. Founders often experience that they are working against the clock in managing both business and human resource challenges, even though they do agree that the entrepreneurial-agile and high-performance-driven culture should not be a substitute for an ethical-courageous-people-friendly culture. Most SMBs at their early stages of development do not believe in investing in a dedicated human resource manager, and most founders themselves lack the proper understanding of human resource practices for their firms, instead they believe that the firm's vision and founders' social capital will be sufficient in compensating the lack of basic human resource practices and procedures. Often it was observed that owners/founders/CEOs/BODs are more attracted towards factors such as holacracy, shiny-agile-culture, or a cool-physical-place to work which do not follow stringent rules, but a place where flexible-business-culture is more appreciated. Most of the time, owners/ founders, investors, or leadership do not agree with what impacts the harmful employment cultures in fast-growth organisations with a race to stay afloat with these operational hacks until a potential crisis occurs. There is a need for these SMB founders to accept that flexible-business-culture should not create hindrance in the performance and development of teams. These businesses believe in fail fast and pivot with minimal concern over which methods to be adopted when teams need to get dissolved because the executives believe that HR will ruin the flexible-work-culture and HRs are the dreadful start-up-work-culture-killers!

On a human level, a basic formal work agreement is the first step to a happy future employee. Human resource as a function in a start-up organisation is as same as in any multinational or corporate organisation. HR should be there to take care of workforce planning, recruiting potential employees, creating employee contracts, onboarding new hires, training, identifying and developing performance standards, retaining and nurturing employees, encouraging proactive and engaging culture, empowering teams and cultivating their career paths, and investing in good human resource information system (HRIS) software to separation or offboarding of employees. Here the role of the HR manager will be very instrumental in managing the employee life cycle in their firms. The human resource manager also has a responsibility in ensuring both personal and professional growth of coworkers, developing workplace culture, and strategising policies that strengthen both founder's and team's vision. Stans (1946, pp. 362–363) described various features for the survival of the small business as an economic factor and listed that apart from lack of adequate initial capital and long-term financing and high-unit costs operation, small business struggles to fit adequate managerial, scientific, and technical skills to develop the "know-how of production and distribution and needs additional costs for extensive research and development activities" (Stans, 1946, p. 363). The question here lies not in attracting these managerial and technical skills but in retaining them so that the business and employees both can sustain. Let us take a hypothetical example of an ambitious youth who, when placed as an employee in a manufacturing unit, will have an urge to operate business differently while dealing with customers/clients, investors, balancing inventory and production capacity, or maintaining good housekeeping, but the disparity in managing high unit costs of production or service can lead to a failure in handling any of these. Precisely, the manufacturer making two hundred pumps a week cannot afford to save labour and facilities without making sure that the workers/employees at the factory are well trained in the know-how of machinery operation and maintaining production levels. The other challenging part is that these business needs to have an expert expeditors, purchasing agent, or other representatives to ensure an adequate supply chain apart from the production. The managing of factory units not only requires a competitive team but an investment in necessary accounting and managerial software. This visualises the need for robust human resource personnel to manage workers and teams and businesses strategically for the sustainability of small businesses and employees.

10.2 Managing Human Resource Leadership Challenges in SMBs

In this section, various challenges and issues faced by SMBs and employees of small business firms at their level are highlighted, and how both the parties collectively are trying to support and overcome these challenges, making the work as effective as possible. To compete globally, these SMBs are required to depend upon external factors and have to engage in joint efforts with their investors, employees, stakeholders, and competitors to gain a competitive advantage. Sustainable competitiveness is the main concern because SMBs face more severe resource constraints. These firms need to be highly innovative adopting various cross-functional practices and at the same time must ensure integration of learning culture and knowledge-sharing within their teams, further ensuring that these interventions are placed in such a way making employees engaged and making work more performance-driven. A knowledge-driven HR practice will ensure that the work does not stop at attracting, recruiting talented individuals, but placing these specific potential individuals in profiles that match their skills which can lead halfway to competitive advantage. The intellectual potential of these skilled employees needs to be channelised in such a way wherein a culture of "matchers" can be cultivated. This matcher culture will help to develop a workplace where work and its output are placed first and teams can collaborate without having a fear of their hard work being snatched away by their team members.

Practitioners too believe that beyond the influence of knowledge and human resource management, intellectual capacity remains as intellectual material. Many scholars advocate the importance of high-performance work systems as a way to gain a competitive advantage. Bendickson *et al.* (2017) explains the importance of high-performance work systems (HPWS) as a necessity for small businesses. The HPWS are a combination of HRM practices that includes staffing, sourcing the best-fit candidates, self-managed work teams, flexible work assignments, decentralised decision making, training and development, open communication, and compensation that can help to establish a system to improve the likelihood for small businesses to meet their goals in a way to "enhance capabilities and ensuring long term survival" (Bendickson *et al.*, 2017, p. 3; Evans & Davis, 2005).

Small businesses that practice HPWS are "more likely to experience a high level of growth, survival, development of capabilities and goal achievement" (Bendickson *et al.*, 2017, p. 8). To survive, young firms need to be competent and develop "internal resources that are often difficult to be replicated by outside organisations and which in turn can promote organisational survival and growth". This sort of level of performance (business and its human resources) is the same as in large established corporations. A superior human capital and social capital is the accelerator of a firm's growth. A well-enhanced high performing human capital will greatly contribute to meeting desirable business outcomes while adding value to firms, employees, customers than competitors (Barney, 1991; Pfeffer & Salancik, 1978).

10.2.1 *Challenges in Human Resource Development (HRD) and Innovation*

SMBs do face multiple challenges when it comes to innovation management for HRD practitioners. A human resource manager has dual pressure: to survive in the shrinking budgets and at the same time allocate sufficient resources to employees so that they can implement the trial and error method for innovations. HRD practitioners stress that though the integration of a culture of creativity, flexibility, and innovation is important in small business, there needs to be a balanced check on other complementary organisational culture such as employee engagement, coaching and mentoring, the amalgamation of social capital within teams, leadership development, etc, which can become very instrumental in HRD effectiveness and those interventions focused on stimulating innovation. Now, this is a tough job to accomplish.

10.2.2 *Small Businesses are Agile When Dealing with Entrepreneurial Decision Making*

When it comes to decision making, the entrepreneurs (or as mentioned in the above section, owners/founders) of small businesses face many operative challenges, and decision making is one of the many operative challenges faced by them. Decision making requires a strategically thoughtful process. These owners/founders many at times have to make decisions amidst ambiguous situations without giving a second thought to its outcome. The success of small firms relies greatly on "a well-thought-strategic-decision" (Robinson & Pearce, 1983). This challenge comes wrapped up with having a high uncertainty and risk associated with it. A phenomenon that is inevitable here is the feeling of fear and ambiguity that revolves around the byproduct of this decision making. Yagnik and Chandra (2019, p. 10) advocate that entrepreneurs work in an environment that has high uncertainty and risk associated with the outcomes of the decision-making process. Further, it was cognised that creativity techniques can be used as a tool to generate multiple options to beat uncertainty and overcome fear and manage decision making in such a way so that it creates a win-win for both owners of young firms and their employees (Yagnik & Chandra, 2019, p. 11).

10.2.3 *The COVID-19 Pandemic and Challenges Faced by SMBs*

When we are discussing the challenges faced by SMBs and referring to the current time, there is a need to also highlight the devastating impact the COVID-19 pandemic has created on small businesses across sectors including start-ups or young organisations, leading to a situation of cash crunch, decline of sales, and negative impact on overall businesses altogether. One of the articles published in *Economic Times* (2020) summarised a survey on 250 Indian start-ups conducted by the Federation of Indian Chamber of Commerce and Industry (FICCI) and Indian Angel Network (IAN) and concludes that about 70% of start-ups have been impacted by the current COVID-19 pandemic, among these, 12% of businesses have to shut their operations and 60% are operating with disruptions; whereas close to 30% of these enterprises have observed administrative and operational challenges and they have to lay off employees during the lockdown period, making it challenging for human resource professionals to identify which of their employees to retain and which to let go. Additionally, small businesses are juggling with other workplace challenges and their impact on economic conditions such as layoffs have also created a decline in employee productivity and morale. In such a time, small businesses have to find ways to boost and motivate their employees' productivity while juggling to manage capital to sustain the business.

A very recent survey released by the regional Federal Reserve Banks has observed that in the US during the year 2020, 44% of small firms have more than $100,000 in debt and, a separate survey by the regional Federal agency observed that 8% of these small firms owe more than $1 million to its investors, a debt which they have to clear soon to function smoothly. The pandemic has created a very devastating impact on small business owners in the US, even the Federal Paycheck Protection Program has provided $525 billion to these small firms as a form of forgivable loans with an additional $284 billion in funding to small businesses in 2020 to survive salary disbursements to the employees of these SMBs. But this programme also requires these businesses to spend at least 60% of funds on payroll to qualify for full forgiveness. Now at the same time, these small businesses are also struggling to resolve disputes involving personal guarantees, attorneys, phone bills, tax obligations, rental payments, paying salary to employees, and other business operative expenses (Simon & Haddon, 2021).

10.3. Solutions and Recommendations for Organisations and Employees

While the initial challenge for small businesses lies in sourcing the right candidate from the pools of active (and most of the times passive) candidates, the human resource manager in small businesses also needs to standardise the process of identifying and focusing on core competencies along with mandatory qualifications that are necessary for success in the job instead of relying on CVs alone for the hiring process. Passive candidates should be engaged in activities like writing SOPs, cover letters, working on case studies, or assigning live short projects. This will help in the assessment of those who are interested in jobs and removing non-serious candidates. Indian firms believe in experience-based recruiting rather than solely relying on competency-based recruitment. During one interview, Lazlo Bock, former Head of People Orientation at Google shares their method to predict employee performance in workplace "work sample", a method of competency-based-work-simulation where candidates were given some job task to be finished within a specified duration to test the sincerity, knowledge, and competency of candidate-fit for the job (Shortlist, 2017). Apart from this, another challenge also lies in the mindset of Indian recruiters/owners is that they take the hiring process as a mere requirement for running a business and not the core requirement of assessing what makes a business successful. Start-ups can resort to Professionals Employer Organisations (PEOs) to help taking care of overall HR practices. These PEOs will not only make sure to consider technology, market, and innovation in the business model, which can be instrumental in overall success.

While considering solutions, some of the tried and tested best practices highlighted in studies are mentioned below:

- A performance-commitment culture needs to be integrated into the system. This will ensure that all human resource functions such as recruitment, selection, and placement of teams/ individual employees should be in such a way that encourages job rotation and flexible-work assignment, an open door communication, and the performance-related-reward system will also enhance this process.
- Training of employees should be carried out after a thorough and careful need-analysis. Training as a method of performance solution has been observed to improve work output and induce innovation many times.
- A well-planned induction programme can help to make new hires get themselves acquaint with the policies, process, and systems. During the onboarding process, the new hires should be made aware of performance indicators, performance evaluation

standards and appraisals, and performance improvement methods. A clear understanding of contingent pay rise will communicate clearly about policies. A tour of the shop floor/plant, and/or a visit to suppliers, clients, and customers can further help to induce knowledge about processes and functions which will help new hires and existing employees to perform as per expectations.

Some studies have highlighted various areas where knowledge-based human resource management practices can prove to be useful in SMEs. Some of these are:

- Knowledge-based recruitment: Identifying and attracting potential human capital, selecting employees not only based on their current skills, knowledge, or experience but also based on the employees' potential, pertinent networking, learning, and knowledge capabilities.
- Knowledge-based performance assessment: Based on employees' contribution and involvement in improving the organisation's knowledge process, e.g., knowledge creation, sharing, and application.
- Knowledge-based training: It is not possible for competent employees to remain competent forever as skills often depreciate and become less (or of no) use in the future. This entails regular development of employees' expertise and knowledge comprehensively, by personalising training to fit employees' peculiar needs and ensuring continuous development.
- Knowledge-based compensation: Managers often use both intangible (such as recognition and status) and tangible incentives (such as one-off rewards and bonuses) to encourage knowledge-sharing, creation, and application among employees. This is recompensing employees based on their contributions to the organisation's key knowledge process involving knowledge creation, sharing, and application.
- Knowledge-based career management: Involves the use of support from top management, skill assessment activities,

knowledge creation, sharing, and application for the career progression of employees.

Other solutions which can be helpful to overcome operative challenges by HRD practitioners of SMBs:

- Small businesses can use incentives such as stock options which may have a greater influence than in large corporates.
- Removing bureaucratic multiple layers and hierarchy of designations and yet having status (or designations) of employees can help to reduce hierarchical differences and can help to create a more conducive work environment.
- SMBs do have flexible culture at their initial phase of development than mature organisations, but along with flexibility, a culture of control, trust between workers, and management control will be more instrumental in developing growth and change.
- Young firms do practice cost-differentiation leadership and hence dedicating enormous resources in human resources alone could be challenging and may lead to disagreements between promotors, but a comprehensive plan aligning the usage of resources and its performance output can be considered.

Apart from all the points stated above, careful analysis on staffing should be done. It should be made sure that job-fit-based staffing after assessing the knowledge, skills, attitudes, and temperament of existing or potential employees may result in selecting the best candidate for the position. For staffing, careful job analysis, selective screening of potential candidates and assessment of technical, administrative, and managerial skills, and analysing the right personality and attitude, temperament, characteristics, general mental ability, cognitive and analytical skills can help to predict good and fast decision making in the system. Lepak and Snell (1999) refer to this as an HR architecture implying appropriate uniqueness in finding an organisation-person-job-fit which leads to enhancement of individual and organisational performance. In a nutshell, human resource is a strategic component. Young firms do not look at human resources as a method to lead to value creation, rather more as a means to maintain legal compliances and regulate costs. This practice needs to change. To develop and enhance human capital and organisational performances, human resources need to be strategised in small and medium enterprises.

References

Acharya, S. R., & Chandra, Y. (2019). Entrepreneurship skills acquisition through education: Impact of the nurturance of knowledge, skills, and attitude on new venture creation. World Academy of Science, Engineering and Technology, International Science Index 146, *International Journal of Social, Behavioral, Educational, Economic, Business and Industrial Engineering, 13*(2), 186–196.

Arthur, J. B. (1994). Effects of human resource systems on manufacturing performance and turnover. *Academy of Management Journal, 37*(3), 670–687.

Audretsch, D. B., & Thurik, A. R. (2001). What is new about the new economy: Sources of growth in the managed and entrepreneurial economies. *Industrial and Corporate Change, 10*(1), 267–315.

Barney, J. (1991). Firm resources and sustained competitive advantage. *Journal of Management, 17*(1), 99-120.

Bendickson, J., Muldoon, J., Liguori, E., & Midgett, C. (2017). High performance work systems: A necessity for startups. *Journal of Small Business Strategy, 27*(2), 1–12.

Bishop, J. (1994). The impact of previous training on productivity and wages. In Lynch, L. (Ed.), *Training and the Private Sector*, pp. 161–200. University of Chicago Press, Chicago.

Blanchflower, D. G. (2000). Self employment in OECD Countries. *Labor Economics, 7*, 471–505.

Blanchflower, D .G., & Oswald, A. J. (1998). What makes an entrepreneur? *Journal of Labor Economics, 16*(1), 26–60.

Bosma, N., Van Praag, M., Thurik, R., & De Wit, G. (2004). The value of human and social capital investments for the business performance of startups. *Small Business Economics, 23*(3), 227–236.

Bourdieu, P. (1985). The social space and the genesis of groups. *Social Science Information, 24*(2), 195–220.

Burt, R. S. (2000). The network structure of social capital. In Staw, B. M. & Sutton, R. I. (Eds.), *Research in Organizational Behavior*, Vol. 22, pp. 345–423. Elsevier, New York.

Economic Times (July 5, 2020). About 70 per cent start-ups impacted by COVID-19: Survey. Available at https://economictimes.indiatimes.com/small-biz/start-ups/newsbuzz/about-70-per-cent-start-ups-impacted-by-covid-19-survey/articleshow/76801147.cms

Evans, W. R., & Davis, W. D. (2005). High performance work systems and organizational performance: The mediating role of internal social structure. *Journal of Management, 31*, 758–775.

Gummer, B. (1998). Social relations in an organizational context: Social capital, real work and structural holes. *Administration in Social Work, 22*(3), 87–105.

Lepak, D. P., & Snell, S. A. (1999). The human resource architecture: Toward a theory of human capital allocation and development. *Academy of Management Review, 24*, 31–48.

MacDuffie, J. P., (1995). Human resource bundles and manufacturing performance: Organizational logic and flexible production systems in the World Auto Industry. *Industrial and Labor Relations Review, 48*(2), 197–121.

Milgrom, P., & Roberts, J. (1992). *Economics, Organization and Management.* Englewood Cliffs.

Mincer, J. (1974). *Schooling, Experience and Earnings.* Columbia University Press, New York.

Nahapiet, J., & Ghoshal, S. (1998). Social capital, intellectual capital, and the organizational advantage. *Academy of Management Review, 23*(2), 242–266.

Pfeffer, J. S., & Salancik, G. (1978). *The External Control of Organizations: A Resource Dependence Perspective.* Harper & Row, New York.

Robinson, R. B., & Pearce, J. A. (1983). The impact of formalised strategic planning on financial performance in small organizations. *Strategic Management Journal, 4*(1), 197–207.

Shortlist (2017). 4 hiring challenges and opportunities facing Indian companies today. Available at: https://shortlist.net/2017/05/20/4-hiring-challenges-and-opportunities-facing-indian-companies-today/

Simon, R., & Haddon, H. (April 4, 2021). Small business owners feel weight of personal debt guarantees. Wall Street Journal. Available at: https://www.wsj.com/articles/small-business-owners-personal-debt-guarantees-coronavirus-pandemic-11617555245?mod=hp_lead_pos7

Spence, M. A. (1974). *Job Market Signaling: Informational Transfer in Hiring and Related Processes.* Harvard University Press, Cambridge.

Stans, M. (1946). What small business needs. *The Accounting Review, 21*(4), 361–371.

Yagnik, A., & Chandra, Y. (2019). Using creativity to defeat fear and manage ambiguity for enhancing entrepreneurial decisions. In Caputo, A., & Pellegrini, M. (Eds.), *The Anatomy of Entrepreneurial Decisions. Contributions to Management Science*, pp. 9–28. Springer, Cham.

Chapter 11

An Influence of Artificial Intelligence on Jobs and HRM in Small Manufacturing Units

Ashwini Sonawane

Vishwakarma University, Pune, India

ashwini.sonawane@vupune.ac.in

Atul Loomba

Rabindranath Tagore University, Bhopal, India

atulloomba121@yahoo.co.in

Johana Paluchova

Slovak University of Agriculture, Nitra, Slovakia

johana.paluchova@gmail.com

Abstract: Artificial intelligence is a tool used by human intelligence and technology to improve various fields' performance. In the simplest sense, AI is a branch of intelligence involved in constructing intelligent machines that can be used for work that usually requires human understanding. Human resources management plays a vital role in the company's management and generally encompasses people and their behaviour. HR policies are a set of guidelines for the organisation's management of its staff. Today, HR managers must examine the skills and talents required by employee artificial intelligence in different departments. The problem identified here is that human limitations, such as biases, preconceptions, and time restrictions, can prevent an HRM process's effectiveness. This is a problem because it can lead an organisation to lose its job and monetary value candidates. The chapter discusses artificial intelligence's influence on job/work and HRM where we are focusing mostly on small manufacturing units.

Keywords: Artificial intelligence, HRM, Machines, Manufacturing units, Small business.

11.1 Introduction

Technology and artificial intelligence (AI) developments in the digital world are rapidly gaining a competitive edge. The exercise and decision making of the various management tasks have changed. There is no new technology and innovation without consequences. The employ of AI across multiple management functions is similar (Merlin & Jayam, 2018). The use of AI for different functional services also involves the management of human resources (HR). HR management will positively and negatively impact the passage of time and AI use because it continuously changes the world we live in (Wall & Wood, 2005).

Human resources management plays a vital role in the company's management and generally encompasses people and their behaviour. HR policies are a set of guidelines for the organisation's management of its staff. Their main functions are recruitment, selection, training, development, etc. It also includes termination, compensation, discipline, and security policy. The impact of AI on HR is related to recruitment, selection, training, performance, and work.

Science and technology innovation, on the one hand, helps create employment and promote employment. However, it eliminates jobs that do not comply with and prevent new technologies; it is difficult to maximise strengths and avoid weaknesses. In recent years, Master Li Shi's victory over AlphaGo, AI, has become an essential part of the field of human visibility, leading us to a new way of thinking.

AI plays an important and useful role in reducing or eliminating the workloads of staff and managers using technology to complete the process using specific mathematical algorithms. Today, HR managers must examine the skills and talents required by employees (Sharma, 2020) through using AI in different departments. Knowing and learning AI instruments is often difficult for new employees. It gives employees a fear of losing their jobs. Therefore, this study aims to investigate AI's impact on work and HRM.

11.2 Conceptual Background

11.2.1 *Concept*

AI addresses rival computer systems' ability to solve human-like, complex reasoning, learning, and self-correction capabilities. These are widespread in various fields, and recent developments in hardware and software technology have strengthened AI systems. It is widely used for optical communication, network planning, programming, transport networks, to name but a few. These systems use various complex algorithms that communicate at high speed and are designed for superior decision making. It is more efficient and effective than computer system experts. It has been used in narrow but well-tested applications, such as specific medical diagnostics and driverless cars. The number of road accidents decreased in these areas of application, and AI systems made medical diagnosis more accurate. AI has opened up several global opportunities, optimising relevant algorithms will help develop a superhuman understanding of multiple automatic processes.

11.2.2 *Definition*

According to John McCarthy — the father of AI — technical and scientific computers are highly innovative software. It's a path to a machine, a computer aid, or a program that wisely thinks the same way as smart people believe.

AI can examine how people think, train, identify, and operate while trying to solve problems. AI can then use the results of this study to build smart systems and software.

11.2.3 *Stages of AI*

Following are the three stages of AI (see Figure 11.1):

- Machine Learning: This is a group of algorithms used to train knowledge systems from experience.
- Machine Intelligence: These are the advanced groups of algorithms used for automatic training. For example, deep neural networks. AI technology is currently at this stage.
- Machine Awareness: Self-education from expertise without external data.

11.3 AI in Manufacturing

AI seems to have travelled rapidly from science fiction to conference room. Besides enabling a robotics work environment, AI is also very important for production. It can be valuable to organisations today. AI helps manufacturers stay competitive, lower costs, optimise their capital, and provide a better environment and service to their employees.

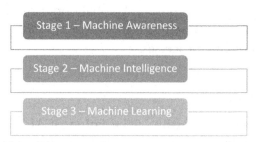

Figure 11.1. Diagrammatic representation types of stages of AI

11.3.1 Aspects of the Supply Chain that are Being Revolutionised by AI

Large production companies start purchasing and allocating materials using AI. The economy develops around shorter invention cycles, globalisation, sustainable development, and mass customisation so that material requirements planning (MRP) can be agile for many businesses every day.

Future factories take over MRP's next level. Machine learning models propose changes to planning parameters, lead times, inventories, quality predictions, chain disruptions, isolation, and end-customer satisfaction in both lead time and price.

AI also helps manufacturers set higher expectations for capacity-based delivery dates, volumes, and unforeseen downtime, and AI can help firms decide what to do with their substitution capabilities, such as early-year seasonal goods production at a reduced retail store price.

11.3.2 AI Adoption in the Manufacturing Sector

Since supervised AI generally requires good data and training, the industry using common data is the most successful. All logistics companies use the same route map, weather, and traffic data. Similarly, virtually every retailer has the same universal product code (UPC) to identify products that many customers benefit from the UPC data AI techniques. In other words, when solutions emerge, industries adopt AI. High-quality data industries are ready to use AI solutions earlier than other industries.

11.3.3 Trends

The impact of AI on production will be varied. Computer vision (CV) improvement has been used for quality assurance for many years by detecting product failures in real-time. However, since manufacturing involves more data than ever before, plant managers do not pay staff to enter AIs for computer vision data to simplify data collection.

The Internet of Things (IoT) or cyber-physical systems are the second areas of AI influence. IoT is remarkable because basic technology is being deployed quickly, even without considering the results and safety aspects. In short, IoT is a tsunami of data that AI can use to understand and develop. This contributes to the improvement of generative processes in product development.

11.4 Industry Aspects

11.4.1 *Introduction*

One of India's growing industries is the manufacturing sector. India's Prime Minister Narendra Modi has launched "Make in India" to put India on a global map and an internationally recognised economic growth. The government intends to create 10 million new employment by 2022.

11.4.2 *Segment*

Manufacturing segments are divided into four parts: basic goods, capital goods, intermediate goods and consumer goods (see Figure 11.2).

11.4.3 *Market Size*

Gross value added (GVA) from India's manufacturing industry grew by 5% at current fundamental prices during FY16 and FY 20, according to the government's annual national revenue. The GVA sector's current cost was projected at 397 crores in FY20PE. In Indian manufacturing, business conditions continue to be favourable. The manufacturing part of the index of industrial production (IIP) for FY20 was 129.8. The recent growth in metal production was 10.8%, intermediate commodities 8.8%, food products 2.7%, and tobacco 2.9%. India's 8th core industry index was 131.9 in FY20. Goods exports declined annually by 4.78% in FY20.

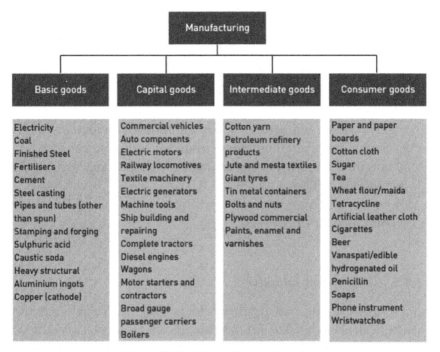

Figure 11.2. Types of manufacturing

11.4.4 *Investments*

Indeed, India is on its way to becoming the hub for hi-tech manufacturing through the "Make in India" push, with worldwide giants establishing plants in India, attracting more than one billion customers, and increasing buying power in an Indian market. According to UNCTAD, India was one of the top 10 recipients of foreign direct investments (FDIs) in 2019, an increase of INR 49 crore (or 16%) over the previous year. In Indian production from 2000 to 2020, cumulative FDI reached INR 88.45 crore. India has become one of the most attractive manufacturing investment destinations. Some of the significant investments and developments are:

- SWSL bagged an INR 260 million building contract in Australia in May 2020.

- Oricon Enterprises concluded a joint venture with Italian-based Tecnocap Group in March 2020 to establish a new lug cap manufacturing company, Tecnocap Oriental.
- Mumbai received its first state-owned Bharat Earth Movers (BEML) metro coach under the "Make in India" initiative.
- STP Ltd., located in Kolkata, acquired a 95.53% interest in the waterproofing and protective coating industry in October 2019.
- In September 2019, OnePlus introduced Indian smart TVs.
- In August 2019, Vivo was planning to increase capacity in India by INR 350 million.
- Capacity utilisation in manufacturing in India was 69.1% in the second quarter of 2019–20.

11.4.5 *Government Initiatives*

- The government had approved the production-linked incentive (PLI) in March 2020 for producing electronics. The scheme proposes an incentive for production to promote domestic production and attract significant investment in mobile and electronic devices, including ATMPs.
- In the defense industry in May 2020, the government automatically increased its FDI by 74%.
- In March 2020, the Union Cabinet adopted a financial support system through Economic Management Council (EMCs) to develop international infrastructure and town facilities and services.
- The number of new members of the Provident Fund in March 2020 reached four lakhs, according to the MOSPI report on payroll reports.
- In the period 2016–20, 73 lakhs were trained under the direction of Pradhan Mantri Kaushal, and 723 lakhs were trained in the period 2020.
- In February 2020, India attended 14,000 Industrial Training Institutes (ITIs).

- In automatic contract manufacturing in August 2019, the government approved 100% FDI.
- The PMKVY 1.0 has been trained for 19 lakh applicants, 13.23% of which were prepared. By June 2019, 59 lakhs, approximately 24%, had been taught by PMKVY 2,0, launched in October 2016.
- In February 2019, the Union Cabinet adopted the National Policy on Education (NPE) and planned to create an e-commerce industry of $400 billion by 2025. The world growth rate of 32% was targeted over the next five years.
- The government aims to increase the producing industry's GDP share to 25% by 2025 under the "Make in India" initiative.
- The Mid-Term Foreign Trade Policy (FTP) Review (2015–20) showed that the Indian administration increased its micro, small & medium enterprises (MSME) export incentive by 2%. Until April 2020, the FTP has been extended.

11.4.6 *Road Ahead*

India is an attractive foreign investment manufacturing hub. Many brands have established or want to set production sites for mobile, luxurious, and automobile applications in their countries. By 2025, Indian production is expected to reach INR 100 million. The Goods and Service Tax (GST) will transform India into an investment-intensified common market with a GDP of 2.5 trillion dollars and a population of 1.32 trillion. The government seeks to ensure its holistic development by stimulating industrial corridors and intelligent cities.

These measures will also contribute to integration, monitoring, and the creation of the industrial development environment.

11.4.7 *Advantage India*

Advantage India talks about Robust Demand, Increasing Investments, Policy Support and Competitive Advantage (see Figure 11.3).

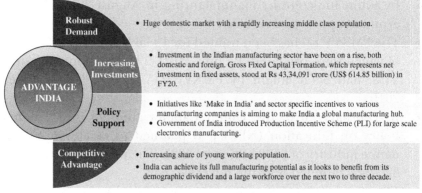

Note: PE — Provisional Estimate.

Figure 11.3.   Advantage India

11.5 Literature Review

Huang and Hayat's (2019) study aimed to measure Pakistan's artificial human resource intelligence while comparing it with Australia's performance. The results showed that HR is implementing AI in both countries. However, Australia is more effective in implementing AI in its HR companies.

Yawalkar (2019) examined artificial human resource intelligence's role and understood the human resources department's challenges. The research concluded that AI's role is more significant in various roles within the human resources department, where robotics companies can handle recruitment, data analysis, data collection, reduced workload, and improved workplace efficiency.

Abu-Khaled (2020) investigated the influence of AI on employment in Jordanian high-tech firms. In conclusion, the results indicated that real AI affects full employment in Jordanian high-tech companies. Automation evaluated the highest work effect followed by efficiency, while ease of use does not affect total job dimensions.

Jauhari's (2017) study assessed AI and machine learning's impact on current practices. AI is becoming increasingly essential, reshaping how companies recruit and perform all recruitment activities, as machine learning technology uses chat and conducts all activities. AI will screen and email candidates with confirmation or rejection.

Iqbal's (2018) study aimed to determine the impact of AI on the recruitment, training, development, and retention of workers within organisations. The study found that AI has a positive impact on company employee management and recommended investments in AI processes to bring HR management to the next level.

Reilly (2018) studied and demonstrated that the near-future application of HR activities in a company is changing dramatically. Although some employees may be affected, they improve company efficiency. Simultaneously, some western organisations' integration of AI into certain human resources practices has become competitive. But the best way to integrate quality control with AI is to engage in all hourly activities.

Srivastava (2018) pointed out that AI plays a vital role in human resource management; it contributes primarily to employee planning and efficiency management, making it difficult for employees to evaluate their work manually so that recruitment can be carried out automatically via AI. Performance evaluation will not discriminate against and will compensate employees and officials. Decisions are made using relatively advanced algorithms, and AI will improve the development of each organisation.

Bhardwaj (2019) said it is clear that all businesses receive many summaries. Introducing AI systems shifts the strategy from recruitment to employee involvement. This method is now being implemented using a search algorithm that shows that many small applications meet a few requirements.

Nunn (2019) studied AI's growing impact on recruitment in almost all industries. Each of the organisation's human resources officers' goal is to employ recruitment, automate contact with candidates, remove prejudices from candidate selection, and participate in screening. AI may offer educational recognition and conduct skill-based interviews, etc. The Human Resource Information System (HRIS) provides a picture of training and development that includes a photo of employees' skills and needs and links their vision.

Tambe *et al.* (2018) reported moving from big data to HRM and AI learning. They also focus on marketing, sales, essential selection, recruitment, training, and growth decisions. Amazon used AI to make critical business decisions in 2018. Collection, training, and development criteria are based on various AI algorithms. Because these algorithms are already implemented in applications, the algorithms are code-based, and AI can significantly benefit. This is one of the best techniques for evaluating employee performance in each organisation.

According to Ahmed (2018), if the organisation's success has increased, it will reduce HR managers' pressure. AI provides more personal interactions with new staff unfamiliar with where to go, and it plays a crucial role in helping them talk. AI also allows staff to see how the company can be run and implemented across the board and how it handles all employee issues and algorithms to make recruiting easier and enhance unbiased services for HR professionals. AI finds pattern and anomalies in data. It allows the company to set its own rules and procedures.

Hussein *et al.* (2016) reviewed and analysed AI conceptualisation components in AI audit history: sensing, implementation, meta-controls, meta-processes, exogenous measurement, rapid detection of phenomena, and integration of evidence in-service analysis. Furthermore, the authors conclude that AI can replace auditors with several automated tasks and automatically identify a complete audit plan based on customer status and existing evidence.

Admin looked at the modern world and how it intimidated multinational workers. AI is the world's most innovative. Since AI is of interest in almost all areas, outcomes such as in banking and insurance are remarkable. However, when most companies worldwide join AI, new companies — especially start-ups — join AI to remain recognisable and competitive.

Surve (2020) investigated human-robot AI interactions (HRI). Even if you can do all your physical work, AI can do it. But AI can't have emotional intelligence — the main downside to human-robot interaction. Only robots can perform pre-instruction, and not being human, their actions cannot be reversed. Independent software modules are difficult to impose, especially architectural challenges.

Van Pay (2018) found out how AI re-invented HR. Companies mainly use AI solutions for its industry and worries if a non-personal entity can handle business practices. Using an organisation's AI to collect data using a multi-candidate test reduces the time needed to complete and interview applicants to find the right candidate. Applicants receive additional details, including expertise and experience. AI interview software like HireVue and Mya are used. In particular, AI technology focuses on the cycle from acquisitions to interviews, significantly reducing recruitment schedules and making it easy and practical to appoint the suitable candidates to play different roles and work.

11.6 Research

11.6.1 *Statement of the Problem*

The study's problem is work reality. After interviewing employees, recruiters complain that their companies are trying to cut costs and make AI available to employees, especially those with weak skills, and feel this threatens their jobs. Since humans have limited skills, keeping up with all the necessary tasks is not easy, and each recruiter usually requires a lot of time. The problem identified here is that human limitations, such as biases, preconceptions, and time restrictions, can prevent the effectiveness of HRM processes. This is a problem because it can lead an organisation to lose its monetary value and candidates (Baron *et al.*, 2018). The study discusses AI's effect on work and HRM. Earlier studies differ between supporters and opponents. Arntz *et al.* (2016) argued that technological unemployment is likely to increase over the years as workers seek new jobs after being laid off due to advances in AI. Frontier Economics (2018) discussed that recent industrial automation is linked to declining employment and manufacturing profits at low and medium-sized formal enterprises. Therefore, this study aims to investigate AI's impact on work and HRM.

11.6.2 *Objectives of the Study*

- To analyse the effect of AI on HRM in the manufacturing sector
- To determine the influence of AI on work in the manufacturing sector
- To evaluate the relationship between AI and HRM in the manufacturing sector

11.6.3 *Research Methodology*

The researcher assesses the corporate culture, employee engagement, and level of company satisfaction. The current research is the analytical version of the analysis process, including qualitative and quantitative knowledge on various aspects. The questions were designed to provide direct responses to the goals of the analysis. Responses were collected from retailers, readers and marketers individually to evaluate the primary outcomes.

11.6.4 *Research Design*

For this project, the form of study will be descriptive in nature. Descriptive work provides a summary of the current state of affairs. The study's key disadvantages are that the investigator does not influence the variables; only what happened or was happening can be recorded.

11.6.5 *Sampling Technique*

For this analysis, respondents were picked based on convenience sampling. Due to time constraints, and lack of awareness of the environment, the key reason the sampling approach should be used is that it is not easy to collect data from all the customers who worked on the project.

11.6.6 *Sample Size*

The survey is conducted among 75 respondents.

11.6.7 Data Collection Method

The investigation is carried out to achieve the study's objective, and data collected from both primary and secondary data are collected. Preliminary evidence is in the form of a questionnaire, which is a useful tool to meet a wide range of people who can read and write independently. The questionnaire contains both open-ended and closed-ended questions. Simultaneously, the first section describes the demographic variables, and the second section demonstrates the impact of AI on work and HRM in the manufacturing sector. In addition to the secondary data used, the material extracts from journals, research papers, blogs, and articles on how AI impact work and HRM in the manufacturing sector.

11.6.8 Tools for analysis

The researcher applies specific statistical tools like percentage, regression, and correlation. Appropriate marketing analytics tools are also applies in the study, which includes descriptive analysis using Excel.

11.6.9 Limitations of the Study

Only a small sample size of 75 may have biased the results. The scope of the analysis is restricted to the manufacturing sector only. The research population applies only to employees in the manufacturing field for convenience purposes. The answers of the respondents determine the accuracy of the data.

11.7 Data Analysis and Findings

Table 11.1 shows the age of the respondents. It reveals that 22.7% of respondents belong to the age group of 25 to 30 years, while 32% belong to the age group of 30 to 35 years, followed by 21.3% belonging to the age group of 35 to 40 years and 24% belonging to the age group of above 40 years. It is concluded that most of the respondents belong to 30 to 35 years of age in this study.

Table 11.1.   Age of respondents

Particulars	No. of respondents	Percentage
25 to 30 years	17	22.7
30 to 35 years	24	32.0
35 to 40 years	16	21.3
Above 40 years	18	24.0
Total	**75**	**100.0**

Table 11.2.   Gender of respondents

Particulars	No. of respondents	Percentage
Female	24	32.0
Male	51	68.0
Total	**75**	**100.0**

Table 11.3.   Education level of respondents

Particulars	No. of respondents	Percentage
Diploma	22	29.3
Undergraduate	23	30.7
Postgraduate	19	25.3
Others	11	14.7
Total	**75**	**100.0**

Table 11.2 shows the gender of respondents. Out of 75 respondents, 32% or 24 respondents were female, and 68% or 51 respondents were male. It is evident that the larger portion of respondents is male.

Table 11.3 shows the education level of respondents. It is found that 29.3% of respondents are educated to diploma level, while 30.7% are undergraduate, 25.3% are postgraduate and 14.7% are others. It is concluded that the majority of respondents in this study are undergraduate (see Figure 11.4).

Table 11.4 shows the designation of respondents. It indicates that 29.3% of respondents are supervisors, while 26.7% are assistant

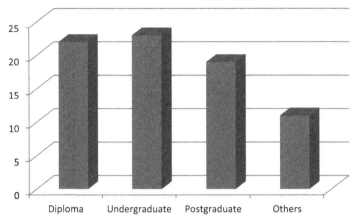

Figure 11.4. Education level of respondents

Table 11.4. Designation of respondents

Particulars	No. of respondents	Percentage
Supervisor	22	29.3
Assistant manager	20	26.7
Manager	17	22.7
Others	16	21.3
Total	**75**	**100.0**

managers, followed by 22.7% managers, and 21.3% others. It is concluded that most of the respondents who are involved in this study are supervisors.

Table 11.5 shows the working experience of the respondents. It finds that 37.3% of respondents have less than 3 years of experience in AI technology, while 33% have work experience between 3 and 6 years, and 30.7% are above 6 years. It is concluded that the highest number of respondents have less than 3 years of experience in AI technology.

Table 11.6 shows the marital status of the respondents. It is observed that 45.3% of respondents are married, and 54.7% are unmarried. It is concluded that most of the respondents who have participated in this study are unmarried (see Figure 11.5).

Table 11.5. Working experience of respondents

Particulars	No. of respondents	Percentage
Less than three years	28	37.3
3 to 6 years	24	32.0
Above six years	23	30.7
Total	**75**	**100.0**

Table 11.6. Marital status of respondents

Particulars	No. of respondents	Percentage
Married	34	45.3
Unmarried	41	54.7
Total	**75**	**100.0**

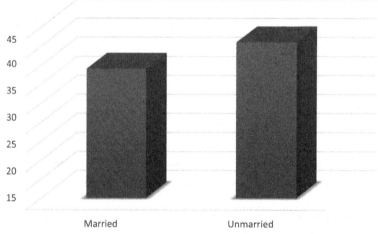

Figure 11.5. Marital status of respondents

Table 11.7 shows the awareness of AI in the manufacturing sector. It indicates that 100% of respondents know about AI in the manufacturing industry. It is concluded that the majority of respondents who participated in this study know about AI in the manufacturing industry (see Figure 11.6).

Table 11.8 shows the descriptive statistics for AI (see Figure 11.7). It indicates that 13% of respondents utilise AI to improve

Table 11.7. Awareness of AI in the manufacturing sector

Particulars	No. of respondents	Percentage
Yes	75	100.0
No	0	0.0
Total	**75**	**100.0**

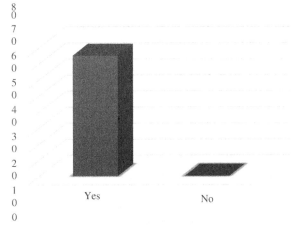

Figure 11.6 Awareness of AI in the manufacturing sector

Table 11.8. Descriptive statistics for AI

Particulars	Mean	Standard deviation
AI applies human-less procedures	3.0933	1.49027
AI replaces them with manual tasks	3.0133	1.39974
AI uses errors to prevent them automatically	2.9067	1.40629
AI utilises improved productivity	3.1600	1.36600
AI is used to accelerate workflows	3.0400	1.49268
AI is used economically by the company	2.9867	1.47496
The staff understand AI quickly	3.0533	1.33450
The employee efficiently uses AI systems	3.0533	1.42272

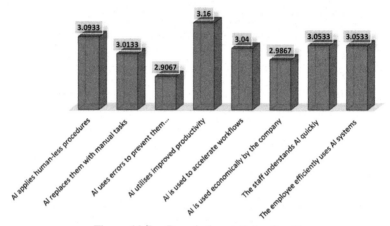

Figure 11.7.   Descriptive statistics for AI

Table 11.9.   Descriptive statistics for recruitment

Particulars	Mean	Standard deviation
Potential candidates are drawn from AI	2.9200	1.37310
AI enhances the recruiter's response time	3.0800	1.48652
AI uses it to find new talents quickly	2.9200	1.44970
AI uses CVs for flattering	3.3600	1.28020
AI forecasts employees' success	2.8667	1.47349

productivity, and 11.96% of respondents use AI to prevent errors. On the other hand, the standard deviation shows that the staff who understand AI technology quickly have high AI accuracy.

Table 11.9 shows the descriptive statistics for recruitment. It suggests that 22.18% of respondents use this AI technology for CVs flattering. The least 18.93% of respondents have used AI technology in recruitment to forecasts employees' success. However, the standard deviation indicates that the recruitment used the AI technology for flattering the CVs, which has a high accuracy (see Figure 11.8).

Table 11.10 shows descriptive statistics for a selection. It indicates that 21.61% of respondents use AI technology to test for a

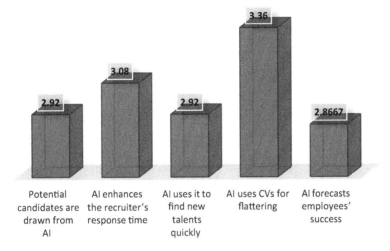

Figure 11.8. Descriptive statistics for recruitment

Table 11.10. Descriptive statistics for a selection

Particulars	Mean	Standard deviation
The company uses AI to assess vacancies	2.8400	1.46158
The company uses AI to test for a specific job	3.0800	1.29197
It uses AI to reduce human distortion	2.7467	1.45280
The company uses AI to identify the right person	2.7467	1.29545
AI is used for company interview planning	2.8267	1.35939

specific job and 19.3% of respondents use AI to reduce human distortion and work with the right person. However, the standard deviation suggests that AI is used for the selection process to identify the right person for the job to have high accuracy (see Figure 11.9).

Table 11.11 showings descriptive statistics for organisation performance. It shows that 17.36% of respondents are using AI for new products/services capacity increased and 15.31% of respondents are using AI to improve the internal process simplification capacity. However, the standard deviation stated that the AI used to enriched

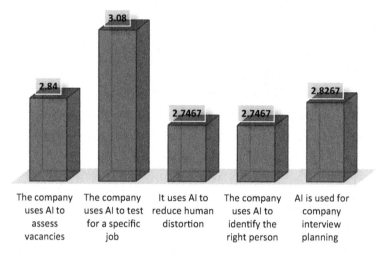

Figure 11.9. Descriptive statistics for a selection

Table 11.11. Descriptive statistics for organisation performance

Particulars	Mean	Standard deviation
New products/services capacity increased	3.0533	1.35461
Improve rapid marketing of innovations	2.9867	1.36058
Enhanced economic responsiveness	3.0000	1.40463
Improved internal process simplification capacity	2.6933	1.39471
Enriched responsiveness to a new industry or market information	2.9733	1.33531
Optimised resource capacity and knowledge redundancy	2.8800	1.42336

responsiveness to a new industry or market information has high organisation performance accuracy (see Figure 11.10).

Table 11.12 shows descriptive statistics for employment. It indicates that 13.04% of respondents use AI for changes to management staff and 11.45% of respondents use AI to create effects that can compensate for a replacement to some degree. However, the

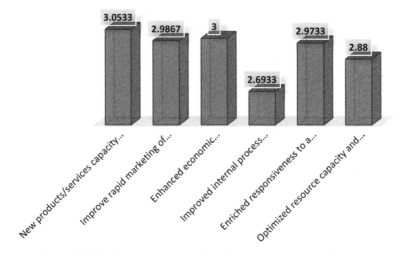

Figure 11.10.   Descriptive statistics for organisation performance

Table 11.12.   Descriptive statistics for employment

Particulars	Mean	Standard deviation
Work methods change	2.9600	1.45602
Changes in labour demand	2.9600	1.38954
Changes to management staff	3.0533	1.45094
Increase resident revenue to boost demand	2.8400	1.38564
New technology itself creates jobs	2.9867	1.54652
Expand economic scope for job creation	2.9733	1.55070
Development is rapid and violent and promotes employment demand	2.9600	1.49268
AI creates effects that can compensate for the effect of replacement to some degree	2.6800	1.40616

standard deviation shows that AI increases resident revenue to boost demand with high employment accuracy (see Figure 11.11).

Table 11.13 shows the descriptive statistics for work behaviour. It shows the descriptive statistics for work behaviour: 15.15% of respondents are enthusiastic about innovative ideas and 12.9% of

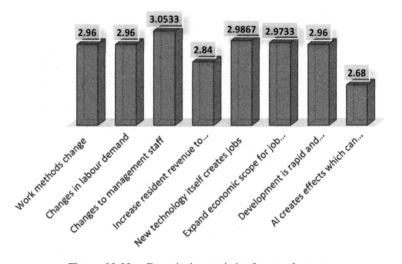

Figure 11.11. Descriptive statistics for employment

Table 11.13. Descriptive statistics for work behaviour

Particulars	Mean	Standard deviation
They discuss problems that aren't part of their everyday work	3.0000	1.28400
They ask how to improve things	2.6667	1.40783
They provide original solutions to problems	2.7600	1.37389
Our staff find new ways to fulfill their tasks	3.0800	1.30239
Enthusiasm for innovative ideas	3.1333	1.49172
Our staffs contribute to implementing new ideas	2.9600	1.39923
Our staff work to develop new things	3.0800	1.52244

respondents are asked how to improve things by using AI. However, the standard deviation states that the staff finds new ways to fulfill their tasks has high work behaviour accuracy (see Figure 11.12).

H0: There is no significant relationship between the HRM variable and AI.

H1: There is a significant relationship between the HRM variable and AI.

Table 11.14 shows the correlation between the variables of HRM and AI. The first variable (Recruitment and AI) shows the correlation value is 0.775 and the P-value is 0.000 and thus concludes that there exists a significant association between the variables.

The second variable (Selection and AI) reveals the correlation value is 0.556, the P-value is 0.000 and hence infers that the selection has a significant relationship with AI.

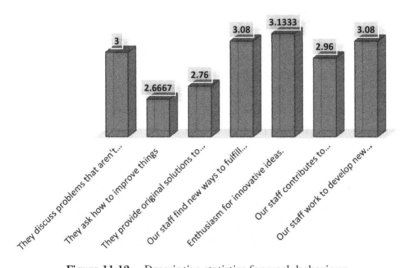

Figure 11.12. Descriptive statistics for work behaviour

Table 11.14. Correlation between the variables of HRM and AI

Particulars	Recruitment	Selection	Organisation performance	Employment	AI
Recruitment	1	.371	.432	.261*	.775
		(.003)	(.005)	(.004)	(.000)
Selection		1	.524	.327	.556
			(.001)	(.002)	(.000)
Organisation performance			1	.263*	.795
				(.003)	(.000)
Employment				1	.720
					(.000)
AI					1

Table 11.15. Correlation between the work and AI

Particulars	Work	AI
Work	1	.558
		(.000)
AI		1

The third variable (Organisation performance and AI) indicated that the correlation value is 0.795, the P-value is 0.000 and then concludes that there is a strong and positive association between the organisation performance and AI.

The last variable (Employment and AI) depicts that the correlation value as 0.720 and the significance value as 0.000. Hence it is evident that employment has a positively significant relationship with AI.

H0: There is no significant relationship between the work and AI.
H1: There is a significant relationship between the work and AI.

Table 11.15 shows the correlation between the work and AI. It finds that the association between the work and AI has a correlation value is 0.558, and the significance value is 0.000. Thus it is concluded that the work has a strong and positive association with AI, and it is statistically significant.

11.8 Suggestions

The organisation identifies the necessary abilities, skills, and capabilities for each job and then uses AI to conduct the resume search based on that criteria. Selecting the right individual is vital to HRM, including recruitment, selection, organisational performance, and employment. An organisation can benefit from AI by leveraging its competitiveness. Organisations should rely on AI for office automation tasks to reduce the need for human labour. HR experts can focus more on strategic planning within the organisation. HR professionals are now tasked with improving their decision making, knowledge of AI, secure work, reducing workloads, and increasing production.

11.9 Conclusion

AI reduces manual analysis and complicated planning in building programs and recommends data rather than relying on gut feeling. Therefore, AI is ready for better, less biased decisions and more effective HR teams and managers' actions. AI has significantly improved human lives, and before its introduction, people are indifferent with AI. It has saved time and resulted in higher output for companies and people every day.

The study aims to assess the effects of AI on HRM and the manufacturing sector. The study's findings show that most survey respondents are between 30 and 35 years of age. However, the larger portion of respondents is male. Respondents' opinions shows that HRM and work are directly and statistically significant to AI. HRM and work behaviour have a positive effect on AI. AI improves life if it is understood and used correctly, thus AI creates a better future. As a result, recruitment has a 60.1% impact, selection has an impact of 30.9%, organisational performance has an impact of 63.2%, employment has an impact of 51.8%, and AI has a 31.1% impact. However, the organisation's performance is strong and positive, and AI is the least affected by selection. The low combination strength of all variables is, therefore, statistically significant.

References

Abu-Khaled, N. K. (2020). The impact of AI on employment in high-tech companies in the Jordanian market. Doctoral dissertation, Middle East University.

Ahmed, O. (2018). Artificial intelligence in HR. *International Journal of Research and Analytical Reviews, 5*(4), 971–978.

Arntz, M., Gregory, T., & Zierahn, U. (2016). The risk of automation for jobs in OECD countries. OECD Social, Employment and Migration Working Papers, No. 189. Available at: https://doi.org/10.1787/5jlz9h56dvq7-en

Baron, I. S., Musthafa, & Agustina, H. (2018). The challenges of recruitment and selection systems in Indonesia. *Journal of Management and Marketing Review, 3*(4), 185–192.

Bhardwaj, R. (2019). How AI is revolutionizing the human resource functions. Entrepreneur. Available at: https://www.entrepreneur.com/article/325715

Frontier Economics (2018). The impact of artificial intelligence on work: An evidence review prepared for the Royal Society and the British Academy. Available at: https://royalsociety.org/-/media/policy/projects/ai-and-work/frontier-review-the-impact-of-AI-on-work.pdf

Huang, W., & Hayat, A. (2019). Impact of artificial intelligence in enterprises HR performance in Pakistan: A comparison study with Australia. *Global Journal of Management and Business Research.* Available at: https://journalofbusiness.org/index.php/GJMBR/article/view/3074

Hussein, H. T., Ammar, M., & Hassan, M. M. (2016). Induction motors stator fault analysis based on artificial intelligence. *Indonesian Journal of Electrical Engineering and Computer Science, 2*(1), 69–78.

Iqbal, F. M. (2018). Can artificial intelligence change how companies recruit, train, develop, and manage human resources in the workplace? *Asian Journal of Social Sciences and Management Studies, 5*(3), 102–104.

Jauhari, A. (2017). How AI and machine learning will impact HR practices. Vccircle. Available at: https://www.vccircle.com/how-ai-and-machine-learning-will-impact-hr-practices/

Matsa, P., & Gullamajji, K. (2019). To study impact of AI on human resource management. *International Research Journal of Engineering and Technology, 6*(8), 1229–1238.

Merlin, R., & Jayam. R (2018). AI in human resource management. *International Journal of Pure and Applied Mathematics, 119*(17), 1891–1895.

Nunn, J. (2019). The emerging impact of AI on HR. Forbes. Available at: https://www.forbes.com/sites/forbestechcouncil/2019/02/06/the-emerging-impact-of-ai-on-hr/?sh=7eeffbb55496

Reilly, P. (2018). The impact of AI on the HR function. IES Perspectives on HR. Available at: https://www.employment-studies.co.uk/system/

files/resources/files/mp142_The_impact_of_Artificial_Intelligence_ on_the_HR_function-Peter_Reilly.pdf

Sharma, N. (2020). Fostering positive deviance: A potential strategy to an engaged workforce. *Strategic Direction, 36*(8), 1–3.

Srivastava, P. (2018). Impact of AI on strategic HR decision making. People Matters. Available at: https://www.peoplematters.in/article/technology/ impact-of-artificial-intelligence-on-strategic-hr-decision-making-17935

Surve, A. A. (2020). Impact of artificial intelligence in human resource management. Doctoral dissertation, University of Mumbai.

Tambe, P., Cappelli, P., & Yakubovich, V. (2019). Artificial intelligence in human resources management: Challenges and a path forward. *California Management Review, 61*(4), 15–42.

Van Pay, B. (2018). How AI is reinventing human resources. HR Leader. Available at: https://archive2.hrmac.org/Full-Article/how-artificial-intelligence-is-reinventing-human-resources

Wall, T. D., & Wood, S. J. (2005). The romance of human resource management and business performance and the case of big science. *Human Relations, 58*(4), 429–462.

Yawalkar, M. V. V. (2019). A study of artificial intelligence and its role in human resource management. *International Journal of Research and Analytical Reviews, 6*(1), 20–24.

Chapter 12

Towards a Framework for Higher Education Curriculum for Small Family Business

David Devins* and Brian Jones[†]

Leeds Business School, Leeds Beckett University, UK

*d.devins@leedsbeckett.ac.uk

[†]b.t.jones@leedsbeckett.ac.uk

Abstract: There is an established policy discourse associated with the role of higher education (HE) in supporting the development of small and medium sized enterprises (SMEs) but far less attention tends to be given to the needs of small family businesses. Given their unique socio-cultural context and the sizeable contribution that family businesses make to society and the economy, this is perhaps surprising. The heterogeneity of family businesses and their preferences for entrepreneurial learning present significant challenges to education providers offering formal courses of study to SMEs. Very few UK university programmes address the knowledge and skills required to start and sustain family businesses and this may be seen to represent a significant market failure in the provision of higher-level learning services to this important sector of the economy. This paper adopts Miller and Seller's (1990) framework that identifies three general educational orientations (transmission, transaction, and transformation) as a theoretical construct to explore the nature of university curriculum and the extent to which it connects with small family firm learning and development interests. This chapter introduces a framework to guide curriculum design influenced by the interests of small family businesses and considers some associated challenges and avenues for further investigation.

Keywords: SMEs, Higher education, Small business, Family business, Employees.

12.1 Introduction

Reforms of higher education (HE) and the integration of industry and labour market interests in the curriculum are seen as a key to achieving the goals of smart, sustainable, and inclusive growth outlined in the Europe 2020 strategy. Across Europe, the knowledge economy brings new challenges for higher level skills and demographic changes forecast a future European labour market which will be simultaneously confronted by an ageing population and shrinking cohorts of young people. This presents a dynamic context for HE where young people need relevant knowledge and skills to successfully enter and progress in the labour market and older workers are increasingly called upon to update and broaden their higher level knowledge and competencies. Enterprise in the form of business start up, sustainability, and growth is seen to be a key driver of economic prosperity and the ways in which HE supports the development of learner knowledge and skills are viewed by policy makers as a key to unlocking productivity and economic growth. Public policy prescription identifies a requirement for more work relevant education, flexible modes of delivery, and new forms of validation of learning (European Commission, 2012). There have been several communiqués from the European Commission calling for the use of innovative and evolving pedagogies to support workforce development and innovation. Many of the flagship initiatives and European funding instruments are actively supporting innovation in education systems and the development of the links between HE institutions (HEIs) and industry.

The White Paper in England, "Success as a Knowledge Economy" makes it clear that HE must embrace their role as drivers of economic progress (BIS, 2016). Improving the quality of teaching features strongly in the White Paper and the extent to which employers are engaged with courses and the degree to which university programmes are industry-relevant are identified as important outcomes that students, taxpayers, and the government expect teaching to deliver. Putting aside a concern that the focus on economic value may be overbearing, the demand for higher-level skills in the labour market both now and in the future presents an opportunity for HE in the UK. The introduction of the Teaching Excellence Framework (TEF) is designed to make better information available to potential learners and the continued development of alternatives to the traditional three- or four-year full time undergraduate degree. These alternatives include; a two-year accelerated degree; studying part time; in modules; from a distance; or in a degree apprenticeship, embedded with an employer. The White Paper says little about Masters level qualification, although one can safely assume that those programmes that connect with the labour market and support student progression are likely to be highly prized. However, the success of these supply-side innovations is largely dependent upon the extent to which businesses create quality job opportunities for graduates as they leave education and provide high quality placements for those studying courses offering work-based learning opportunities. In order to further these interests, universities need to understand economies, the businesses that operate in them, and work in partnership to inform the design of curriculum that addresses their interests.

It would appear that enterprise and entrepreneurship education offer powerful tools for personal empowerment and for small business growth and development. The debate around the nature, purpose, workings of, and rationale for Enterprise and Entrepreneurship Education (Gibb, 1987, 1993, 2002; Pittaway & Cope, 2007; Jones & Iredale, 2010) provides part of the context for exploring family business influenced curriculum. In particular, it can shed light on the learning that takes place within such contexts. Much good work has been done in Enterprise and Entrepreneurship Education at policy (European Commission, 2006; OECD, 2001; Ofsted, 2004; Volkmann *et al.*, 2009), practitioner, (Young Enterprise, 2021) and academic (Hytti & O'Gorman, 2004; Kuratko, 2005) levels. Enterprise and Entrepreneurship interventions with young people (Young Enterprise, 2021; Jones & Iredale, 2006), women (Treanor, 2012), ethnic minorities (Hussain *et al.*, 2010), as well as those operating in specific regions and localities (Matlay, 2001; Jones & Iredale, 2008) serve to underline the importance attached to these concepts and practices. However, the role of Enterprise and Entrepreneurship Education in helping support and sustain small family businesses has in large part been noticeable by its absence and this chapter seeks to redress this research gap by detailing and outlining the potential for HE to develop curriculum and teaching and learning strategies that connect with the world of the small family businesses.

The choice of family businesses as a vehicle to explore these issues may seem idiosyncratic. However, family businesses are an important part of local, national and global economies, operating in all industrial sectors of the economy. The European Union network of family businesses (EFB) representing long-term family owned enterprises estimates that there are more than 14 million (the vast majority of them small enterprises) that account for around 50% of GDP and employ 60 million workers across Europe. In the UK alone, the Institute for Family Businesses (IFB) referring to research by Oxford Economics suggest that there are an estimated 4.6 million family businesses (87% of all private sector firms) employing 11.9 million people (36% of all private sector employment) and contributing the equivalent of 19% of the Government's total tax receipts (IFB, 2016). About 97% of them are small organisations employing less than 50 employees. Family businesses are by any measure an important element of most economies; however they are increasingly a concern to European policy makers who recognise the challenge of family business sustainability in the long run. This has led the EFB to identify the greatest challenge facing family businesses as the transfer of ownership and/or management of the business to the next generation which manifests itself in different ways in different European states. In the UK, the Department for Business Innovation and Skills estimates that around 266,000 family businesses anticipate closure and over 500,000 full transfer in the five years to 2018. A natural desire to keep the business within the family means business owners have to make decisions relating to when and how to transfer management and ownership of the company to the next generation. As with firms more generally, many family businesses will be looking to the future to build their business strategy in a world that is increasingly complex, and both family leaders and their successors are accused of being culprits in succession failure, with many failing to anticipate or plan for succession (Kraus *et al.*, 2011; IFB, 2008). The extent to which HE is able to support leadership and management in these businesses will go a long way to determining the success of the economy.

In this exploratory chapter we draw on the literature to describe what family business influenced curriculum could look like in HE. Having briefly outlined the context in and against which this chapter is set, the theoretical foundations are outlined and relevant literature is discussed through an exploration of different education perspectives that have implications for teaching and learning strategies. The chapter then explores issues around curriculum design and discussion is centred on the nature, purpose, function, working, and delivery of enterprise education. The analysis of the literature is extended towards a framework to explore small family business influenced curriculum. The chapter concludes by restating the importance of the family business sector to the economy and identifying the need for curriculum design that draws on action oriented, work-based, and work-related pedagogy that reflects the interests of students and business. This leads to a number of fundamental questions and avenues for further investigation.

12.2 Theoretical Underpinnings

The introduction of the Teaching Excellence Framework (TEF) is as much about learning as it is about teaching with the terms often used in tandem in the White Paper. Learning however is the ultimate goal (whereas teaching can be seen as a means to achieve this end) and may be described as a process by which people acquire new knowledge, including skills and specific competencies and assimilate and organise them with prior knowledge in memory to make them retrievable for use in both routine and non-routine action (Anderson, 1982). It can also be defined as an emergent, sense-making process in which people develop the ability to act differently, through knowing, doing, and understanding why (Mumford, 1995). By learning, people construct meaning through experience and create new reality in a context of social interaction (Weick, 1995). It is a dynamic process of awareness, reflection, association, and application that involves transforming experience and knowledge into functional learning outcomes (Rae, 2006). Small business learning is hence complex and interconnected with a somewhat ad hoc approach to formal learning and a heavy reliance on experiential learning (Warren, 2004). It is frequently reported that small business managers have a preference for informal learning, characterised by doing, exploring, experimenting, copying, problem solving, and learning from mistakes made in the process (Gibb, 1997; Dalley & Hamilton, 2000). The important features of such learning are that while it is often very meaningful and directly relevant to issues in the workplace, it is not recognised explicitly as learning remains to all intents and purposes invisible. Mumford (1995) suggested that such learning while direct and focused on work can also be accidental and unstructured. What's more, it may result in unreflective and uncritical learning which fails to move the learner or the organisation forward. Reference to the seminal work of Kolb (1984) and Schön (1983) and formulations that argue that what is embodied as knowledge is revealed through reflection and deliberation either in action or after action are relevant here. An early and influential contribution by Gibb (1997) draws on the work of Argyris and

Schön (1978) and Senge (1990) which go some way to explaining why many small organisations fail in the first few years or get "stuck" in a cycle of adaptive learning (in order to cope with change) rather than the generative learning (the active integration of new ideas which results in a change in the learner's or organisations existing schemata) necessary to meet the aspirations of policy makers in terms of sustainability, economic competitiveness, and lifelong learning.

The nature of organisational and individual learning in the small business context has been subject to much discussion and debate. Much of the literature assumes individual learning focused on "the entrepreneur" through cognitive processes (Deakins, 1996; Rae & Carswell, 2000; Cope, 2003) and neglects the context in which the learning takes place. Devins and Gold (2002) argue that a socio-cultural approach is a useful way to frame learning in the small business context. They argue that the "world" of small business can be explored through a consideration of Vygotsky's (1978) socio-cultural theory of learning and particularly what he referred to as the Zone of Proximal Development (ZPD). This is described as the distance between the actual development level as determined by independent problem solving and the level of potential development as determined through problem solving under guidance or in collaboration with more capable peers. For a small business manager, what is known requires a consideration of present concerns, existing capacities, and understandings and skills to find solutions to problems faced. These interests provide the starting point for learning at a particular moment in time and it is through interaction with others that thoughts, feelings, and behaviour can advance. In a related domain, Hamilton (2011) explores entrepreneurial learning in family business and challenges the understanding of learning as principally an individual phenomenon, invoking situated learning and the conception of the family business as "communities of practice" (Lave & Wenger, 1991). In this context, understandings are developed, negotiated, and shared with others operating in a range of overlapping "family" and "business" communities of practice. Translating and transferring practice from one community of practice to another brings innovation and the potential for transformational change. Applying these notions of learning to the design of university curriculum raises some interesting questions in relation to the nature of education as we work towards establishing a theoretical framework to guide HE curriculum design for small family businesses. In order to explore this further, we draw on the framework proposed by Miller and Seller (1990) that identifies three general orientations implemented by educational systems to support learning. These orientations are classified as transmission, transaction, and transformation and each has implications for the curriculum that are developed by HEIs to reflect the needs and interests of small family businesses.

The primary purpose of education from the transmission perspective is to ensure that knowledge, skills, and values are transmitted from academy to the student body. The learner has a largely passive role as a recipient of knowledge provided by the academy. Through this transmission lens, learning focuses on the content of the curriculum that the student must master (Fink, 2003) and the educators function is to design the curriculum to enforce correct behaviour (Van Gyn & Grove White, 2004). In contrast to the emphasis on acquiring necessary knowledge which lies at the heart of transmission, a transaction perspective emphasises the development of skills needed to acquire knowledge. Integral to this perspective is an emphasis on learning programmes associated with problem solving and the development of cognitive skills to support further knowledge acquisition. From this perspective, both educators and students are partners in the learning process and this reciprocal relationship means that students must become active learners (Fink, 2003). This perspective is heavily influenced by the pragmatic philosophy of Dewey (2009), first published in the early 1900s, which draws on a collaborative rational problem solving approach as a critical education methodology. Through this lens, the educator remains responsible for structuring the learning environment, although the associated pedagogy differs radically from that envisaged by the transmission models. Collaborative learning with other students and group processes are encouraged, teachers remain the content experts but they also model the cognitive problem-solving skills their students are expected to develop by addressing with them the ambiguities and dilemmas inherent in the subject matter as a means of teaching students how to construct knowledge for themselves. The transformation perspective in education is a rich intersection of views and traditions drawn from humanistic psychology, philosophy, and from post-modern and post-colonial theory (Van Gyn & Grove White, 2004). Mezirow (1991) argues that the role of the transformational educator is to assist the learner in identifying and examining assumptions that underlie his or her feelings, beliefs, and actions while remaining at all times conscious of how their teaching practice aligns with their learner's personal and social location. The educator acts as an "empathetic provocateur, gently creating dilemmas by encouraging learners to face up to contradictions between what they believe and what they do" (p. 366).

Whilst the way in which higher education curriculum is understood and theorised may be contested, there is some consensus that the concept of curriculum has become broader, increasingly changing from a text or document indicating the subject knowledge to be acquired by a learner towards a more dynamic, comprehensive framework. Educational orientation influences the nature of curriculum and in the transmission orientation, discipline centred content defines the knowledge that the student must acquire. Educators can articulate specific learning outcomes and pedagogy based on instructional strategies that will lead to desired learning outcomes. Assessment mainly requires reproduction of the prescribed curriculum content with a relatively low level of real world application (Fink, 2003). By way of contrast, a transaction-oriented curriculum is often based on resolving "real" problems where academics perform roles as facilitators, advisors, or as an expert resource as opposed to working in a more traditional academic role as a transmitter of knowledge (Boud, 2001). This orientation addresses the learner's ability to demonstrate higher-order thinking skills, including their ability to assess a problem, their capacity to draw upon resources including the knowledge they have constructed over the course of their learning, their creativity in providing solutions, and their ability to make informed choices among various possible options. This perspective emphasises learning rather than teaching, and learner-centred outcomes such as critical thinking, self-directed learning, or reflective practice are highly valued (Boud, 2006; Workman, 2009). Teaching and learning strategies informed by this perspective include problem-based or inquiry-based learning, collaborative learning, reflective practice, and life-long learning that appear to connect more closely with the action oriented learning preferences of owner-managers working in smaller enterprises. Curriculum from the transformation perspective is integrated and interdisciplinary, allowing for significant input from learners as knowledge holders and recognising their role as agents of change with teaching, learning, and workplace practice underpinned by pedagogical practices such as critical dialogue, interdisciplinary study, communities of practice, and critical pedagogy and with assessment practices tending to be holistic and qualitative in nature (Miller & Seller, 1990). The integrated, multidisciplinary, and learner-informed approach appears to be suited to the situational, action oriented learning context likely to be found in many family businesses.

12.3 Curriculum Design

It is vital when designing curriculum to understand the differences and similarities between enterprise and entrepreneurship education as well as the different purposes, learning and teaching strategies and outcomes associated with these terms from an HE perspective. Before we turn to this, it is important to recognise that all higher education curriculum design takes place within a wider institutional context which is influenced by the National Regulatory environment. The UK Quality Code for Higher Education is the definitive reference point for all UK higher education providers (Quality Assurance Agency for Higher Education or QAA, 2021). Whilst critical review of these substantial regulations is beyond the scope of this chapter, it is important to note that they make it clear what higher education providers are required to do, what they can expect of each other, and what the general public can expect of them and that the processes of curriculum design, development, and approval are an essential element of higher education bureaucracy associated with internal quality assurance and enhancement. They ensure that appropriate academic standards are set and maintained and that the programmes offered to learners enable the intended learning outcomes to be achieved. Curriculum design depends on reflection and critical self-assessment by individuals, groups, and HE providers working together in an iterative process of development dependent upon feedback from a range of sources which may include other staff, students, employers and professional statutory and regulatory bodies. Curriculum design therefore provides opportunities for HE providers to innovate alongside a culture of continuous improvement and to design and develop programmes that reflect wider socio-economic needs of the economy and society. We suggest that work-based learning and enterprise and entrepreneurship education share theoretical and conceptual design and in a number of ways are similar in their practice. There are of course differences between the two educational concepts but they are nevertheless closely related in terms of their history and heritage. They share a common educational genetic code but are nevertheless distinct entities in their own right.

The QAA also provides guidance for the provision for enterprise and entrepreneurship education that has been developed by representatives drawn from, and acting on behalf of, the enterprise education community (QAA, 2012). It is intended to be of practical help to those working with students in higher education to foster their skills in enterprise and entrepreneurship and is our point of departure for the consideration of curriculum design in this chapter. The guidance recognises that enterprise and entrepreneurship education is structured differently across different institutions. Some offer standalone degree programmes in the subject area, while others offer parts of awards, and others still offer training and development as part of careers education and preparation for employment. It also recognises that learners may gain practical skills and experience through participation in extra-curricular activities, such as participation in "start-up" schemes. The QAA identifies a distinction between enterprise and entrepreneurship education where "enterprise education is defined as the process of equipping students (or graduates) with an enhanced capacity to generate ideas and the skills to make them happen. Entrepreneurship education equips students with the additional knowledge, attributes and capabilities required to apply these abilities in the context of setting up a new venture or business" (QAA, 2012, p. 2). The difference between the two concepts has also been discussed by Gibb (1993) as well as Jones and Iredale (2010 and 2014). Enterprise education seeks to equip people — school children, students at colleges and universities, as well as those in training — with the life skills needed to enable them to operate as well rounded citizens in the community but also as employees in the workplace. Using the pedagogy of enterprise education inevitably involves handing over a degree of ownership of learning to those doing the learning and this is achieved by careful design and delivery of the learning environment. In keeping with the transaction perspective, it can involve introducing a degree of uncertainty into teaching, learning, and assessment as the "fixed points" of traditional learning are called into question and in some cases removed. Challenging, questioning, and calling into doubt the established order — be that education, business or society/community — and that which is "known" helps to prepare enterprise learners for the fast changing, complex, uncertain, and insecure environments in which their futures will operate.

The QAA proposes a four stage model (Figure 12.1: Developing entrepreneurial effectiveness) that moves from "Enterprise Awareness" to "Developing an Entrepreneurial Mindset" through to "Developing Entrepreneurial Capability" before finally resulting in "Entrepreneurial Effectiveness". The figure/model is useful as it sets out in a clear way the entrepreneurship education journey from the

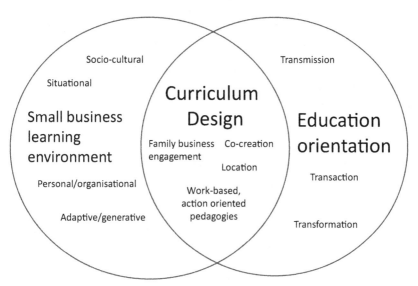

Figure 12.1. Towards a framework for family business influenced curriculum

learners' perspective. However, in practice, the journey is not always as smooth or as linear as conveyed by the QAA (2012, p. 12). There is undoubtedly some duplication and repetition with regards to what is learned at different educational phases and between and within subject areas. The model is an ideal type and is not fully or always reflective of enterprise and entrepreneurship education reality on the ground. There is a degree of movement back and forth between the various stages outlined in the QAA model. The QAA model is conceptually succinct but does not fully convey the complex realities of enterprise and entrepreneurship education in practice. The actual practice is of movement and constant change whilst the model is largely static which is perhaps simply indicative of the difference between the written word and life as it is lived and experienced — figures/models can only capture and convey so much.

The enterprise and entrepreneurship education problem which we define here and with which enterprise educators wrestle with in the design of curriculum is the translation of abstract conceptual ideals into meaningful enterprise and entrepreneurship teaching, learning, and assessment practice. Teaching, learning, and assessment of enterprise and entrepreneurship education takes on a number of guises but perhaps the defining characteristic is that of active (enterprise) as opposed to passive (traditional/didactic) learning (for a fuller discussion on this, see Jones & Iredale, 2006 and 2010). Real world practice of enterprise and entrepreneurship can be brought to life in and away from the traditional classroom environment through guest lectures, case studies, projects, consultancy, and other forms of business engagement. In line with transformational orientations, the trainer, teacher, or lecturer becomes a partner in the learning process and does not possess a monopoly of knowledge or necessarily have the "right answer". The opportunity to experiment and try things out and to experience uncertainty in a bounded learning environment helps create and to some extent simulates the experience of entrepreneurship. The QAA guidance sets out what it is enterprise educators should seek to do by specifying eight tasks. By way of example, one task states: "enable students to relate their learning to their subject or industry context and to personal aspirations" (QAA, 2012, p. 22). Linking education with business, especially small businesses, is a key aspect of enterprise and entrepreneurship education throughout all educational phases. The QAA guidance also draws a distinction between owner-managers of small businesses and entrepreneurs: "An entrepreneur demonstrates enterprising approaches and attributes, such as creativity, vision, responsiveness to opportunity, and ambition for business growth, which are distinct from business skills and knowledge" (QAA, 2012, p. 9). Undoubtedly entrepreneurs need to know of and be familiar with functional areas of management (finance, accountancy, law, marketing, and among other things human resources) and some of these feature in entrepreneurship education but less so in enterprise education. What is conveyed through either enterprise or entrepreneurship education depends in part on whether the course being studied is "learning for" or "learning about" enterprise. The QAA (2012, p. 9) notes that "About" courses "... tend to draw upon a more traditional pedagogy involving lectures and set texts to explore the theoretical underpinning of enterprise and entrepreneurship". In contrast, "For" courses "… are normally delivered via experiential learning opportunities that engage and enhance the student's abilities and skills, set within a meaningful and relevant context" (QAA, 2012, p. 9).

The nature of enterprise and entrepreneurship education shifts the emphasis of teaching and learning strategies away from traditional pedagogical approaches associated with knowledge transmission towards those associated with transaction and transformation. The pedagogy of enterprise education involves a degree of negotiation over what is learnt and how learning takes place. The balance of power and control of learning is more fluid than in a traditional (didactic) classroom learning environment. Active learning, by doing, trying things out, experimenting, giving it a go, making mistakes, learning from mistakes, learning to fail and learning from that, as well as having fun and creating something from nothing all feature as aspects of enterprise education practice. As part of the process, security gives way to insecurity and from this a sense of personal as well as business resilience emerges. Knowing one's way is replaced by having to find one's way. The certainties of the world as it is known are somewhat diminished and the resultant uncertainty allows for the creation of new ways of seeing problems as well as identifying solutions. Also, as part of the enterprise education process, attitudes and opinions change and new ways of working deliver new and unintended results. Working with others as part of a group task or project helps develop teamwork and negotiation skills. Central to the enterprise education pedagogy is the opportunity it affords to find out, engage, and work with, as well as to better understand the importance of and workings of small businesses. Prioritising and placing small businesses at the centre of enterprise education serves a number of purposes. It draws attention to the importance of small businesses to the economy and society. It challenges the view that big business and big government are all pervasive and know best. Small is shown to be not only beautiful but also liberating and empowering. In facilitating a can-do attitude, students have their eyes opened to the possibility it affords them of working for themselves, and of starting, growing, managing, and exiting a business. Empowered enterprise learners are better placed to spot opportunities, solve problems (individual, community, or business), do something as opposed to waiting for something to be done, be creative and innovative, and to take better charge of their own futures. Enterprise education adds value to the traditional classroom teaching and learning experience and ultimately can result in more wealth creating individuals and businesses — be that for- or not-for-profit.

The pedagogy of enterprise education presents new challenges to the role of the teacher. Teachers are expected to act as facilitators of learning and to learn in partnership with their students. Learning is gained from real world experience and small business owner managers act as acknowledged experts and give presentations, talks, and contribute to debates and other forms of business-education engagement. This serves to validate the learning and to demonstrate what can be achieved. Learning from textbooks does have a place but this is lessened somewhat when learning through the pedagogy of enterprise education. Teachers' perceptions of themselves as acknowledged experts in their field is challenged and so too are the educational props (textbooks) they use to confirm their sense of self, power, and their role of teacher. For some teachers, enterprise education can present challenges and it is important for teachers to reflect on that experience and see how they might incorporate aspects of it into their everyday classroom teaching.

In terms of learning outcomes, enterprise and entrepreneurship education can enable and empower learners and give them options by opening their eyes to their own potential as well as new opportunities. Creativity, autonomy, and independence are the positive enterprise and entrepreneurship education outcomes. Their ultimate purpose is to allow people to live fuller, more rewarding, and richer lives as citizens, employees, small business owner-managers, and entrepreneurs. This is done by helping people move from a state of being dependent and disempowered to being independent and empowered. Instead of being dependent on the teacher or lecturer for information and knowledge, independent (enterprising) learners seek out opportunities and learn from and through them. Particular emphasis is placed on developing the knowledge domains of know-how, know-what, know-who and know-why. Instead of citizens being dependent on government, agencies, or others to find solutions to social and community problems, independent (enterprising) citizens speak up, act, take the initiative and champion causes, re-frame the problem, and find novel/innovative ways to address the societal and community issues. Moving employees, especially those working in small businesses, from a state of being dependent (waiting for someone — a line manager — to tell them what to do) to a state where they can act independently by acting in an enterprising way and take on and embrace multiple tasks is seen as another positive. Enterprise and entrepreneurship education can help people solve problems in their own lives and from these solutions come new products or services that can be made into for-profit self-sustaining businesses. In other words, nascent entrepreneurs are equipped with the skills and tools they need to move from a position in which they are dependent on others for answers to a situation where they can independently find their own answers.

12.4 Towards a Framework for Family Business Influenced Curriculum Design

Issues of educational orientation, curriculum design, and pedagogy are intertwined with the social and historic contexts of HE and the wider world in which institutions are situated. Government reports, leaders in industry, and others in the wider society urge that the world is one of change. Often this observation is a preliminary remark to the suggestion that students should be better prepared for the world that they are going to encounter and that success for the student should be measured in terms of their progress in the labour market and their subsequent salary and influence (Reich, 2000). The implication, and it is often asserted outright, is that HEIs have insufficiently taken account of the character of the wider world and need to be redesigned so that they address the challenges that it brings (Barnett & Coate, 2005). Curriculum design that takes account of the wider interests of the economy and its constituent organisations, such as that offered by enterprise education, is one response to this challenge and at the core of approaches to join the worlds of education and work.

On the surface, an emphasis on family businesses may appear peculiar; however, we argue that they represent an important part of local, national, and international economies. Some have described them as the dominant form of business organisation in the world (Miller *et al.*, 2008) and research in the UK suggests that there are over 4 million in the UK (IFB, 2016). Bearing in mind that a large proportion of these are micro businesses, the size and contribution of the sector as a whole would appear to provide legitimate justification for small family firm interests to be taken into consideration in the design of higher education university curriculum that seeks to reflect economic considerations.

A further justification for the development of HE curriculum to prepare students for work in a family business or to support the development of leadership and management capability amongst those already working in family businesses lies in their distinctiveness, not least in the relationship between the social systems of the family and the firm where the blending of family and business social systems provide a unique context for work and learning (Kraus *et al.*, 2011). "Familiness" is created by the interactions between the founder, family members, generations of the family, and the business and is offered as an explanation for both the superior and suboptimal performance of family businesses. Habbershon and Williams (1999) distinguish between "distinctive" (where family involvement provides a firm with competitive advantage) and "constrictive" familiness (where family involvement becomes an encumbrance to the firm). Nicholson (2008) suggests that family businesses able to achieve an unusually high degree of cultural control through high-trust relationships with various stakeholder groups are able to gain tangible competitive advantage. However, at the same time a less positive picture is painted in line with public prejudices, media horror stories, and fictional sagas about the dangers of psychological overspill from dysfunctional families into the businesses they run. The concept of socio-emotional wealth, defined as "non-financial aspects of the firm that meet the family's affective needs, such as identity, the ability to exercise family influence, and the perpetuation of the family dynasty" has also become influential in the study of family businesses (Gómez-Mejía *et al.*, 2007, p. 106). At the same time, the financial relations between the family and the business are often complex and uncertain where disentangling family and business related assets and sharing the liabilities and benefits of success are often contested issues (Habbershon & Pistriu, 2002).

The need to join the worlds of business and academia to provoke deeper transformations in curriculum as academics design and implement more active methods of teaching, learning, and assessment to align learner, business, and policy interests leads us to present an initial framework to inform family influenced curriculum design.

In order to reflect on the implications of this framework for the development of curriculum, we briefly consider the QAA guidance for the provision of enterprise and education before considering some pedagogical implications. Applying a family business lens to the QAA guidance, it would appear that the interests of small firms more generally may have influenced the guidance for the provision for enterprise and entrepreneurship education, through for example the contribution of Institute for Small Business and Entrepreneurship (ISBE) and acknowledgement of the excellent work of Allan Gibb. However, there is little mention of the unique learning context of small businesses, let alone family business context within the guidance. The QAA guidance conceives of teaching, learning, and assessment being both "For" (how to work for, manage, or start a business) and "About" (gaining insight to conceptual and theoretical issues) businesses. We would like to supplement this with "In" as a further dimension that takes into account the situated nature of learning and communities of practice that dominate much of the small business literature associated with learning. In particular, we argue that a case exists for the re-orientation of situated "in" context learning so that learning becomes more differentiated, detailed, specific, and sophisticated. At the simplest level, this could include mention of the small family businesses context within the QAA guidance. To do so would enhance curriculum, enrich provision, further and deepen understanding of needs, and most importantly build and strengthen links between HE and small family businesses. The teaching and learning strategies most likely to feature in such curriculum include action based modes such as problem-based learning, action learning, inquiry-based learning, cooperative learning, critical thinking, and reflective practice (Van Gyn & Grove-White, 2004; Costley & Armsby, 2007). A key characteristic of these approaches is that learners are expected to play a more active role in their learning experience, often addressing "real world" problems and contributing to "solutions" to be applied in the work context.

Research suggests that a key to encouraging learning in small businesses that appears to be transferable to the family business context is to join them in their world, providing opportunities that reflect personal aspirations and ambitions that enable the entrepreneur to take ownership of their own development (CEML, 2002). It has long been argued that educationalists and others who design small firm learning opportunities should not enforce their own curriculum on small firms (Gibb, 1997). Whilst traditional transmission orientations may work in some circumstances, our central argument is that HE should look towards the development of transactional and transformational approaches in the form of, for example, the co-production of knowledge to engage smaller businesses and embed learning in the family business context. The co-creation of educational value is realised by employers in the workplace and by individuals taking responsibility for their own futures (Vargo et al., 2008). The theoretical emphasis on a socio-cultural and situated approach to learning has led some to consider action learning as an appropriate pedagogical response (Choueke & Armstrong, 1998; Clarke *et al.*, 2006). In particular, the emphasis of action learning on relational and conversational practices, contextualised action, and critical reflection is likely to be of particular relevance to leadership and management development in smaller businesses. It also presents an opportunity to enter the murky waters of familiness and to surface and address some of the personal issues that impact on the sometimes idiosyncratic decision making that occurs in family business (although referral to professional counselling may be a more appropriate option for some participants facing particularly wicked family problems) (Camillus, 2008).

Does joining the small family business world mean shifting the delivery of learning opportunities away from the university campus? For some time, university curriculum has been influenced by the need to recognise self-driven learning gained through the workplace or social activity (Silverman, 2003). This learning is often grounded in experience, and HEIs are now offering many work-based and work-related interventions (Kettle, 2013). These influence the curriculum in many ways and include cooperative and work integrated learning, student placements, graduate internships, observation of practice, and simulated experience. The idea of the flipped classroom (Bergman & Sams, 2012) would appear to be becoming more prevalent in HE as a means of increasing student engagement (Millard, 2012), which may have some transferability to the small family business context. The flipped classroom inverts the traditional transmission approach of education predominantly delivered through lectures on campus towards one where academics provide learning direction (online or through personal communications) with academic input emphasising the progression of prior learning and contextualising it in academic and practical terms through facilitation. Programmes delivered in the workplace with learners problem solving whilst at work and the university campus playing a relatively small role may help to overcome some barriers to learning (such as time away from the workplace and the contextualisation of learning) faced by small business managers. However, others have found that the opportunity to reflect and question real world issues at a distance through removing themselves from the context of the business can be highly beneficial to small business leaders and managers (Clarke *et al.*, 2006). At the same time, family business leaders may benefit from the wide array of information, digital and technical resources, and social networks that universities have at their disposal and may lie beyond the reach of many small family businesses but have wider application in the workplace.

Much of the learning taking place in the small firm environment is informal and the challenge associated with the recognition of this activity in the workplace is a longstanding one (Bjornavold, 2000). One of the solutions to this is the recognition of learning achieved through assessment which can form two main purposes in higher education. Firstly, as an aid to the learning process providing feedback on what are sometimes referred to as learning deficits associated with achieving a specific level of learning. Secondly, as "proof" of an accomplished learning programme that aids transfer between different levels and contexts. Learning agreements can be a key element of pedagogy and these have traditionally been formal written agreements between a learner and a supervisor usually detailing what is to be learnt, the resources and strategies available to assist it, what will be produced as evidence of the learning, and how that output will be assessed (Anderson *et al.*, 1998). One form of a family business informed curriculum can be the inclusion of the employer in the development and implementation of these agreements serving to underpin learning in the workplace for students or workers. This can be a complex negotiation process between the employer, student, and university with the development and implementation of pedagogical approaches often led by university academics with the expectations of employers and students exerting a powerful influence on learning outcomes and how they are to be delivered and assessed (Devins *et al.*, 2015). Critical reflection formalised into reports, essays, journals, logs, diaries, or professional artefacts are often valuable and central parts of assessment (Nottingham & Akinleye, 2014; Helyer, 2011), however it should be recognised that challenges associated with motivation producing these outputs (once the action has been achieved) and grading and evaluation of such artefacts remain (Crème, 2008).

In today's environment, the design of university curricula is shaped and formed by stakeholders with competing interests and agendas including students, external and internal academic advisers, QAA, businesses, senior university management, and governors. If family business interests are to be reflected in curriculum, their voice has to be heard in this milieu. At the micro-level of the institution, each university will have its own ways of engaging businesses in curriculum design. One of the most common mechanisms is the use of Industrial Advisory Boards (or similar) where middle and senior management representatives from several relevant organisations influence the design process helping to provide industry and sector insights, a sounding board for new ideas, gather feedback on modules and medium term curriculum developments, or inform the design of pedagogy including work placements. If the interests of small family businesses are to influence curriculum design through this mechanism, family businesses themselves need to be willing to engage and participate in such activity. Universities need to invite them and more probably proactively target engagement activities to encourage them to enter into the world of higher education, whilst at the same time family businesses will need to open their doors to university interests. Through establishing dialogue, family business issues and recurring themes likely to have a bearing on curriculum design such as socio-emotional wealth, familiness, survivability capital (Wilson *et al.*, 2013), and the social and psychological implications of ownership and transition (Pierce *et al.*, 2005) may start to feature in specialised courses or become part of mainstream curriculum. Many of the distinctive features of family businesses rest on the nature of the relationship within and between the family and the business. Understanding, explaining, and accounting for the complexities of this relationship is what would set a family business learning programme apart and mark it out as distinctive from other generalist business courses.

12.5 Conclusions

The sheer size and economic importance of the family business sector would appear to provide a rationale for the development of HE curriculum seeking to develop student employability and improve leadership and management capability in the economy. However, the heterogeneity of the sector, the prevalence of informal, situated learning, and the difficulties of engaging small family businesses in the design of curriculum pose many challenges for HE. The evidence suggests that an emphasis on action oriented, work-based, and work-related pedagogy with learning outcomes reflecting the tri-partite interests of learners, employers, and the academy should lie at the heart of a family business informed curriculum resulting in the requirement for a more sophisticated, differentiated, and tailored HE curriculum. However, reflecting the interests of family businesses to this degree represents a relatively new and dramatic reshaping of academic practice that is likely to be contested to varying degrees in different HE institutions and raise fundamental questions and avenues for further investigation. For example, to what extent should curriculum content and pedagogy be influenced by external stakeholders such as family businesses? Should HE curriculum for small family businesses be directed at undergraduate or postgraduate students, at owners or managers, family members or others? Is the curriculum to be influenced by start-up and/or more mature family business development? What role is there for accreditation of prior-learning and assessment of the expertise of students who elect to undertake a programme of study? What learning outcomes are relevant and how are they specified and assessed? Which teaching and learning strategies yield the best results (and for whom)? Are university quality assurance systems flexible enough to accommodate the interests and expectations of external stakeholders such as family businesses? Are universities and small family businesses willing to invest the time it takes to design curriculum? Do academic staff possess the knowledge and skills to engage external stakeholders and develop the required transactional or transformational orientation towards learning? These and other questions would appear to provide fertile ground for further research and development.

References

Anderson, J. R. (1982). Acquisition of cognitive skill. *Psychological Review, 89*(4), 369–406.

Anderson, G., Boud, D., & Sampson, J. (1998). Qualities of learning contracts. In Stephenson, J. & Yorke, M. (Eds.), *Capability and Quality in Higher Education*, pp. 162–173. Kogan Page, London.

Argyris, C., & Schön, D. (1978). *Organizational Learning: A Theory of Action Approach.* Addison Wesley, Reading, MA.

Barnett, R., & Coate, K. (2005). *Engaging the Curriculum in Higher Education.* The Society for Research into Higher Education and Open University Press, Maidenhead.

Bergman, J., & Sams, A. (2012). *Flip Your Classroom: Reach Every Student in Every Class Every Day.* International Society for Technology in Education/American Society of Continuing Education, Washington, DC.

BIS (2016). Success as a knowledge economy: Teaching excellence, social mobility and student choice. Available at: https://www.gov.uk/government/uploads/system/uploads/attachment_data/file/523396/bis-16-265-success-as-a-knowledge-economy.pdf

Bjornavold, J. (2000). *Making Learning Visible: Identification, Assessment and Recognition of Non-Formal Learning in Europe.* European Centre for the Development of Vocational Training, Thessaloniki.

Boud, D. (2001). Creating a work-based curriculum. In Boud, D. & Solomon, N. (Eds.), *Work-Based Learning: A New Higher Education?* pp. 44–58. Society for Research into Higher Education and the Open University Press, Buckingham.

Boud, D. (2006). Combining work and learning: The disturbing challenge of practice. In Edwards, R., Gallaghar, J. & Whittaker, S. (Eds.), *Learning Outside the Academy: International Research Perspectives in Lifelong Learning*, pp. 77–89. Routledge, London.

Camillus, J. (2008). Strategy as a wicked problem. Harvard Business Review. Available at: https://hbr.org/2008/05/strategy-as-a-wicked-problem

CEML (2002). Joining entrepreneurs in their world. Council for Excellence in Management and Leadership, London.

Choueke, R., & Armstrong, R. (1998). The learning organisation in small and medium-sized enterprises: a destination or a journey? *International Journal of Entrepreneurial Behaviour and Research, 4*(2), 128–140.

Clarke, J., Thorpe, R., Anderson, L., & Gold, J. (2006). It's all action, it's all learning: Action learning in SMEs. *Journal of European Industrial Training, 30*(6), 441–455.

Cope, J. (2003). Entrepreneurial learning and critical reflection: Discontinuous events as triggers for higher-level learning. *Management Learning, 34*(4), 429–450.

Costley, C., & Armsby, P. (2007). Work-based learning assessed as a field or mode of learning. *Assessment and Evaluation in Higher Education, 32*(1), 21–33.

Crème, P. (2008). Student learning journals as transitional writing. *Arts & Humanities Higher Education, 7*(1), 49–64.

Dalley, J., & Hamilton, B. (2000). Knowledge context and learning in small business. *International Small Business Journal, 71,* 51–59.

Deakins, D. (1996). *Entrepreneurship and Small Firms.* McGraw-Hill, Maidenhead.

Devins, D., Ferrandez-Berrueco, R., & Kekale, T. (2015). Educational orientation and employer influenced pedagogy. Practice and policy insights from three programmes in Europe. *Higher Education, Skills and Work-Based Learning, 5*(4), 352–368.

Devins, D., & Gold, J. (2002). Social constructionism: A theoretical framework to underpin support for the development of managers in SMEs? *Journal of Small Business and Enterprise Development, 9*(2), 111–119.

Dewey, J. (2009). *Democracy and Education: An Introduction to the Philosophy of Education,* WLC Books, New York (original work published 1916).

European Commission (2006). Implementing the community Lisbon programme. fostering entrepreneurial mindsets through education and training. COM (2006) 33 final, Commission of the European Communities, Brussels.

European Commission (2012). The European higher education area in 2012. The Bologna process implementation report. Education, Audiovisual and Culture Executive Agency, Brussels.

Fink, L. D. (2003). *Creating Significant Learning Experiences. An Integrated Approach to Designing College Courses.* Jossey-Bass, San Francisco, CA.

Gibb, A. A. (1987). *Enterprise Culture: Its Meaning and Implications for Education and Training.* MCB University Press, Bradford.

Gibb, A. A. (1993). The enterprise culture and education: Understanding enterprise education and its links with small business, entrepreneurship and wider entrepreneurial goals. *International Small Business Journal, 11*(3), 11–34.

Gibb, A. A. (1997). Small firms' training and competitiveness, building upon small business as a learning organisation. *International Small Business Journal, 15*(3), 13–29.

Gibb, A. A. (2002). Creating conducive environments for learning and entrepreneurship: Living with, dealing with, creating and enjoying uncertainty and complexity. *Industry and Higher Education, 16*(3), 135–148.

Gómez-Mejía, L. R., Haynes, K. T., Núñez-Nickel, M., Jacobson, K. J., & Moyano-Fuentes, J. (2007). Socioemotional wealth and business risks in family-controlled firms: Evidence from Spanish olive oil mills. *Administrative Science Quarterly, 52*(1), 106–137.

Habbershon, T., & Pistrui, J. (2002). Enterprising families domain. Family influenced ownership groups in pursuit of transgenerational wealth. *Family Business Review, 15*(3) 223–238.

Habbershon, T. G., & Williams, M. L. (1999). A resource based framework for assessing the strategic advantages of family firms. *Family Business Review, 12*, 1–25.

Hamilton, E. (2011). Entrepreneurial learning in family business: A situated learning perspective. *Journal of Small Business and Enterprise Development, 18*(1), 8–26.

Helyer, R. (2011). Aligning higher education with the world of work. *Higher Education, Skills and Work-Based Learning, 1*(2), 95–105.

Hussain, J. G., Scott, J. M., & Matlay, H. (2010). The impact of entrepreneurship education on succession in ethnic minority family firms. *Education & Training, 52*(8/9), 643–659.

Hytti, U., & O'Gorman, C. (2004). What is "enterprise education"? An analysis of the objectives and methods of enterprise education programmes in four European countries. *Education & Training, 46*(1), 11–23.

IFB (2008). *The UK family business sector.* A report by Capital Economics, London.

IFB (2016). *The state of the nation.* Oxford Economics, London.

Jones, B., & Iredale, N. (2006). Developing an entrepreneurial life skills summer school. *Innovations in Teaching and Learning International, 43*(3), 233–244.

Jones, B., & Iredale, N. (2008). Case study: International development in Ukraine. *Journal of Enterprising Communities: People and Places in the Global Economy, 2*(4), 387–401.

Jones, B., & Iredale, N. (2010). Enterprise education as pedagogy. *Education & Training, 52*(1), 7–19.

Jones, B., & Iredale, N. (2014). Enterprise and entrepreneurship education: Towards a comparative analysis. *Journal of Enterprising Communities: People and Places in the Global Economy, 8*(1), 34–50.

Kettle, J. (2013). *Flexible Pedagogies: Employer Engagement and Work-Based Learning.* Higher Education Academy, York, UK.

Kolb, D. A. (1984). *Experiential Learning: Experience as the Source of Learning and Development.* Prentice Hall, Englewood Cliffs.

Kraus, S., Harms, R., Fink, M., & Pihkala, T. (2011). Family firm research: Sketching a research field. *International Journal of Entrepreneurship and Innovation Management, 13*(1), 32–47.

Kuratko, D. F. (2005). The emergence of entrepreneurship education: Development, trends and challenges. *Entrepreneurship, Theory and Practice, 29*(5), 577–597.

Lave, J., & Wenger, E. (1991). *Situated Learning. Legitimate Peripheral Participation.* Cambridge University Press, Cambridge.

Matlay, H. (2001). Entrepreneurial and vocational education and training in central and Eastern Europe. *Education & Training, 43*(8/9), 395–404.

Mezirow, J. (1991). *Transformative Dimensions of Adult Learning.* Jossey-Bass, San Francisco, CA.

Millard, E. (2012). Five reasons flipped classrooms work: Turning lectures into homework to boost student engagement and increase technology-fuelled creativity. University Business. Available at: https://margopolo04.files.wordpress.com/2013/12/flipped-classroom-reasons.pdf

Miller, D., Le-Breton-Miller, I., & Sholnick, B. (2008). Stewardship verses stagnation: An empirical investigation of small family and non-family businesses. *Journal of Management Studies, 45*(1), 51–78.

Miller, J. P., & Seller, W. (1990). *Curriculum Perspectives and Practice.* Copp Clark Pitman, Mississauga.

Mumford, A. (1995). *Effective Learning.* Institute of Personnel & Development, London.

Nicholson, N. (2008). Evolutionary psychology and family business: A new synthesis for theory, research and practice. *Family Business Review, 21*(1), 103–118.

Nottingham, P., & Akinleye, A. (2014). Professional artefacts: Embodying ideas in work-based learning. *Higher Education, Skills and Work-Based Learning, 4*(1), 98–108.

OECD (2001). *Putting the Young in Business: Policy Challenges for Youth Entrepreneurship.* Organisation for Economic Co-operation and Development, Paris.

Ofsted (2004). Learning to be enterprising: An evaluation of enterprising learning at key stage 4. HMI 2148, Ofsted, Manchester.

Pierce, J. L., O'Driscoll, M., & Coghlan, A. M. (2005). Work environmental structure and psychological ownership — the mediating effects of control. *Journal of Social Psychology, 144*(5), 507–534.

Pittaway, L., & Cope, J. (2007). Entrepreneurship education: A systematic review of the evidence. *International Small Business Journal, 25*(5), 479–510.

QAA (2012). Enterprise and entrepreneurship education: guidance for UK higher education providers. Quality Assurance Agency for Higher Education, Gloucester.

QAA (2021). UK quality code for higher education. Available at: https://www.qaa.ac.uk/en/quality-code

Rae, D. (2006). Entrepreneurial learning: A conceptual framework for technology-based enterprise. *Technology Analysis and Strategic Management, 18*(1), 39–56.

Rae, D., & Carswell, M. (2000). Using a life-story approach in researching entrepreneurial learning; The development of a conceptual model and its implications for the design of learning experiences. *Education and Training, 42*(4/5), 220–227.

Reich, R. (2000). *The Future of Success.* A. Knopf, New York.

Schön, D. (1983). *Educating the Reflective Practitioner; Towards a New Design for Teaching and Learning in the Professions.* Cambridge University Press, Cambridge.

Senge, P. (1990). *Systems Thinking.* Bantam Doubleday Dell, New York, NY.

Silverman, M. (2003). *Supporting Workplace Learning.* The Institute for Employment Studies, Brighton, UK.

Treanor, L. (2012). Entrepreneurship education: exploring the gender dimension: A gender and enterprise network, HEA sponsored, discussion workshop. *International Journal of Gender and Entrepreneurship, 4*(2), 206–210.

Van Gyn, G., & Grove-White, E. (2004). Theories of learning in education. In Coll, R. K. & Eames, C. (Eds.), *International Handbook for Cooperative Education. An International Perspective of the Theory, Research and Practice of Work Integrated Learning,* pp. 27–36. World Association for Cooperative Education, Boston, MA.

Vargo, S. L., Maglio, P. P., & Akaka, M. A. (2008). On value and value cocreation: A service systems and service logic perspective. *European Management Journal, 26*(3), 145–152.

Volkmann, C., Wilson, K. E., Mariotti, S., Rabuzzi, D., Vyakarnam, S., & Sepulveda, A. (2009). Educating the next wave of entrepreneurs: Unlocking entrepreneurial capabilities to meet the global challenges of the 21st century. A report of the Global Education Initiative, World Economic Forum, Geneva, April.

Vygotsky, L. S. (1978). Interaction between learning and development. In Cole, M., John-Steiner, V., Scribner, S. & Souberman, E. (Eds.), *Mind and Society: The Development of Higher Psychological Processes*. Harvard University Press, Cambridge, MA.

Warren, L. (2004). A systemic approach to entrepreneurial learning: An exploration using storytelling. *Systems Research and Behavioral Science*, *21*(1), 3–16.

Weick, K. (1995). *Sensemaking in Organizations*. Sage, Newbury Park.

Wilson, N., Wright, M., & Scholes, L. (2013). Family business survival and the role of boards. *Entrepreneurship Theory and Practice*, *37*(6), 1369–1389.

Workman, B. (2009). The core components: Teaching, learning and assessing. In Garnett, J., Costley, C. & Workman, B. (Eds.), *Work Based Learning Journeys to the Core of Higher Education*, pp. 189–203. University Press, Middlesex.

Young Enterprise (2021). Available at: https://www.young-enterprise.org.uk/

https://doi.org/10.1142/9789811239212_0013

Chapter 13

Using Influencers as Sales Professionals: A Strategy for SMEs & Start-ups

Megha Sharma*,† and Vinod Kumar Singh‡

Faculty of Management Studies, Gurukula Kangri (Deemed to be)
University, Haridwar, India

†meghaas663@gmail.com

‡drvksingh1969@gmail.com

Abstract: Every marketer is aware of the growing importance of influencers, and undoubtedly, social media influencer marketing is on the top priority list for every marketing and sales professional. Small and medium enterprises and start-ups are the backbones of the global economy; they still face tough competition from large companies. This chapter aims to explore and define the importance of influencer marketing for SMEs and start-ups. Researchers analysed the systematic literature review from past research. They found that influencer marketing can be the key to making SMEs and start-ups succeed in their marketing campaigns with minimal capital and funds. Thus, by finding the right influencer and recognising their engagement relations with consumers, the

---

*Corresponding author

sale of the business is boosted. This chapter concluded that SMEs and start-ups should strategise to conduct influencer marketing to target large audiences and consumers' trust.

Keywords: SMEs, Start-ups, Influencers, Sales professionals, Sales employees.

13.1 Introduction

Small and medium-sized enterprises (SMEs) and start-ups play an essential role in the business domain (Ozgulbas *et al.*, 2006; Han *et al.*, 2018). About 90% of businesses fall in the category of SMEs and start-ups, and they reflect a huge part of the consumer economies globally (Konstantopoulou *et al.*, 2019). With the growing use of technology and digital aspects, the competition for SMEs and start-ups has increased with growing opportunities. Therefore, it is possible, if not unavoidable, for SMEs to examine elements such as changing technology and developing communication strategies as paths to competitiveness (Gradzol *et al.*, 2005).

The crucial success impact for SMEs and start-ups is to contact customers for future effective performance (Dulewicz & Higgs, 2003). To increase the effectiveness in the global market, SMEs and start-ups must boost conversations and contacts with the customers (Gończ *et al.*, 2007). As SMEs and start-ups lack capital funds compared to large organisations, it is essential to understand and explore the need to boost their sales with minimum and limited capital investment. This chapter aims to provide insights into the importance of influencers in a marketing campaign with minimum investments, especially regarding SMEs and start-ups.

Without a doubt, social media is one of the leading marketing tools for organisations of contemporary times. Social media marketing (SMM) is a wise decision any marketer takes to promote their brands in an existing competitive market. SMM helps the brand reach new, potential, and current customers quickly, compared to traditional marketing techniques. By getting through to a large audience with a cost-effective approach, SMM is exerting its importance in the modern marketing field. Academic research also provides significant evidence for SMM to be a vital medium for businesses to reach their potential customers and get feedback about their products or services (Rockendorf, 2011).

Celebrities and social media influencers use their online presence as their new medium of brand endorsement. An account directly maintained by a brand/organisation on social media might not affect consumers' buying decisions the same way an individual is discussing that brand in their videos, posts, and photograph might. These individuals with considerable following share their own experience of using a brand, which develops a factor of trust between a consumer and the brand (Lou & Yuan, 2019). These individuals who can create, generate trust and interest among their online followers are thus recognised as social media influencers.

Many SMEs assume that social media is a more expensive mode of promotion. But the fact is, social media provide abundant opportunities for businesses to engage with customers. Fashion and beauty was the first industry to experiment with the influencer market (Matveeva, 2019). But with the growing pace of influencer marketing, every industry is investing in influencers. This chapter aims to explore and discuss how SMEs and start-up businesses may be involved in influencer marketing through their marketing plan, as it is a cost-effective method. As SMEs and start-ups, managerial forces have started investing in Web 2.0 technologies to make promotional activities (Abrahamsson *et al.*, 2018). As companies are shifting their advertising most of their budget towards social media and more on influencer marketing for effective sales, SMEs and start-ups need to know that higher sales revenue can be achieved in low-budget marketing.

13.2 Materials and Methods

This analysis is based on a survey of the literature from research articles published between 2005 and 2021. The studies were chosen from leading journals of Scopus and Web of Science. We also refer to particular publisher databases like Emerald, Springer, Elsevier, and so on. Furthermore, website publications were examined to obtain data about the issue. This chapter examines the previously unknown impact of social media and emerging social media personalities known as influencers and their impact on SMEs and start-ups.

13.3 Analysis of Literature

13.3.1 *Influencer Marketing*

On social media platforms, various individuals are gaining fame and trust from the audience because of their unique and promotional content shared on their social media accounts, and they are called influencers. On their respective social media accounts, promotional activities done by influencers are explained as social media influencer marketing. Since the last decade, influencers have gained massive popularity on social media by endorsing products and services and sharing their experience after using them. Social media influencer marketing can be defined as "choosing a famous non-celebrity for endorsing the specific company's brand in social media platform to drive consumers purchase decision" (Glucksman, 2017). Social media gives a chance to followers of social media influencers to interact with their favourite influencers directly. This give-and-take interaction between influencers and their followers has brought a new element to the advertising field. Therefore, this helps influencers endorse the product and turn a follower into a brand consumer (Glucksman, 2017). An influencer should be very creative to promote a specific product, as the consumer wants to get entertained with some new imaginations because they are tired of all the old and boring content. As per past research, social media influencer marketing is way cheaper than celebrity endorsements, which every entrepreneur undoubtedly wants to adopt. Influencers are found in every field, such as fashion, traveling, food, health, fitness, etc. Organisations are also concerned about choosing an influencer to promote their products, as findings by Abrahamsson *et al.* (2018) suggest that consumers and companies consider two factors, "ideal" and "trust" while deciding on choosing an influencer.

13.3.2 *Types of Influencers*

Influencers are often categorised based on the number of their followers or subscribers. The usual differentiation for influencers are nano-influencers, micro-influencers, macro-influencers, and mega-influencers (Estay, 2020).

- Influencers who have up to 10k (10,000) followers/subscribers are called nano-influencers. Such influencers are budget-operational for brands, and consumers consider them as their friends and family, which shows that they are trustworthy in the eye of consumers; hence, ROI would be superior and probable while investing in them.
- Influencers who have between 10k to 100k followers/subscribers are called micro-influencers. Companies and brands favour them more because they are more functional and robust than nano-influencers and provide a significant ROI to the brand. Also, they have a substantial impact on consumers.
- Influencers who have between 100k to 1M (1 million) followers/subscribers are called macro-influencers.
- Influencers who have more than 1M followers/subscribers are called mega-influencers. Such influencers are also popularly recognised as celebrities or super-stars of the social media platform they are using.

13.3.3 *How to Boost Sales through a Marketing Campaign?*

Generally, SMEs and start-ups are run by an individual or a small team of members, and they play multiple roles in the business. Due to this reason, sales of the business, unfortunately, are set backward. Research conducted by Influencer Marketing Hub (2020) on 1,000

SMEs owners revealed that only 56.9% of owners recruit marketing professionals, and 49.7% spent an average of two hours a week to market themselves. Without the marketing campaign, SMEs and start-up owners face difficulties in boosting their sales.

Thus, to boost the sales of SMEs and start-ups, the following tips are concluded to be helpful to them (Influencer Marketing Hub, 2020):

- **Properly research the consumer base**

  This may sound basic, but it is the most crucial point that the majority of SMEs and start-ups ignore. They lack in analysing the actual needs of their customers. The products developed by them are mostly not needed by the market. Therefore, by properly researching customers' needs in the market, products may experience great sales. For instance, Uber, a start-up, recognised that customers need ride-sharing services as people are concerned about cleanliness, hygiene, safety, and comfort at affordable prices, thus Uber was invented. They provided assistance and marketed themselves as per customer needs and are one of the successful start-ups.

  After some time, Uber invented "earn by endorsing friends" and "travel package for workers". These features helped companies to get all services in one bag as the companies were able to manage the travel account of their employees on Uber.

  After Uber's service became a success, they discovered other needs in the services market — people desired experienced construction workers who were accessible on-demand and paid on a provisional basis. Uber capitalised on the chance by launching the Uber Works app. It has a considerable array of contractors who have been certified by Uber. The launch of the app was a huge success.

- **Building the trust of customers is a top priority**

  For SMEs and especially for start-ups, earning the customer's trust is needful. Once customers trust their products, the demand increases, and businesses/brands experience repeated sales for their products. The experts have named this phenomenon the "Trust Economy" (Sahoo, 2014).

The following ways will help SMEs and start-ups to earn the trust of customers:

- By making a reliable identity for their brands at their business's website, social media account, and other electronics and print media.
- By publishing the customer experience and recommendations as proof at the website, social media, or their apps and rankings at Playstore.
- Creating business accounts on digital media like social media, and being identifiable through Google search by posting the address, name, etc.
- The easy-return policy is a great attraction to gain customers' trust.
- Businesses may show a softer side by publishing honest content from consumers and staff.

- **Generating striking marketing messages**
  Customers deal with a large bulk of advertisements daily. Many customers avoid the ads by simply switching to either ad-free networks or by blocking ad messages. The solution is to create a strategic message that attracts and retains customers' memory. For instance, after the release of Star Wars, Duracell threw an ad campaign. They showed Darth Vader, a fictional character, putting their batteries into his sword. As the fictional character always amuses people, the company experienced a considerable linkage with customers.

- **Investing in social media**
  Social media has become a strong market and the most extensive channel to sell. Companies now choose social media for market research and new product launch. SMEs and start-ups should not ignore social media platforms.

For example, updating stories on social media is becoming a powerful tool for market professionals. Many researchers have identified that posting stories on social media is effective in increasing the business's sales.

- **Collaboration with influencers**
  Influencers are the most incredible content creator since the last decade. There would not be a good choice other than influencers to spread the good words about the brand. Influencers have large numbers of followers. These followers trust the recommendations given by the influencers more than celebrities. Therefore, selecting an appropriate influencer with the same niche as the business's products would be the best opportunity for any business.

13.4 Importance of Social Media Marketing for SMEs And Start-ups

Until the last decade, social media for enterprises was new and was assumed to be expensive. It was mostly developed countries that used social media as a primary mode to promote their businesses. In the recent era of digitisation, where everything has turned online, organisations and brands have increased social media usage. With the rising growth of Instagram, YouTube, Twitter, Facebook, Pinterest, Snapchat, LinkedIn, etc., many businesses and brand owners see the opportunity for their promotional activities. With the increased use of social media, various content creators known as influencers have made their presence by promoting the brands. Thus, social media influencers have successfully grown into authentic promoters where brands use them to reach entire social media customers.

By this mode, it has been observed by enterprises and brands owners that social media and influencers help them to boost the sales of the company and helps to generate a handsome income. However, other than influencer marketing, social media has also opened up another excellent investment platform, especially for

SMEs and start-ups. There is another world for such business holders where they get a great opportunity in the growing fame of hashtags, likes, and comments, etc. (Fountain, 2021).

Therefore, social media marketing has three strategic ways that can help SMEs and start-ups, given as follows (Fountain, 2021):

- Creating brand awareness — Social media marketing has benefits distinct from traditional media. Social media is more vital than media like TV, print media, radio, etc. Social media helps spread information at a fast speed compared to traditional platforms of media. Contents on social media spread to approximately more than 1 million people in a short period in a cost-effective manner. This helps to generate a large number of followers for the business. It has been observed that this sort of promotional campaign is successful.
- Increase in website traffic — When a business generates their websites, they might use social media to divert traffic to their websites uninterruptedly. Through this way, the website of the particular company is trafficked other than Google search.
- By direct selling — Through social media, a business can directly market its products and services. This creates awareness amongst the customers about the business's upcoming or existing product and service. For example, Indian start-up Meesho advertised itself on social media platforms like Facebook and Instagram by displaying the products and prices.

Big brands like Adidas, McDonald's, BMW, and others use Snapchat to brand awareness. Similarly, SMEs and start-ups may also use Snapchat to run campaigns by using custom filters and creating ads on stories of Snapchat. Likewise, Instagram also has the feature of posting stories. In a day, 2–3 stories posted by SMEs' and start-ups' managers or marketing professionals will keep it at the top of the customers' feed. Thus, posting regular stories helps a lot. Zomato, a start-up, is an example for using social media as a great source of advertisement.

Similarly, social media influencers using content creation and sharing will help drive the traffic of the start-ups' and SMEs' websites. Collaborating with influencers is the most effective way to reach a large audience in lesser time. But this is only operative if the business knows how to get the right influencer. As every influencer has their uniqueness, managers and business professionals need to find the right influencer for their brand.

13.5 Results and Discussion

13.5.1 *How to Choose the Right Influencer?*

In the digital period, it is very competitive for companies to become a strong pillar in the market, especially for SMEs and start-ups. Where SMEs & start-ups deal with limited funds, investing in influencer marketing would be the best strategy. However, they should know how to invest in influencers without wasting their funds (Ozgulbas *et al.*, 2006).

- Engagement plays a vital role in the number of followers — For assessing actual results derived from a successful marketing campaign, followers' attention is more important than the number of followers. When influencers promote a particular brand, the rate of likes and comments on influencers' posts shows the engagement rate of the influencers. Mainly, influencers with a large number of followers have less engagement rate than influencers with fewer followers. Consumers find micro-influencer and nano-influencers more trustworthy as compared to others.
  - ○ Ozgulbas *et al.* (2006) reported the recommendation of an influencer marketing platform named The Yoke Network; most companies are not aware that nano-influencers are not likable by brands for promotional activities. Hence, SMEs and start-ups shall not neglect them as they tend to have an excellent engagement rate. Also, they promote the brand in exchange of the product and services.

- Focus and start with the fans — For choosing the right influencer, SMEs and start-ups first shall pick them out by looking at the existing lists of their fans. It can be done by finding out the people from the business's social media who love the products and their peer group who are influenced. By picking out the fans of the company, SMEs and start-ups marketing professionals can use them as their promotional faces, unlike the celebrities and more like influencers. This would increase brand awareness among other people.
  - With a zero marketing investment budget, a business may achieve a heart-warming response.
- Giving rewards to the performance rather than posts — Surprisingly, paying influencers as per the number of posts they would update to make promotions would be a total waste of money and resources. The influencers will generally post the brand's product on their feed the number of posts they got paid without making much effort to make it a successful campaign. This technique would be similar to traditional promotional activities like TV ads, print media, etc. This would not increase the effort of influencers to make the campaign a success.
  - Therefore, it would be more creative and beneficial for SMEs and start-ups to pay them based on their performance rather than paying them per post. The Yoke Networks, which mainly work on influencers' campaigns, suggested that they provide brands excessive interest, activities, and opinions targets when paid as per their performance.
  - Thus, consumers are becoming aware and intelligent, so choosing the right influencer who may upgrade the sale of the brand and business is the key to success for SMEs and start-ups with the limited fund and more reach of audience.

13.5.2 *Methods to Run Influencer Marketing*

The first stage of running influencer campaign is to know the right influencer to target for the particular type of business. There are three methods through which SMEs and start-ups could follow to run a successful influencer marketing campaign (Geyser, 2019):

- The gradual way. Previously, to launch influencer marketing was to find influencers gradually. With the gradual method, a business has to handle all the selection, administration, and analysis. In the initial stage, the company does not have much ability to pay for advertisements, thus connecting with social media influencers is the priority.

  Thus, marketing professionals shall spend their time researching social media platforms each day to finalise who may attract the target market for their company. Slowly, marketers will get to connect more with the influencers.

  Once the business establishes the goals, marketers need to know the type of influencer they want to engage. Influencers that do not match the demographic target may be ignored.

  There are some free of cost tools that help in selecting the right influencer for the business:
  - LinkedIn — It provides an excellent search engine feature. Marketers just need to find and select the influencer of their niche by typing into the search bar. There are other options available too that make the search easy by modifying it.
  - Twitter — It also has a skilled search bar. It is easy to find people of the preferred interest.
  - Tweetdeck — Influencers can be found by related hashtags that particular area of influencers use.
  - MozBar — It is capable of finding websites related to influencers. It has two sites named Domain Authority (DA) and Page Authority (PA). DA mainly helps in defining the importance of a website importance.
- Platforms. There are plenty of platforms available for functioning influencers campaigns. These platforms provide numerous services such as, discovering influencers, managing relationship,

amplifying content of influencers, analysing third-parties, marketplace for influencers, promotion management, etc.

By using specific platforms, the selection of influencers becomes mandatory. It will help to find the type of influencers a business set-up or brand wants to work with. Platforms provide a list of influencers according to the particular work area, and marketer may finalise the influencer which suits them best.

Several platforms work in other directions. By posting the influencer's requirement by establishing an engagement, influencers make an offer with the company after getting engaged in the company's network.

- Influencer networks. Several businesses, like conventional advertisers, embrace a practical learning strategy towards influencer marketing. Linking with influencer marketing agencies gives opportunities to find out effective influencer which suit best to the business.

Such agencies perform the majority of their job in finding the suitable influencer which suits the best for the particular brand and manages the business's campaign on their behalf, although SMEs and start-ups sales and marketing professionals would still have to establish their goals and objectives for their business.

Influencer marketing agencies will organise and help achieve the influencer marketing campaign for the business, but still every business needs to set its goals appropriately.

13.5.3 *Different Ways for SMEs & Start-ups to Collaborate with Influencers*

Sincere influencers only collaborate with the business if they feel their followers will benefit from the products. Influencers, if they promote inappropriate products, may lose their credibility concerning their followers. Hence, it is pointless to try collaborating with influencers having different target audiences from the particular business.

To work with influencers cost-effectively, it is essential to know the different ways through which SMEs and start-ups could collaborate (Geyser, 2019):

- By providing free samples to the influencers, they post the experience and quality on their social media accounts. But most influencers nowadays look for paid promotions instead.
- Asking influencers to review the products on their social media account.
- Providing ample amount of products to influencers so they could give them to their followers, as per the demand.
- By making the influencer campaign challenging for the influencers, they could use more of their more skills and efforts.
- Paying the appropriate amount for the advertised product and article.
- Posting blog posts — this is especially important for influencers who run a popular blog.

13.5.4 *Influencer Marketing and Small Businesses*

Social media has revolutionised the reach for non-celebrities in the world. Today, more and more people can express themselves online without incurring any high cost and, through the virtue of their knowledge and talent, possess the power to influence their followers. This opens up a significant opportunity for SMEs and start-ups. Such businesses cannot do marketing at such a scale, unlike more prominent organisations/market leaders who can hire celebrities for their branding and promotion exercise. Social media marketing, especially influencers marketing, gives these SMEs and start-ups a fighting chance today to create awareness about their product and services at a minimal cost. Most of the influencers, especially nano and micro-influencers, do not ask for a significant amount for their endorsement and, in many cases, are willing to do so based on the barter system as well. While there are several other ways of promoting products and services online, influencers marketing has the following key advantages:

- Most influencers based on their interest also strictly follow a particular segment of followers such as automobile enthusiasts, foodies, fashion, etc. thus, it ensures that promotion through these influencers is reaching only to the right audience and potential customers of the business.
- Other forms of online marketing usually involve digital ads that pop up abruptly, leaving the audience irritated/frustrated and often trying to skip or block those ads. However, to the followers of social media influencers (whom they trust), every post has some value associated with it, so they will be more likely to pay attention to it and explore it a bit further.
- Building trust among consumers is a difficult task in the initial stages of any business and is significantly much harder for small businesses. Influencers with sufficient credibility make this task easier for SMEs and start-ups as the trust between the influencer and followers will help the product gain better awareness and recognition, which other digital marketing techniques may not achieve without incurring a high cost.
- The ROI on influencers marketing (especially in the barter system) would be way higher than any other traditional social media marketing.

13.6 Concluding Remarks

Though social media marketing has been practiced for quite some time now, influencers marketing has provided SMEs and start-ups with an excellent opportunity to get heard by their potential customers without shelling out a significant amount for that purpose. This appears to be a substantial strategy for them as they can reach out to their targeted audience and save their expenses to be utilised for other essential processes such as product development, quality controls, etc. With the increasing popularity of social media influencer marketing and the growth of influencers in social media platforms, SMEs and start-ups should immediately opt for the influencer's marketing. They should understand the growing power of influencers in market. The key is to select the right influencers with significant reach to the potential customers, which can help gain quick traction for the firm in the competitive market.

References

Abrahamsson, C., Lezis Israelsson, J., & Nilsson, V. (2018). Identifying influencers on Instagram: Important factors to consider when identifying influencers to use for sponsorships and collaborations. Masters thesis.

Balakrishnan, B. K., Dahnil, M. I., & Yi, W. J. (2014). The impact of social media marketing medium toward purchase intention and brand loyalty among generation Y. *Procedia-Social and Behavioral Sciences, 148,* 177–185.

Dulewicz, V., & Higgs, M. (2003). Leadership at the top: The need for emotional intelligence in organisations. *The International Journal of Organisational Analysis, 11*(3), 193–210.

Estay, B. (2020). Instagram influencer marketing: The organic superfood you need to fuel your ecommerce store. Available at: https://www.bigcommerce.com/blog/nstagram-influencer-marketing/#what-is-an-influencer

Fountain, M. T. (2021, January 25). Why small businesses and start-ups should invest in social media marketing. Forbes. Available at: https://www.forbes.com/sites/forbesbusinesscouncil/2021/01/25/why-small-businesses-and-start-ups-should-invest-in-social-media-marketing/?sh=43985b94563e)

Geyser, W. (2019, August 21). How to use influencer marketing to grow your business. Influencer Marketing Hub. Available at: https://influencermarketinghub.com/how-to-use-influencer-marketing-to-grow-your-business/

Glucksman, M. (2017). The rise of social media influencer marketing on lifestyle branding: A case study of Lucie Fink. *Elon Journal of Undergraduate Research in Communications, 8*(2), 77–87.

Gończ, E., Skirke, U., Kleizen, H., & Barber, M. (2007). Increasing the rate of sustainable change: A call for a redefinition of the concept and the model for its implementation. *Journal of Cleaner Production*, *15*(6), 525–537.

Gradzol, J. R., Gradzol, C. J. & Rippey, S. T. (2005). An emerging framework for global strategy. *International Journal of Manufacturing Technology Management*, *7*(1), 1–19.

Han, L., Xiang, X., & Yang, X. (2018). Emerging economies and financing of SMEs. *Financial Entrepreneurship for Economic Growth in Emerging Nations*, 22–45.

Influencer Marketing Hub. (2020, May 14). 8 sales and marketing tips for start-ups. Available at: https://influencermarketinghub.com/marketing-tips-start-ups/

Konstantopoulou, A., Rizomyliotis, I., Konstantoulaki, K., & Badahdah, R. (2019). Improving SMEs' competitiveness with the use of Instagram influencer advertising and eWOM. *International Journal of Organisational Analysis*, *27*(2), 308–321.

Lou, C., & Yuan, S. (2019). Influencer marketing: How message value and credibility affect consumer trust of branded content on social media. *Journal of Interactive Advertising*, *19*(1), 58–73.

Matveeva, S. (2019, May 28). Working with influencers: Advice for start-ups. Forbes. Available at: https://www.forbes.com/sites/sophiamatveeva/2019/05/28/working-with-influencers-advice-for-start-ups/?sh=4cd3c6bd2935

Ozgulbas, N., Koyuncugil, A. S., & Yilmaz, F. (2006). Identifying the effect of firm size on financial performance of SMEs. *The Business Review*, *6*(1), 162–167.

Rao, M. (2017, December 30). Rise of the trust economy: 6 steps for start-ups to earn trust, create value, win customers. Your Story. Available at: https://yourstory.com/2017/12/rise-of-the-trust-economy-6-steps-for-start-ups-to-earn-trust-create-value-win-customers/amp

Rockendorf, D. (2011). Continental 2011 social media strategy. [Interview] Personal Communication.

Sahoo, S. R. (2014). An empirical investigation of social media as a marketing tool in micro, small and medium enterprises in India. *International Journal in Management & Social Science*, *2*(12), 233–246.

Chapter 14

'PREFACE' Leadership in Times of Crises: Evidence from Indian SME Sector

Ekta Sinha

SP Jain School of Global Management, Mumbai, India

ektasinha26@gmail.com

Abstract: The study has been taken up with a purpose to understand how a leader can behave during the times of crises. Such times may demand situational and unplanned decisions. Every crisis has different internal and external context; thus, leadership competences which can be useful in "normal" circumstances may not be fruitful in times of crises. However, there could be certain approaches/competences of leadership which can be generalised. The work is based on the review of literature and in-depth interviews with leaders from 23 organisations representing the Indian small and medium-sized enterprise sector. Lived experiences of the participants were captured in the form of narration to understand their role as a leader to keep their businesses alive during the COVID-19 pandemic. With the help of thematic coding, lessons were drawn to develop an understanding of the underlying key competences of a leader that can help to take firm actions during challenging situations. The findings of the study suggest that seven identified leadership competences (PREFACE) can be applied during a crisis to achieve a balance between people and organisational economy. These leadership competences can help in overcoming unforeseen situations to gain competitive advantage and survive challenges. The study holds some important practical implications. Such times like the one where the world is battling a deadly virus, agile and effective decisions need to be made. It should be noted that the post crisis world would also be filled with challenges, such as: lack of demand, lack of jobs, changed work habits and raised inequality. With the help of the suggested competences, one may find a ground to base his/her actions to overcome trials posed due to a crisis. This study addresses an important gap in the literature by presenting an overarching framework for the crisis leadership in the small and medium enterprise sector. This chapter, with the help of in-depth interviews, highlights some important leadership competences which can be helpful in handling crisis situations in small and medium enterprises.

Keywords: Crisis leadership, COVID-19, Resilience, Emotional intelligence, Small business.

14.1 Crisis as a Specific Context for Leadership?

Leadership is not a novel area of research and has attracted the attention of practitioners and academics since long. There is a large pool of literature available on leadership. However, there is comparatively limited information available as to how a leader should behave in the times of a crisis. COVID-19 has presented the world with unprecedented challenges; hence opportunities. But recognising opportunities in the times of crisis takes a lot of hardship, which only a true leader can display. The survivors would certainly agree that this crisis has divided the world into two distinct eras: pre and post COVID-19. Between these two lies the current COVID-19 period, which is full of challenges. Handling these challenges is imperative for survival in the post COVID-19 era. Leaders across globe are trying their best to fight this crisis and overcome the ill effects. Such tough times requires tough decisions and tough decisions require true leaders. It is evident from past instances that its often how the crises have been handled which leads to positive or negative consequences and not the crisis per se (Sinha and Ajgaonkar, 2021). Past evidences suggest that leadership behaviour varies across different context (e.g., Osborn *et al.*, 2002). Thus, it becomes very important to understand the significant leadership competences in light of a context (Liden & Antonakis, 2009). Some leadership competences may co-vary in one context and may not co-vary in another (Antonakis *et al.*, 2003). Crisis presents a very different context to leaders which is not usual or "normal". Hence, leadership competences which are considered effective during "normal" times may not be significant during the times of crisis (Haslam *et al.*, 2001; Hunt *et al.*, 1999). According to James and Wooten (2005), crisis could be sudden (like COVID-19 or a terrorist attack) or smoldering (those events that start out as small and gradually escalates to crisis). In both these situations a leader's role takes a center stage. A crisis can have most devastating impact on organisations and their stakeholders, thus, requires both immediate and urgent attention (Haddon *et al.*, 2015). However, till date, due to lack of focused literature in this context, there lies limited understanding and clarity regarding effective leadership practices (James *et al.*, 2011). Thus, there is no comprehensive framework which explains effective leadership competences during a crisis. In this study we present one such framework by examining the extant literature and drawing from the in-depth interviews conducted with leaders from India small and medium-sized enterprise (SME) sector.

14.2 Leadership Styles and Dilemmas during Crisis

Literature looks somewhat divided when it comes to required competences during the times of crisis. Where one set of literature advocates the idea of authoritative leadership style during a crisis (Gartzia *et al.*, 2011; Mulder *et al.*, 1986) in order to coordinate efforts in one direction, as identified by the leader, other set of literature suggests that there is a preference for more transformational competences when a leader is required to manage people through a crisis (Ryan *et al.*, 2011). Such transformational competences may include higher emotional intelligence, open communication, motivation, and giving hope to people. While leaders having these competences may demonstrate higher degree of care for their people and may handle contingencies better (Hannah *et al.*, 2009), leaders with authoritative competences may demonstrate higher degree of self-confidence, decisiveness, analytic ability, willingness to assume responsibility, and the ability to delegate (Van Wart & Kapucu, 2011; Mulder *et al.*, 1986). Further, the extant literature either talks about personality traits (Kottika *et al.*, 2020) or presents a narrow view of characteristics necessary for a leader to deal with a crisis specifically for SMEs. The fragmented nature of the existing literature, calls for a closer examination of leadership in a crisis situation to gain deeper insights into the key competences of a leader required to survive complicated situations.

There are also some dilemmas associated with a leader during a crisis management. A leader may have some legitimate concerns other than safety (Sagan, 1994). Wildavsky (1998) found a positive correlation between economic growth and safety. Simply put, a dollar is better spent on the economy than on prevention and that preventative policies suppress growth. Leaders need to somehow reconcile these dilemmas (Boin & Hart, 2003). While handling a crisis, a leader has to take decisions related to resource allocation that can result in negative or positive learning and change (Marcus & Goodman, 1991). Pre COVID-19 era leaders were involved in innovation, greater top and bottom lines, larger market share, and expansion for the organisations. But today, the same set of leaders are making rapid decisions to control the adversities and maintain liquidity. They are facing unforeseen redblocks such as changed workplace, issues related to supply chain, and operational challenges (Nichols *et al.*, 2020). Supporting all the stakeholders is certainly not an easy job for leaders. This transition is not easy and requires competences that can handle the situation of crisis well. An effective crisis management by leaders can make huge impacts on organisations and can help them swim through it (Boin *et al.*, 2013). While the existing literature provides some vital insights on crisis leadership competences from large organisations, investigations from the small and medium-sized enterprises (SMEs) is very limited. This blocks our understanding of crisis leadership for this significant sector as unlike large organisations, SMEs function on informal relations and unstructured HR making it tough for them to win stakeholders' support (Jiang *et al.*, 2012). The existing literature does not offer a clear understanding as to how a leader should act in the times of crisis and overcome the adversities specially when it comes to the SME sector. Through this work, we introduce a framework to crisis leadership in the SME sector.

14.3 Introduction to the Indian SME Sector with Special Reference to the Food Processing Industry

In India, the SME sector has been classified based on the investment on plant & machinery and annual turnover (Table 14.1). The SMEs sector has emerged as a significant sector in the Indian economy over the last five decades. It contributes to employment generation, innovation, exports, and comprehensive growth of the economy and society by encouraging entrepreneurship.

The sector accounts for 45% of total industrial production, 40% of total exports and contributes significantly to the GDP with a share of 7.09 % of manufacturing segment and 30.5% of service (SME Chamber of India, n.d.). SMEs are complementary to large industries as ancillary units and this sector contributes significantly in the

Table 14.1. SME classification in India

Classification	Small	Medium
Manufacturing enterprises and enterprises rendering services	Investment in plant and machinery or equipment: Not more than Rs. 100 million and annual turnover: not more than Rs. 500 million	Investment in plant and machinery or equipment: Not more than Rs. 500 million and annual turnover: not more than Rs. 2.5 billion

Source: https://msme.gov.in/know-about-msme.

inclusive industrial development of the country. The micro, small, and medium enterprises are widening their domain across sectors of the economy, producing diverse range of products and services to meet demands of domestic as well as global markets (Ministry of Micro, Small and Medium Enterprises, 2020).

Specifically, the food processing industry is considered the "sunrise industry" in India indicating huge growth potential. It has an important role to play in linking Indian farmers to consumers in the domestic and international markets. The industry engages approximately 1.93 million people in around 39,748 registered units with fixed capital of US$32.75 billion and aggregate output of around US$158.69 billion. Major industries constituting the food processing industry are grains, sugar, edible oils, beverages, and dairy products (Invest India, n.d.). While India's food processing sector is one of the largest in the world and its output is expected to reach US$535 billion by 2025–26, during COVID time it too faced some harsh scenarios. The rationale for choosing SME food processing units for examination lies in the fact that it is complex and involves multiple stakeholders with significant characteristics of quality, compliance and cost-effectiveness (Ziggers & Trienekens, 1999). The entire production chain, product/service, pricing, and distribution processes are also characterised by quality concerns and market competition (van der Vorst, 2000). Guidelines and norms may not be clear or adequate in many cases, especially in the SME industry. Proactive leadership is essential to curb the negative impacts of any crisis. Thus, this sector makes a good choice to study the leadership competences during the times of crises.

14.4 Contextualisation of Leadership

There are studies to suggest that appraisals of effective leadership vary across contexts, and there exists no one prototype for a "good leader" (Osborn *et al.*, 2002). Therefore, to understand leadership, one should understand the context in which it exists and crisis in the SME sector provides one such context. Crises in general can be extremely detrimental for business as they threaten business goals, erode trust, destroy company value, exert pressure on management by providing limited time for management to respond, and may even lead to business failure (Lerbinger, 2012). Extant literature suggests that small and medium-sized firms may be more vulnerable to crises events due to lower levels of preparedness, resource constraints, relatively weak market positions, and higher dependence on government and local agencies (Herbane, 2013). SMEs usually suffer from financial loss, reduced sales volume, incapability of meeting contract terms, cash flow difficulty, reduction in staff number, and even closing down of the business during or after crises events. Crises events may also bring emotional and psychological stress to victims and the leaders of SMEs (Doern, 2016).

The goal of any organisation is to undergo and maintain its identity via improving their performance. Subsequently, the role of a leader in ensuring excellent organisational performance cannot be ignored. Especially with regards to SMEs, leadership is even more important given the constraints and dependencies the sector has. SMEs cannot successfully develop new small businesses without the presence of effective leadership. In times of crisis, the role of a leader becomes more critical as given the existing unfavourable conditions, developing alternative approaches to survive and recovering crisis adversity could be challenging (Kottika *et al.*, 2020). Dent and Cudworth (2018) indicated that the effective decision-making and teamwork can be critical challenges to effective crises responses in SME sector. Leaders in SMEs should be able to provide proper training for managers on crisis stress management (Ferris *et al.*, 2007) and resolving conflicts in the workplace. Robustness and flexibility are again very critical when managing any crisis. Leaders need to consider rapid customisation of their strategies and timely reorganising of their courses of action (Ansell *et al.*, 2010). However, it would be interesting to understand the core leadership competences in the SME sector for crises management from the perspective of a leader.

14.5 Identifying Crises Leadership Competences

In times of crises, leaders at all levels should go hand in hand with stakeholders (Janssen & Vroot, 2020). The COVID-19 pandemic broke the inertia and brought a sense of urgency in the SME sector across the world to quickly respond to the challenges thrown upon by the pandemic. This situation put high demands on leaders to respond to the crisis effectively and restoring the trust and livelihood of the stakeholders.

In order to identify competences related to crisis leadership, in-depth interviews were conducted with leaders from 23 organisations functioning in the food processing industry in India. The criteria for selecting interviewees involved their survival through the COVID-19 pandemic. This helped the researcher understand the strategies adopted by them to tackle the challenges of the COVID-19 crisis. By analysing the narratives and following the process of thematic coding, we identified seven critical competences which can help SME leaders to fight, survive and recover the challenges of crises. Figure 14.1 shows the key relating behaviours to a particular competence for successful handling of the unforeseen situations by leaders in the SME sector.

14.6 Towards the Comprehensive Framework of Crisis Leadership

The seven identified competences — PREFACE — represents a framework of crisis leadership in the SME sector (Figure 14.1). Let us discuss each of these competences necessary to traverse through a crisis, one by one.

14.6.1 *Proactive*

Proactiveness emerged as a core competency during our interview. During our interview it was revealed that to survive the challenges of any crisis it is important to identify the firm's vulnerabilities. Although crises are uncertain and sudden but careful analysis of the market and

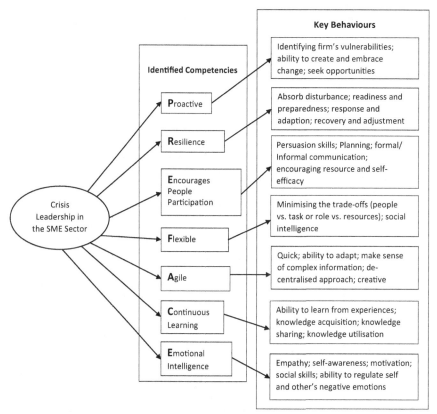

Figure 14.1.   Framework for crisis leadership in the SME sector

business environment by leaders can equip the firm with necessary guards to mitigate the ill-effects of a crisis. In general, there are two main elements of leadership proactiveness: the anticipatory element, where a leader acts upon something that he/she believes is happening in the future; and the element of creating change and shaping one's environment in present times (Parker & Collins, 2010). Proactive leaders seek out opportunities and act upon them. Our study revealed that proactive leaders were able to manage the crisis situation by reducing costs, avoiding taking loans and by reducing prices for their products/services. More than 50% of the leaders also identified opportunities in the crisis. For example, one of the leaders mentioned that due to the increased demand of natural and organic products they used their facility to produce dehydrated ginger, onion, and garlic powder and sold natural cold-pressed juices, thus, creating value for the organisation and other stakeholders. Some of them benefitted from the help provided by the government and deployed necessary technology to manage operations effectively during the crisis, like, developing an app to receive orders easily from the customers.

14.6.2 *Resilience*

SMEs operate in a highly unstructured environment and any crisis — internal or external—may put organisations in a dire need to relook their strategies and take decisions in a very short time. A leader should prepare his/her organisation to "absorb a disturbance and reorganise while undergoing change while retaining the same function, structure, identity and feedback (Walker *et al.*, 2004)". This is called resilience. Starr *et al.* (2003) suggested that resilience is the ability of an individual (or organisation) to withstand systematic discontinuities in order to adapt to new environments put forth by a crisis. Ponomarov and Holcomb (2009) identified three major elements of resilience: readiness and preparedness, response and adaption, and recovery or adjustment. These elements of resilience help leaders to effectively respond to a crisis and re-establish business operations. Leaders articulated during the interview that the ability to handle and absorb disturbance caused by the pandemic allowed them to prepare well in time to adapt to the changing environment so that recovery and stability is achieved with minimum fluctuation of the system. A resilient leader is capable of linking available resources to desired outcomes so that state of equilibrium could be achieved (Norris *et al.*, 2008).

14.6.3 *Encourages People Participation*

There are many stakeholders in a small and medium-sized organisation. While managing a crisis it becomes very difficult to protect the interest of every stakeholder. In order to avoid dissatisfaction among people involved in the organisational activities, it becomes significant for a leader to encourage peoples' participation in managing situations under crisis. A leader in times of crisis may persuade his/her people to collaborate formally (structured) or informally (unstructured). Formal collaboration may involve planning related to resource utilisation across departments and informal collaboration may involve transmitting important information timely without delay across departments. Rowe and Frewer (2000) suggests that there are number of ways in which stakeholders can be involved in decision making during a crisis. At the lowest level, relevant information (e.g., about how the risk estimates were calculated) can be passed on to the stakeholders. Similarly, at higher levels, their views may be solicited through consultation exercises, focus groups discussions, or questionnaires surveys in order to facilitate the decision-making process (Samaddar *et al.*, 2015). Besides decision making, peoples' participation can be very helpful in implementing the required processes to overcome a crisis. SME leaders indicated during the interviews that such collaborations can increase the level of psychological resources available such as means-efficacy and self-efficacy which is based on an individuals' belief in the quality and utility of the tools available for task performance (Eden, 2001) and belief in one's abilities to mobilise resources to meet situational demands (Wood & Bandura, 1989) respectively.

14.6.4 *Flexible*

Flexibility is regarded as a social intelligence, where a leader tailor his/her responses by assessing the demands, needs, and affordance of an organisation in a crisis situation (Zaccaro *et al.*, 1991; Kaiser *et al.*, 2007). The Multiple-Linkage Model by Yukl (1989) draws from contingency theories of leadership and describes how certain short-term and long-term efforts of a leader can turn a crisis situation into a favourable one (Yukl & Mahsud, 2010). It says that a strategic leadership involves flexibility, where a leader minimises the trade-offs associated with an organisation caught in a crisis. The trade-offs could be related to role and resources or people and task objectives. The ability of a leader to assess these trade-offs and make a win-win decision has been regarded as flexibility. For instance, our respondents mentioned that during a crisis situation the need of direct supervision may be compensated by assigning the work to a more experienced subordinate. This will save the precious time that can be utilised for working out strategy to overcome a crisis. A crisis situation sometimes demands behaviours that are opposite, such as: directive vs. empowering. Only a flexible leader can balance between such orthogonal behaviours and competing values to handle a crisis smoothly (Kaiser *et al.*, 2007).

14.6.5 *Agile*

Ability of a leader to quickly adapt can be an important competence in extreme contexts. Agility involves the ability to change during periods of contextual shifts and uncertainty (Lengnick-Hall & Beck, 2005). Agility is made more difficult in the crises due to rapidly evolving situations with imperfect information. In such contexts, a leader's level of agility is tied directly to its ability to adapt, collect and make sense of complex information in his/her environment and adjust accordingly (Chakravarthy, 1982). As noted by Dutton and Duncan (1987, p. 291), threats to agility can occur when a leader becomes "locked into current patterns of responses not because they have become routine and habitual, but because the issues are perceived as non-resolvable due to a resource shortage". Therefore, a leader's agility competence in extreme and novel contexts requires adequate resources and effective organisational communications systems that give them the ability to share timely information and coordinate (Dunn *et al.*, 2002) with stakeholders. In line with Seifert (2007), in our research also more than 50% of the leaders supported the fact that to survive any crisis flatter, more adaptive organisational structures will be more effective, to reduce rigidity, centralisation, and formalisation. An agile leader makes sure that their members are allowed to solve problems creatively (Hatano & Inagaki, 1986) to cope with uncertain and unpredictable work situations (Edwards & Morrison, 1994).

14.6.6 Continuous Learning

The length of a crisis may affect the ability of a leader, team, or an organisation to counter, learn from, and adjust to the crisis. When a crisis is prolonged, leaders have the advantage of learning from the experiences and steering that knowledge back into ongoing operations to survive and recover from the crisis (Hannah *et al.*, 2009). Prolonged crises situations, however, can add bigger load to a leader or organisation and result in deteriorating an organisation's psychological, social and material resources. Thus, it is important to learn continuously to take the right decisions. Learning as a strategy has three components: knowledge acquisition, knowledge sharing or dissemination and knowledge utilisation (Nevis *et al.*, 1997). During the interview, leaders from the SME sector indicated that in the time of crisis it is even more important to carefully analyse and take clues from the environment so that diffusion of knowledge can be done in the right direction to direct the corrective actions which can be critical to the firm's survival. Leaders also mentioned that continuous learning helped them to foster psychological, economic, and social well-being.

14.6.7 Emotional Intelligence

Emotional intelligence (EI) has been regarded as higher order skill to achieve life goals (Goleman, 1995), and becomes even more important for managing a crisis. Empathy, motivation, self-awareness, regulation, and social skills have been regarded as basic tenets of EI (Goleman, 1995). While EI enables us to understand and manage our panic and reactions, it also helps to understand the emotional state of others (Sinha, 2021). Because a leader can understand and see situations with empathy and mindfulness, making strategies and communicating them to the stakeholders becomes less complicated in the times of crises. During our interviews, we found several instances where leaders displayed EI to survive the challenges to COVID-19. In times of crises, fear can be experienced specially in the SME sector which is already unstructured. During the interview leaders mentioned that, threats due to extreme and unexpected events may supersede one's personal resources. This is consistent with research on the broaden and build theory (Fredrickson *et al.*, 2003), which revealed that left unchecked, negative emotions such as fear limit the scope of cognition and attention, restraining potential thought-action; while positive emotions broaden such potential range of thought-action, facilitating greater adaptability under stress. Only an empathetic leader can address his/her followers concerns/threats/fears and help them to keep their calm.

14.7 Implications

Through this chapter the author has highlighted seven key competences of a leader to manage a crisis situation with special reference to the SME sector in India. Any crisis presents leaders with a high level of uncertainty and complexity where classical management tools can turn out to be impractical (Stacey, 2010). The study emphasises that crisis situations demand specific leadership competences as "drivers" for survival than focusing only on financial strength of the firm in SME sector which already function in complex and unstructured environment. Thus, leaders should keep in mind how they directly impact important aspects of the SME strategy such as entrepreneurial and market orientations which, in turn, affect the business performance in the times of crises. In uncontrollable situations like the COVID-19 pandemic that seems to be leading many companies into a recession, an understanding of key leadership competences may guide leaders of SMEs towards aspects which can be worked upon to ensure the survival and revival from the uncertain and sudden situations of crises.

A better understanding of leadership competences in extreme contexts will "apprise a deeper appreciation of the ontology of leadership processes" (Hannah *et al.*, 2009). By observing behaviours relating to the identified competences, we expect to gain a deeper understanding of how leadership operates in crises situation specifically in SME sector. Highlighting these competences will perhaps provide additional evidence for further validity of supposition and boundaries of current models of crisis leadership. However, this work at this point does not believe that studying leadership competences in the context of a crisis will necessarily change the basic understandings of the essence of leadership. Nor do we emphasise that the competences currently in the literature will become irrelevant. But this work will likely contribute to most extant theories applicable to extreme contexts such as directive and transformational. Finally, with the help of this work we uncovered significantly more applicable competences that can be used to inform leadership in the extreme contexts. The work also indicated that when leaders ignore the problems, fail to take charge of the resources and blame others rather than taking meaningful steps to solve a crisis situation then it results into making the crisis situation worse.

14.8 Conclusion

The study showed how the food processing industry of SMEs managed to survive the COVID-19 pandemic while facing one of the most distressing and prolonged economic crises. Leaders survived the challenging times by closely inspecting environmental developments, coordinating with stakeholders, escalating efforts, improving efficiency & productivity, steering financial management, taking appropriate marketing measures, and investing in needed technologies. It is evident that leaders with a proper set of competence not only withstand financial storms that appear unmanageable, but also significantly improve the psychological and social health of the stakeholders, thus, ensuring survival. In Chinese, the word "crisis" is composed of two characters — one represents danger, and the other represents opportunity. In Greek, it stems from "κρίνω" (krínō), which means to pick out, choose, decide, judge (Kottika *et al.,* 2020). In combination, the two translations demonstrate how a leader's competences determine whether the focus will be on loss or on gain. A leader's capability to respond firmly and positively to crises situations can help reduce costs and align stakeholders to focus on the potential benefits of the crisis.

References

Ansell, C., Boin, A., & Keller, A. (2010). Managing transboundary crises: Identifying the building blocks of an effective response system. *Journal of Contingencies and Crisis Management, 18*(4), 195–207.

Antonakis, J., Avolio, B. J., & Sivasubramaniam, N. (2003). Context and leadership: An examination of the nine-factor full-range leadership theory using the multifactor leadership questionnaire. *The Leadership Quarterly, 14*(3), 261–295.

Boin, A., & Hart, T. P. (2003). Public leadership in times of crisis: Mission impossible? *Public Administration Review, 63*(5), 544–553.

Boin, A., Kuipers, S. and Overdijk, W. (2013). Leadership in times of crisis: A framework for assessment. *International Review of Public Administration, 18*(1), 79–91.

Chakravarthy, B. S. (1982). Adaptation: A promising metaphor for strategic management. *Academy of Management Review, 7,* 35–44.

Dent, P., Woo, R., & Cudworth, P. (2018). *Crisis Management for the Resilient Enterprise.* Deloitte Insights.

Doern, R. (2016). Entrepreneurship and crisis management: The experiences of small businesses during the London 2011 riots. *International Small Business Journal, 34*(3), 276–302.

Dunn, J. C., Lewandowsky, S., & Kirsner, K. (2002). Dynamics of communication in emergency management. *Applied Cognitive Psychology, 16,* 719–737.

Dutton, J. E., & Duncan, R. B. (1987). The creation of momentum for change through the process of strategic issue diagnosis. *Strategic Management Journal, 8,* 279–295.

Eden, D. (2001). Means efficacy: External sources of general and specific subjective efficacy. In Erez, M., Kleinbeck, U. & Thierry, H. (Eds.), *Work Motivation in the Context of a Globalizing Economy,* pp. 65–77. Lawrence Erlbaum, Hillsdale, NJ.

Edwards, J. E., & Morrison, R. F. (1994). Selecting and classifying future naval officers: The paradox of greater specialization in broader areas. In Rumsey, M. G., Walker, C. B. & Harris, J. H. (Eds.), *Personnel Selection and Classification,* pp. 69–84. Erlbaum, Hillsdale, NJ.

Ferris, G. R., Hochwarter, W. A., & Matherly, T. A. (2007). HRM After 9/11 and Katrina. In S. Werner, S. Jackson & R. Schuler (Eds.), *Current issues in North American HRM:172-185.* Taylor and Francis, New York.

Gartzia, L., Ryan, M. K., Balluerka, N., & Aritzeta, A. (2011). Think crisis-think female: Further evidence. *European Journal of Work and Organizational Psychology, 21*(4), 603–628.

Goleman, D. (1995). *Emotional intelligence.* Bantam Books, Inc.

Haddon, A., Loughlin, C., & McNally, C., (2015). Leadership in a time of financial crisis: What do we want from our leaders? *Leadership & Organization Development Journal, 36*(5), 612–627.

Hannah, S. T., Uhl-Bien, M., Avolio, B. J., & Cavarretta, F. L. (2009). A framework for examining leadership in extreme contexts. *The Leadership Quarterly, 20*(6), 897–919.

Haslam, S. A., Platow, M. J., Turner, J. C., Reynolds, K. J., McGarty, C., & Oakes, P. J. (2001). Social identity and the romance of leadership: The importance of being seen to be "doing it for us". *Group Processes and Intergroup Relations, 4*(3), 191–205.

Hatano, G., & Inagaki, K. (1986). Two courses of expertise. In Stevenson, H., Azuma, H. & Hakuta, K. (Eds.), *Child Development and Education in Japan,* pp. 262–272. Freeman, New York.

Herbane, B. (2013). Exploring crisis management in UK small-and-medium-sized enterprises. *Journal of Contingencies and Crisis Management, 21*(2), 82–95.

Hunt, J., Boal, K., & Dodge, G. (1999). The effects of visionary and crisis-responsive leadership. *Leadership Quarterly, 10*(3), 423–448.

Invest India (n.d.). Food processing. Available at: https://www.investindia.gov.in/sector/food-processing

James, E. H., & Wooten, L. P. (2005). Leadership as (un)usual: How to display competence in times of crisis. *Organizational Dynamics, 34*(2), 141–152.

James, E. H., Wooten, L. P., & Duskek, K. (2011). Crisis management: Informing a new leadership research agenda. *The Academy of management Annals, 5*(1), 455–493.

Jiang, K., Lepak, D. P., Hu, J., & Baer, J. C. (2012). How does human resource management influence organizational outcomes? A meta-analytic investigation of mediating mechanisms. *Academy of Management Journal*, 55(6), 1264–1294.

Kaiser, R. B., Lindberg, J. T., & Craig, S. B. (2007). Assessing the flexibility of managers: A comparison of methods. *International Journal of Selection and Assessment*, 15, 40–55.

Kottika, E., Ozsomer, A., Ryden, P., Theodorakis, I. G., Kaminakis, K., Kottikas, K. G., & Stathakopoulos, V. (2020). We survived this! What managers could learn from SMEs who successfully navigated the Greek economic crisis. *Industrial Marketing Management*, 88, 352–365.

Lengnick-Hall, C. A., & Beck, T. E. (2005). Adaptive fit versus robust transformation: How organizations respond to environmental change. *Journal of Management*, 31, 738–757.

Lerbinger, O. (2012). *The Crisis Manager: Facing Disasters, Conflicts, and Failures*, 2nd Ed. Routledge, New York.

Liden, R. C., & Antonakis, J. (2009). Considering context in psychological leadership research. *Human Relations*, 62(11), 1587–1605.

Marcus, A. A., & Goodman, R. S. (1991). Victims and shareholders: The dilemmas of presenting corporate policy during a crisis. *Academy of Management Journal*, 34(2), 281–305.

Ministry of Micro, Small and Medium Enterprises (2020). Annual report 2020-21. Available at: https://msme.gov.in/sites/default/files/MSME-ANNUAL-REPORT-ENGLISH%202020-21.pdf

Mulder, M., de Jong, R. D., Koppelaar, L., & Verhage, J. (1986). Power, situation, and leaders' effectiveness: An organizational field study. *Journal of Applied Psychology*, 71(4), 566–570.

Nevis, R., DiBella, A., & Gould, A. (1997). *Understanding Organizations as Learning Systems*. The Society for Organizational Learning, Cambridge, MA.

Nichols, C., Hayden, C. S., & Trendler, C. (2020). 4 behaviors that help leaders manage a crisis. Harvard Business Review. Available at: https://hbr.org/2020/04/4-behaviors-that-help-leaders-manage-a-crisis

Norris, F. H., Stevens, P. S., Pfefferbaum, B., & Wyche, K. (2008). Community resilience as a metaphor, theory, set of capacities, and strategy for disaster readiness. *American Journal of Community Psychology*, 41(1), 127–150.

Osborn, R. N., Hunt, J. G., & Jauch, L. R. (2002). Toward a contextual theory of leadership. *The Leadership Quarterly*, 13(6), 797–837.

Parker, S. K., & Collins, C. G. (2010). Taking stock: Integrating and differentiating multiple proactive behaviors. *Journal of Management*, 36(3), 633–662.

Ponomarov, Y. S., & Holcomb, M. (2009). Understanding the concept of supply chain resilience, *International Journal of Logistics Management, 20*(1), 124–143.

Rowe, G., & Frewer, L. J., (2000). Public participation methods: A framework for evaluation. *Science, Technology and Human Values, 25*(1), 3–29.

Ryan, M., Haslam, S. A., Hersby, M., & Bongiorno, R. (2011). Think crisis — think female: The glass cliff and contextual variation in the think manager — think male stereotype. *Journal of Applied Psychology, 98*(3), 470–484.

Sagan, S. D. (1994). Towards a political theory of organizational reliability. *Journal of Contingencies and Crisis Management, 2*(4), 228–40.

Samaddar, S., Yokomatsu, M., Dayour, F., Oteng-Ababio, M., Dzivenu, T., Adams, M., & Ishikawa, H., (2015). Evaluating effective public participation in disaster management and climate change adaptation: Insights from northern Ghana through a user-based approach. *Risk, Hazards & Crisis in Public Policy, 6*(1), 117–143.

Seifert, C. (2007). Improving disaster management through structured flexibility among frontline responders. In Gibbons, D. E. (Ed.), *Communicable Crises*, pp. 83–136. Information Age Publishing, North Carolina.

Sinha, E., & Ajgaonkar, M. (2020). The Infosys Saga: An Indian IT giant faces a leadership crisis. *Asian Case Research Journal, 24*(01), 13–34.

Sinha, E. (2021). Towards an integrative framework of intrapreneurship by focusing on individual level competencies. *Journal of Asia Entrepreneurship and Sustainability, 17*(1), 106–163.

SME Chamber of India (n.d.). About SME in India. Available at: https://www.smechamberofindia.com/about-msme-in-india.php

Stacey, R. D. (2010). *Complexity and Organizational Reality: Uncertainty and the Need to Rethink Management after the Collapse of Investment Capitalism.* Routledge, London.

Starr, R., Newfrock, J., & Delurey, M., (2003). Enterprise resilience: managing risk in the networked economy. *Strategy and Business, 30*, 70–79.

van der Vorst, J. G. A. J. (2000). Effective food supply chains: Generating, modelling and evaluating supply chain scenarios. Doctor of Philosophy, S.l.

Van Wart, M., & Kapucu, N. (2011). Crisis management competencies. The case of emergency managers in the USA. *Public Management Review, 13*(4), 489–511.

Walker, B., Holling, S. C., & Carpenter, R. S., (2004). Resilience, adaptability and transformability in social–ecological systems. *Ecology and Society,* *9*(2), 5.

Wildavsky, A. (1988), *Searching for Safety.* University of California Press, Berkeley, CA.

Wood, R., & Bandura, A. (1989). Impact of conceptions of ability on self-regulatory mechanisms and complex decision making. *Journal of Personality and Social Psychology, 56,* 407–415.

Yukl, G. (1989). *Leadership in Organizations,* 2nd ed. Prentice Hall, Englewood Cliffs, NJ.

Yukl, G, & Mahsud, R. (2010). Why flexible and adaptive leadership is essential. *Consulting Psychology Journal: Practice and Research, 62*(2), 81–93.

Zaccaro, J. S., Gilbert, A. J., Thor, K. K., & Mumford, D. M. (1991). Leadership and social intelligence: Linking social perspectiveness and behavioral flexibility to leader effectiveness. *The Leadership Quarterly, 2(4),* 317–342.

Ziggers, G. W., & Trienekens, J. (1999). Quality assurance in food and agribusiness supply chains: Developing successful partnerships. *International Journal of Production Economics, 60,* 271–279.

Chapter 15

How "Big" Can Big Data Analytics Be in SMEs: Influence on Rational Decision Making and Organisational Performance

Nidhi S. Natrajan* and Rinku Sanjeev[†,‡]

Symbiosis Centre of Management Studies, Noida, India

[Constituent of Symbiosis International
(Deemed University), Pune]

*nidhi.natrajan@scmsnoida.ac.in

†drrinkusanjeev@gmail.com; rinku.sanjeev@scmsnoida.ac.in

Mitu G. Matta

Lingaya's University, Faridabad, India

mitu.matta@gmail.com

Abstract: In the present competitive and disruptive arena, big data analytics has emerged as a revolutionary approach enabling sound decision making leading to enhanced organisational performance. However, extant studies on big data analytics in organisational perspective is limited, specifically in the case of

‡ Corresponding author

SMEs. The tenet is that organisations bank on superior decision-making capabilities through data-driven insights, like big data analytics. So, it is imperative to explore the intertwined themes from organisational perspectives. In this backdrop, this chapter addresses the key concerns with focus on the enablers and deterrents in big data and its analytics in the context of SMEs and mainly to decipher the ways it contributes to their enhanced organisational performance It investigates the moderating role of big data analytics on the relationship between decision making rationality and organisational performance. So, it adopts a cross-sectional research approach, based on primary data collected from the SMEs firms in Delhi NCR. The key finding of the study emanating from the regression and interaction effect of big data analytics reinforce the use of big data analytics as the moderator, which affects the relationship between decision making and organisational performance. Thus, it reinstates that the use of rational decision making model in the organisation to result in higher performance. The chapter thus presents important insights for developing data-driven insights using the BDA in context of SMEs for driving organisational performance.

Keywords: Rational decision making, Big data analytics, Organisational performance, SMEs, DSS.

15.1 Introduction

In today's competitive and disruptive environment, the role of big data analytics (BDA) is indispensable and far reaching and this spells out aptly in the Industry 4.0 dictum. Industry 4.0 envisages a firm's transition from low-risk entry strategy to an adapted digitisation strategy. In bigger firms, digitisation is already intertwined with the mainstream corporate strategy, but this is not easy for small and medium-sized enterprises (SMEs) in actual sense. It is rightly asserted by Matt *et al.* (2018) that "while many of the emerging Industry 4.0 technologies and tools can be applied in large companies, this may not apply for small and medium establishments". But it is important for SMEs to combat the fast paced competition through digital reformations and big data analytics implementation.

As the backbone of the economy, SMEs provide immense opportunities fostering economic growth and sustainable competitiveness. SMEs are resource constrained and face many challenges and opportunities. As per the SME Chamber of India, micro, small, and medium enterprises (MSME) contribute a lot to the GDP of the country and currently it is around 8%. An *Economics Times* article reported that there are 42.5 million SMEs in India right now and of these around 43% are based on digital platforms. The use of social media and gadgets related to the Internet of Things (IoT) generates a lot of data which leads to big data. SMEs can harness big data analytics for better business prospects. Considering this, it is important to understand the role of data analytics in SMEs and the challenges related to its implementation. Such an understanding will help SMEs to predict their target audience and changing preferences of the customers. The salience of big data & big data analytics is also captured in the Industry 4.0 norms and is imperative for all firms, regardless of their size.

15.2 Benefits & Challenges of Big Data Analytics in SMEs

Specifically, the following are the benefits of incorporating big data analytics in SMEs:

- Understanding customer needs. Use of online platforms and social media can help small organisations focus on manufacturing as per the needs of the customers. The sentiment of the customers around the product or service offered can be easily analysed with the help of analytics.
- Identify trends. Understanding consumer behaviour and identifying the emerging trends can be easily and quickly done with the help of data analytics.
- Understanding market competition. Before the internet age and social media usage, it was difficult for SMEs to understand existing competitions. But now it is very easy to analyse the data and take care of market competition.

- Process improvement. With the use of big data analytics there is high scope of collecting data from machines, sensors, and other processes. The analysis of such data helps in optimising the operations further.
- Changing business model. The data that is getting generated through various processes and touch points helps in generating revenue in innovative ways.
- Acquiring appropriate workforce. Data analytics supports SMEs to recruit suitable workforce. Apart from this, understanding employee's problems is also possible through analytics, thus reducing attrition rate and enhancing employee engagement.
- Cost effective. Most of the technology tools in analytics are based on open source and hence the total cost of implementing it is overall lower and is affordable by SME's.

The challenges in implementing big data analytics in MSMEs:

- Transforming the process and IT based working. There is a lot of effort required to transform legacy data to create a data warehouse and make it usable for further analysis. This sometimes leads to low performance in the initial stages.
- Lack of required skill. Use of big data analytics requires a certain set of technical knowledge and a workforce trained in the same. Acquiring new technical staff and upgrading the existing staff require time and have associated cost.
- Investment in technology and related infrastructure. Although the running cost of using data analytics is low, the onetime investment in implementing this technology is inevitable.

15.3 Big Data Analytics in Organisational Context

In order to thrive through these challenges and grab the opportunities to enhance organisational performance, effective decision making is very critical. Information and digitisation are radically changing how the business is run, specifically decision making.

Information and data-driven decision making is the key to success. The voluminous big data and data analytics have changed the way leaders or managers take decisions. The voluminous data is difficult to handle with traditional database management system. Hence, data warehouse is a special data base which supports multidimensional data set, which is historical in nature. The data mining tools support analysis of such huge and aggregated data (Fan *et al.*, 2015). Big data analytics is required to find hidden trends in the large volume of the data. Decision support systems give insightful analysis, assisting the mangers to base their decisions on facts and not just intuition. Analytics provides intelligent access to the required information and knowledge and support intelligent choice from various alternatives in a given decision-making scenario. As per the Market Watch report (2019), the analytics market is expected to have a value of US$77 billion by 2023. Most of the organisations have strategised to use predictive analytics to plan for the future.

The NASSCOM Big Data & Analytics Summit 6th edition, held in July 2018, highlighted the transformation of enterprise decision making through analytics and AI. NASSCOM (2018) also highlighted that there is an employability gap in the industry in this area. The organisations have come out with a report as an initiative to bridge the gap between the requirements of the industry and the existing talent. In 2021, the estimated manpower requirement in the area of analytics would be between 510,000 and 800,000.

Machine learning is the upcoming trend in analytics for predicting future trends using past data. Not only managers but all the stakeholders including executives and investors have started using big data analytics for weekly, monthly, quarterly, or yearly forecasts. Companies like Google and Facebook are huge success stories with respect to big data analytics usage. Social media has further enhanced the volume of data and organisations would not like to miss online consumer trends. Thus, both online and offline functions in organisation generates terabytes and zettabytes of data, which can be analysed in real time through the application of big data analytics.

Decision support system (DSS) is not only used for large organisations but also for SMEs. The cloud based analytical applications can be accessed on a on demand basis for forecasting and decision making (Chiroma *et al.*, 2015). There is also a need to develop a culture of data-driven decision making in the organisation at all levels. Every organisation large and small can get equal benefit by implementing analytics based decision making. This will help them to understand their customer in a better way, have operational efficiency and effective decision making, further contributing to organisational success. The purpose of the study is to understand the moderating role of data analytics in enhancing organisational performance through effective decision making.

15.4 Previous Work/Theoretical Background

The roots of big data analytics can be traced to the late 19th century during the US census which required processing and analysis of 50 million citizens. The voluminous data was difficult to process manually and took around seven years for processing. One of the major projects related to big data handling was in the context of social security. The US government had in its care 26 million people and the data was managed by IBM. This was one of the largest card reading and digital book keeping project. Another striking example is during World War II, where signals were intercepted by the device called Colossus, in which 5000 characters were searched every second for hidden patterns. During 1965, the US government had to manage data from 742 million tax returns and around 175 million biometric records. The origin and use of big data is quite old, however the amount of big data emerged only in early 2000. Big data analytics supports the analysis of a large amount of data and helps to reveal hidden patterns and unknown trends for better decision making. It is a multidisciplinary field involving application of mathematics, statistics, predictive modelling, and machine learning for finding meaningful patterns and associations.

15.4.1 *Role of Rational Decision Making in Organisational Performance*

Every organisation wants to move ahead in this VUCA environment and perform better. In order to improve continuously and constantly strategise in the midst of changing business and customer needs, organisations need to make many decisions. Decision making is a process, which is based on going through multiple choices available in a particular situation and choosing the best one. The rational decision-making process comprises of multiple steps, from the initial step of problem identification and to the end result of solution to the problem. Individual perception and emotions may guide the decision-making process, which is undesirable from the organisational perspective. Thus, rational decision making is based on facts, data, and logic, instead of the decision maker's individual perception. It is a scientific step by step model to reach to the best solution (Uzonwanne, 2016).

Researchers have emphasised that fact based analysis is required for rational decision making, minimising personal intuition and perception (Oliveira, 2007). Rational decision making also supports the economic theory in terms of finding cost effective solutions. Managers and leaders are responsible for the progress of the organisation. Good decision making is one of the desired qualities for them to do so (Hsiung, 2012).

The selection of the most suitable option during the decision-making process can be very challenging. The complexity increases with the increasing uncertainty in the business environment. The entire process can be divided into three different approaches: the basic one is based on the problem solving angle, the other two are based on the process of decision making itself and technology supported decision making.

The oldest model of rational decision making has been highlighted during late 1950s. The model is based on rational choice and the behaviour of the leader taking the decision. In order to make decisions, it was important to know about choices, probable outcome, and the risk involved with each choice. However, some of the older theories were based on the theory of optimisation. There were also arguments regarding the way in which the human brain makes decisions, which may not be a linear process or be descriptive in nature. There are certain shortcuts as opposed to the step wise decision process which are considered by the human brain to take the decision — this is known as heuristics. Although this kind of decision is based on a low volume of information, often the outcome is precise. In another approach, the decision is made on the basis of biases and errors. It is considered that biases are part of every day life and are also involved in every business situation. This approach centers on minimisation of biases and reduction of error for any decision making in order to achieve a better outcome. There are certain generic biases associated with any decision-making process — over confidence, anchoring, confirmation, availability, and escalation biases.

Rational decision making leads to low chances of inaccuracies and hence supports better organisational performance. The decision based on data and facts result into maximisation of profit while minimising the cost. Rational decision making also expedites the decision-making process, thus supporting effective decision making in less time (Herrmann, 2017).

15.4.2 *Decision Support System (DSS)*

Decision making is an integral part of the organisational operation and requires managers to invest much effort. It is a branch of information system that supports decision making. DSS is a technology-supported decision-making technique (Najib *et al.*, 2010; Chiroma *et al.*, 2015). It makes use of data-driven decision-making process based on the rational decision-making model. The visualisation of the result generated enables managers to take appropriate course of action within the stipulated time frame. Broadly, DSS can be divided into five different types: communication focused, data driven, document driven, knowledge based, and model driven. Depending upon the need of the organisation, either one of the approaches is used or a hybrid method utilising multiple categories is adopted. Around the mid 2000s, business intelligence (BI) and business analytics (BA) emerged as the new way of decision making. There is an integration of enterprise resource planning (ERP), DSS, and big data analytics for cost effective, fast, and accurate decision making (Arnott & Pervan, 2014).

15.4.3 *Role of Big Data Analysis*

From the last three decades, technology has been impacting business and business processes in a very powerful way. The work place is becoming increasingly complex and with the high level usage of ERP software and internet, huge volume of data is getting generated. The real time response to all business needs is creating a time crunch and posing huge challenge for leaders and managers. The global workforce also requires collaboration across the globe and technology has the ability to deal with all these situations (Maté *et al.*, 2015; Budikova *et al.*, 2016).

Big data and big data analytics have emerged as the new technology tool to support decision-making process. The following points highlight how BDA supports the rational decision making:

- High data processing ability. BDA expedites decision making through the facility of slicing and dicing the huge amount of data (in zettabytes) with the help of data warehousing and data mining tools.
- Speedy decision making. Voluminous data can be seamlessly and sophisticatedly processed in real time while enabling quick response rate to the business needs. This is possible due to support in quick decision making. The alternatives generated and the corresponding risks can be quickly evaluated as compared to the manual process.
- Collaborative decision making. Most of organisations have a global workforce and comprise of virtual teams. Such organisations and teams deal with geographical and cultural disparity. However, technology supports what is known as group DSS.

Through analytical tools connected through fast telecom infrastructure (like OLAP — online analytical processing) these group based decisions can be made in less time and accurately (Wang & Byrd, 2017).

BDA is a set of systems and technologies that provides integration of large amount of varied data within the organisation and reveals the hidden patterns in the data. This hidden data helps in taking future decisions with accuracy and within a short time frame (Moffitt & Vasarhelyi, 2013; Davenport, 2014). The magnificence of BDA lies in the variety and velocity of the data integrated in the warehouse. In terms of variety, the data warehouse contains both legacy data and transactional data. With the popularity of social media and its benefit in business, the data can also be text, email, semi structured, audio, video, and social media posts. These data types are not supported by classical relational data base and hence a multidimensional data container, i.e., data warehouse is used to store it (McAfee & Brynjolfsson, 2012; Frisk & Bannister, 2017). The real time data interpretation and analysis facilitates the agile organisation. The organisations today are aiming for BI where both quantitative and qualitative data are analysed using data mining for better decision making. BDA supports descriptive, predictive, and prescriptive needs of business (Chen *et al.*, 2012; Holsapple *et al.*, 2014). Descriptive analytics facilitates decision making by analysing past data highlighting current trends. Predictive analytics facilitates forecasting for long term decision making and prescriptive analytics indicate the best course of action to be taken for best results (Sappelli *et al.*, 2017).

As per the study of Hagel (2015), BDA supports organisations in gaining competitive edge through identifying new opportunities through trend analysis. A new branch of analytics called sentiment analytics uncovers the hidden thought process of the workforce and thus supports the better handling through HR based decision. Thus, BDA is a vehicle for business success through the use of cost effective and real time decision making.

15.5 Objectives

- To study the effect of decision-making process on organisational performance
- To study the moderating role of big data analytics

15.5.1 *Proposed Research Framework*

The conceptual framework comprises of decision making as predictor, big data analytics as moderating variable, and the outcome is the organisation performance, as shown in Figure 15.1.

15.5.2 *Hypothesis*

H1: There is a significant positive relationship between rational decision making and organisational performance.
H2: Big data analytics moderates the relationship between rational decision making and organisational performance.

15.6 Design/Methodology/Approach

15.6.1 *Research Instrument*

To measure big data analysis, there were four items selected from Capgemini (2012), i.e., (i) do you agree/believe that the use of big data has improved your organisation's overall performance

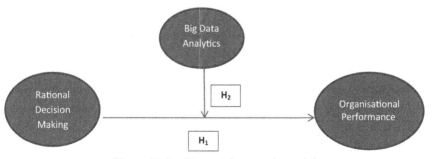

Figure 15.1. Proposed research model

already, and can improve overall performance, (ii) big data management is not viewed strategically at senior levels of the organisation, (iii) there is not enough of a "big data culture" in the organisation, where the use of big data in decision-making is valued and rewarded, and (iv) most operational/tactical decisions that can be automated, have been automated. Respondents were asked to rate their opinions on a seven-point Likert scale in terms of agree or disagree of use of each item, with 1 = Strongly Disagree and 7 = Strongly Agree. Rational decision making were measured by seven items taken from the rational decision-making scale adapted from Uzonwanne (2016), i.e, (i) rational decision making is helpful for identifying the problem that requires a solution, (ii) rational decision making is helpful for identifying the solution scenario, (iii) rational decision making is helpful for carrying out a gap analysis, (iv) rational decision making is helpful for gathering facts, options, and alternatives, (v) rational decision making is helpful for analysing option outcomes, (vi) rational decision making is helpful for selecting the best possible options, (vii) rational decision making is helpful is for implementing decision for solution and evaluate, and final outcome. Respondents were asked to rate the level of their decisions relying on insights derived from data analysis/analytics on a seven-point Likert scale, in which 1 = Strongly Disagree and 7 = Strongly Agree and to measure Organisational Performance, seven items were used: (i) Organisational innovativeness, (ii) Organisational creativeness, (iii) Organisational competitiveness, (iv) Organisational effectiveness, (v) Organisational efficiency, (vi) Organisational productiveness, and (vii) Organisational profitability mentioned by Antony and Bhattacharya (2010) to measure the performance of organisations. A seven-point Likert Scale (1 = Not At All, 7 = Extremely) was used for scoring.

The proposed research model in Figure 15.1 highlights the importance of rational decision making in enhancing organisational performance. It further tries to emphasise that when big data analytics is used as the technological advancement in the organisation to support better decision making. The data was collected through a survey from ten SMEs in Delhi NCR, constituting sample of 390 respondents.

As per the model, the dependent variable (DV) is organisational performance (OP) and the independent variable (IV) is rational decision making (RDM). Here the use of BDA has been considered as moderator (Mo). Both the dependent and the independent variables are measured on the seven-point Likert Scale. However, use of BDA has been represented through dummy variable (Yip & Tsang, 2007). The use of BDA has been represented through "1" and the decision making done without BDA has been coded as "0". The further analysis of the above model will be analysed through dummy variable regression. The effect of RDM on OP can be interpreted through simple regression, which is one step model (Okeh & Oyeka, 2015).

But the moderating role of BDA cannot be deduced from single model regression. Thus, after proving significance of moderator in prediction of dependent variable, it is important to show the moderating effect of BDA. The use of BDA has been coded as a dummy variable and the independent variable is measured on a scale of one to seven. The interaction term gives the interpretation for moderating effect. New variables are created in Statistical Package for the Social Sciences (SPSS) through transformation. Model 1 treats independent variable and use of BDA as simple predictors, whereas in Model 2, apart from these predictors interaction terms are also considered (Agresti & Finlay, 2008).

15.6.2 *Two Stage Regression Model*

The findings are presented in Tables 15.1, 15.2 and 15.3. Table 15.1 indicates that the value of R square increases for the second model from 0.732 to 0.866. This reflects that the model including interaction effect of rational decision making and big data analytics gives better explanation of the variation in organisational performance. Likewise, Table 15.2 shows that both the model is significant, i.e., the model with and without interaction are significant. Further, Table 15.3 shows that the interpretation of the independent variable

Table 15.1. Regression output

Model Summary[a]

Model	R	R square	Adjusted R square	Std. error of the estimate
1	.812[b]	.732	.727	.438
2	.930[c]	.866	.854	.440

[a]Dependent Variable: OP.
[b]Predictors: (Constant), BDA, RDM.
[c]Predictors: (Constant), BDA, RDM, Int_RDM_BDA.

Table 15.2. ANOVA table

ANOVA[a]

Model	Sum of squares	df	Mean square	F	Sig.
1 Regression	301.010	1	43.143	208.894	.000[b]
Residual	49.980	242	.207		
Total	351.982	249			
2 Regression	305.041	13	23.465	117.968	.000[c]
Residual	46.940	236	.199		
Total	351.982	249			

[a]Dependent Variable: OP.
[b]Predictors: (Constant), RDM, BDA.
[c]Int_RDM_BDA.

present in two stage regression is done in the same way as for the simple regression table and the positive coefficient for interaction terms Int_RDM_BDA shows that the variable use of big data analytics act as a moderator and hence if the organisation needs to take better decision, it is through the use of big data analytics which further leads to better organisational performance.

Thus the regression equation for the dummy variable regression considering interaction effect will as follow:

Table 15.3. Coefficient table

Coefficients[a]

Model	Unstandardised coefficients		Standardised coefficients		
	B	Std. error	Beta	t	Sig.
1 (Constant)	.586	.152		3.858	.000
RDM	.226	.049	.225	4.621	.000
BDA	.505	.135	.168	3.728	.000
2 (Constant)	.208	.295		.367	.014
RDM	.289	.107	.287	2.708	.007
BDA	.083	.204	.028	.408	.004
Int_RDM_BDA	.089	.120	.055	.744	.028

[a] Dependent Variable: OP.

Organisational performance
$$= \beta 0 + \beta 1 \text{ Rational decision-making} + \beta 2 \text{ (Big data analytics * Rational decision making)}$$

The analysis of data in two stages and dummy variable conform the hypothetical model.

The current study emphasises the importance of decision making in organisations for better performance. The proposed research model highlights that effective decision making results in better organisational performance and this is further enhanced by using big data analytics. The independent variable (IV) in the study is the rational decision making model, which represents the decision-making process based on the model suggested by Sprague and Carlson (1982). The dependent variable (DV) of the study is organisational performance based on the study of Capgemini (2012) on big data and decision making. The use of big data analytics is the moderator, which affects the relationship between decision making and organisational performance. The catalytic effect of moderator (Mo) enhances the relationship between the independent variable and the dependent variable. The study is cross sectional in approach, based on primary data collected from IT companies in Delhi NCR. All the variables are measured on a seven-point Likert scale. Regression analysis with the interaction effect of moderator was applied to analyse the data.

15.7 Findings

The key finding of the study are based on the result analysis after applying regression and interaction effect of big data analytics. The result indicates that use of rational decision making model in the organisation result into higher performance. The organisations have become digitised and hold huge amount of data for which manual decision making based on the intuition of the manager is ineffective. Use of big data analytics for assisting strategic decision making enhances the quality of decision making and further to enhanced organisational performance. The use of big data analytics supports rational decision making and leads to organisational performance. This happens through cost saving, time reduction, new product development, gaining better insight into market trends and managing social media trends.

15.8 Practical Implications

The decision-making process needs to be drastically changed in the global era where the customer is empowered and the business environment is highly dynamic. This requires SMEs to respond quickly to the fast changing market trends. Thus, decision making has to be fast, based on facts, and effective for intelligent moves in the business. This study will be able to create emphasis on the implementation of data analytics in the organisations for better organisational performance. It is important for leaders and managers to create a culture of data-driven process and decision making. Automation has changed the way organisation is run; currently the big data analytics is used to assist the managers for better decision making, and automated decision process is adopted for less critical or risky decisions. In this case, decision making is machine supported but the ultimate responsibility rests with the human element. However, machine learning with predictive analysis is guiding the future for large percentage of automated decision making.

15.9 Originality/Value

The study is unique in terms of area of research and the methodology adopted. Although much work has been done in the area of DSS and big data, there are few studies on SMEs in the Delhi NCR area. The moderating influence of big data analytics on organisational performance is a new approach to understand the importance of analytics based decision making.

References

Agresti, A., & Finlay, B. (2008). *Statistical Methods for the Social Sciences*, 4th ed. Prentice Hall, Upper Saddle, New Jersey.

Antony, J. P, & Bhattacharyya, S. (2010). Measuring organizational performance and organizational excellence of SMEs. Part 1: A conceptual framework. *Measuring Business Excellence, 14*(2), 3–11. https://doi.org/10.1108/13683041011047812

Arnott, D., & Pervan, G. (2014). A critical analysis of decision support systems research revisited: The rise of design science. *Journal of Information Technology, 29*(4), 269–293. doi:10.1057/jit.2014.16

Budikova, P., Batko, M., Novak, D., & Zezula, P. (2016). Inherent fusion. *Journal of Database Management, 27*(4), 1–23. doi:10.4018/jdm.2016100101

Capgemini (2012). The deciding factor: Big data & decision making. Available at: https://www.capgemini.com/resources/the-deciding-factor-big-data-decision-making

Chen, H., Chiang, R. H. L., & Storey, V. C. (2012). Business intelligence and analytics: From big data to big impact. *MIS Quarterly, 36*(4), 1165–1188.

Chiroma, H, Zavareh, A. A, Baba, M. S., Abubakar, I. A., Gital, Y. A, & Zambuk, F. U. (2015). Intelligent decision support systems for oil price forecasting. *International Journal of Information Science and Management*, 2015: Special Issue (ECDC), 47–59.

Davenport, T. H. (2014). *Big Data @ Work: Dispelling the Myths, Uncovering the Opportunities*. Harvard Business Review Press, Boston, Massachusetts.

Fan, S., Lau, R. Y. K., & Zhao, J. L. (2015). Demystifying big data analytics for business intelligence through the lens of marketing mix. *Big Data Research*, 2(1), 28–32. doi: 10.1016/j.bdr.2015.02.006

Frisk, J. E., & Bannister, F. (2017). Improving the use of analytics and big data by changing the decision-making culture: A design approach. *Management Decision*, 55(10), 2074–2088. https://doi.org/10.1108/MD-07-2016-0460

Hagel, J. (2015). Bringing analytics to life. *Journal of Accountancy*, 219(2), 24.

Herrmann, J. W. (2017). Rational decision making. In *Wiley StatsRef: Statistics Reference Online*, pp. 1–9. Wiley Online Publisher, USA.

Holsapple, C., Lee-Post, A. & Pakath, R. (2014). A unified foundation for business analytics. *Decision Support Systems*, 64, 130–141.

Hsiung, H.-H. (2011). Authentic leadership and employee voice behavior: A multi-level psychological process. *Journal of Business Ethics*, 107(3), 349–361. doi:10.1007/s10551-011-1043-2

Market Watch (2019). Data analytics market 2019. Available at: https://www.marketwatch.com/press-release/data-analytics-market-2019-size-business-growth-regional-trends-development-status-sales-revenue-and-comprehensive-research-study-till-2023-2019-01-15

Maté, A., Llorens, H., de Gregorio, E., Tardío, R., Gil, D., Muñoz-Terol, R., & Trujillo, J. (2015). A novel multidimensional approach to integrate big data in business intelligence. *Journal of Database Management*, 26(2), 14.31. doi:10.4018/jdm.2015040102

Matt, D. T., Rauch, E., & Riedl, M. (2018). Knowledge transfer and introduction of Industry 4.0 in SMEs: A five-step methodology to introduce Industry 4.0. In *Analyzing the Impacts of Industry 4.0 in Modern Business Environments*, pp. 256–282. IGI Global, Pennsylvania, USA.

McAfee, A., & Brynjolfsson, E. (2012). Big data: The management revolution. *Harvard Business Review*, 90(10), 60–68.

Moffitt, K. C., & Vasarhelyi, M. A. (2013). AIS in an age of big data. *Journal of Information Systems*, 27(2), 1–19. doi:10.2308/isys-10372

Najib, M., Boukachour, H., Boukachour, J., & Fazziki, A. E. (2010). Multi-agent framework for hazardous goods transport risk management. *International Journal of Information Science and Management*, Special Issue 2, 27–34.

NASSCOM (2018). Concept note. Available at: https://www.nasscom.in/bigdata/img/about/concept_note.pdf

Okeh, U. M., & Oyeka, I. C. A. (2015). One factor analysis of variance and dummy variable regression models. *Global Journal of Science Frontier Research: F Mathematics and Decision Sciences, 15*(7), 1–12.

Oliveira, A. (2007). A discussion of rational and psychological decision making theories and models: The search for a cultural-ethical decision making model. *Electronic Journal of Business Ethics and Organization Studies, 12*(2), 12–13.

Sappelli, M., de Boer, M. H. T., Smit, S. K. & Bomhof, F. (2017). A vision on prescriptive analytics. In *ALL DATA 2017: The Third International Conference on Big Data, Small Data, Linked Data and Open Data* (includes KESA 2017).

Sprague, R. H. Jr., & Carlson, E. D. (1982). *Building Effective Decision Support Systems.* Prentice-Hall, Englewood Cliffs, NJ.

Uzonwanne, F. C. (2016). Rational model of decision making. *Global Encyclopedia of Public Administration, Public Policy, and Governance,* 1–6. doi:10.1007/978-3-319-31816-5_2474-1. https://link.springer.com/ referenceworkentry/10.1007%2F978-3-319-31816-5_2474-1#toc

Wang, Y., & Byrd, T. A. (2017). Business analytics-enabled decision-making effectiveness through knowledge absorptive capacity in health care. *Journal of Knowledge Management, 21*(3), 517–539. https://doi. org/10.1108/JKM-08-2015-0301

Yip, P. S. L., & Tsang, E. W. K. (2007). Interpreting dummy variables and their interaction effects in strategy research. *Strategic Organization, 5*(1), 13–30. doi:10.1177/1476127006073512

Chapter 16

Effective HR Practices in Family Business in Technology Disruption Era

Senthil Kumar Arumugam*,† and Aarti Mehta Sharma‡

Department of Professional Studies, Christ University,
Bangalore, India

†senthilkumar.a@christuniversity.in

‡aartimehta.sharma@christuniversity.in

Abstract: Today's world of 21st-century business is said to be a VUCA (Volatility-Uncertainty-Complexity-Ambiguity) world. VUCA describes the fast pace of change in the business environment. It has largely been led by the disruption brought about by technology-led human resources departments within organisations to revise strategy approaches and methods to face these emerging challenges. Research studies show that more than two-thirds of the companies in the world belong to family businesses. In the family business, the owners and HR should see what is going on in the business environment and update the situation. As most family businesses have family members in key positions, the tricky issues faced by

---

*Corresponding author

family businesses are mostly about handling family and non-family members and creating effective HR policies. The COVID-19 pandemic in 2019 and 2020 has disrupted their business in unexpected ways. This chapter explores different HR practices adopted by the family business and suggests effective HR practices and procedures to meet the multiple challenges in the family business. The chapter also analyses the strategies of HR practices followed by some top family business firms worldwide. The chapter is formed as a meta-synthesis. It provides more qualitative inputs related to recent challenges and effective HR practices adopted in the technologically competitive era and during the COVID-19 pandemic period.

Keywords: Effective HR, Family business, Digital HR, Family firms, HR practice.

16.1 Introduction

"It is not what you leave your children that matters,
It is what you leave in them"
— Shannon L Alder

The United States Bureau of the Census says that approximately 90% of businesses in the U.S. are either owned by family or controlled by family (Inc., 2021). In India, a report by Deloitte research in the year 2013 says that family businesses stood at 85% out of total companies. A *Business Today* article quoted in the same report says that family businesses contribute to "18 per cent of India Inc's assets, 25 per cent of sales, 37 per cent of reserves and 32 per cent of profits after tax" (Chahal & Sharma, 2020). A PwC report defines "family business as one in which the person who has founded or acquired the business holds the majority of the shares (or by his/her parents, spouse, child, or direct heir of the child), and at least one representative of the family is involved in the management or administration of the business" (PwC, 2013). The same report lauds the efforts put in by family businesses in India in creating employment and pushing growth in the economy. As the name implies, a family business is possessed, maintained, and managed by single-family members (Advicoach, 2018). These members may be connected via blood, marriage, or adoption. Fundamentally, in a family business, most of the shares held by a single family have the majority of voting rights and more power in making strategic decisions. Top-level management usually comes from the same family because of several generations' continuous involvement in a single entity. The single-family business plays a vital role in the economy of their nations and other countries. A significant part of every country's GNP (Gross National Product) and exports are contributed by the single-family business. The family business is characterised by family members acting as members, their position in a company, controls over the company, solid principles, honesty towards company goals and transparency, exercising policies suitable for the interest of the family and business, involvement of multiple generations, and mutual trust with each other. This business has a common origin, set of values, ethics, and business orientation.

Today's world of business is said to be a VUCA (Volatility-Uncertainty-Complexity-Ambiguity) world. VUCA describes the fast pace of change in the business environment (D'Amato & Tosca, 2021). It has largely been led by the disruption brought about by technology and has led to a new generation of employees. In addition, it has led HR departments within organisations to revise strategy approaches and methods to face these emerging challenges. In a family business, the owners and HR should see what is going on in the business environment and update the situation. The COVID-19 pandemic in 2019 and 2020 has disrupted their business in unexpected ways. There are a few challenges presently face by HR professionals in family businesses in the COVID-19 pandemic. They are changing supply chain, remote workings, meeting demands, managing human resources during government announced lockdown periods, compensation payment, unforeseen lock-down, restriction in cross-border exchange of goods and services, less production, etc. Family company executives can learn from the best practices of another firm that specialises in VUCA circumstances to effectively manage VUCA issues like COVID-19 (Castoro & Krawchuk, 2020).

As most family businesses have family members in key positions, the tricky issues faced by family businesses are mostly about handling family and non-family members. This has many layered nuances, and how these situations are addressed influences the company's culture and performance. For any enterprise to succeed, it is crucial to get the best talent available, retain them in the organisation, keep them motivated, and develop desirable behaviours. The business can take advantage of the competitive human resources market to meet its short and long-term goals (Telford, 2020). However, family firms sometimes have difficulties recruiting and retaining other than family talent, mainly because of few HR practices and negative observations of interviewees about the company's professional expertise (Schuman *et al.*, 2016; Tabor & Vardaman, 2001). Another general observation among non-family candidates and workers of the family business is that the entity would favour more family employees, undermining their sense of organisational fairness (Ramadani, 2020). This is coupled with negative stereotypes about family firms having limited resources, low wages and compensation payment, lack of professionalism and integrity, and an increase in nepotism (Samara, 2020). The above perceptions need not be accurate, and in India, large and respected houses like the Tatas, Reliance, Godrej, etc., have been managed very professionally. They are highly respected within the country as well as overseas. However, for other smaller companies to change negative perceptions about family businesses, HR exercises in the family businesses should improve their game and make working environments satisfying and motivating and surpass the expectations of non-family members. The CEO of a family firm also has her work cut out as it is difficult to be objective and unbiased with family members (Ramadani *et al.*, 2020). It is imperative to make the human resource function effective by keeping in mind the organisational well-being of the family and non-family members (Rondi *et al.*, 2021).

16.2 Chapter Objectives

This chapter aims to explain the different methods of current HR practices adopted in family businesses and their various issues. It suggests effective HR practices and procedures to meet the multiple challenges in the family business. The chapter also analyses the strategies of HR practices followed by a few top family business firms worldwide and future challenges in HR practices in the technology disruption and pandemic period.

16.3 Research Design

The chapter is formed as a meta-synthesis. Secondary data sources such as journals and news articles, reports of family business forums, and financial statements of family business firms were collected and analysed. In addition, interviews with HR officials of family businesses were conducted to derive more qualitative inputs related to recent challenges and effective HR practices adopted in the technologically competitive era and during the COVID-19 pandemic period.

16.4 Nature of Family Business

Conventionally HR is involved in the recruiting, selection, on-boarding, training, development, and exit of an employee. However, these functions do not solely fall in the realm of HR only. Whether the manager is in sales, production, or quality, he is equally responsible for the HR lifecycle of the employee reporting to him. To understand the HR function in the family business, one must better understand the nature of family business. Figure 16.1 depicts a circular model that shows the degree of effect/significance that a family component may have. Renato Tagiuri and John Davis of Harvard Business school created a simple game-changing prototype in 1978. It consists of three intersecting areas that are, ownership, business, and family. The diagram shows the impact of family on business and ownership. The circles demonstrate the roles, different groups'

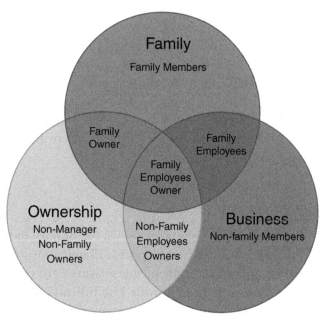

Figure 16.1.   Family business: A circular view
Source. Andrews (2020).

needs, and the interaction of diverse persons within business and family. These three hallmarks of a family business, each having its structures, need to interact with moving forward. The three circles intersect to form seven areas, i.e., anyone involved in a family business will fall in at least one of these seven areas (Andrews, 2020). The first and overarching circle is of course, family and their members, or participation in the organisation. Each of the following seven categories have their viewpoints and goals, and these should be respected; only then can the family business move forward. The people participating in the family firm can be categorised as:

- Members of the family who are not involved in the company
- Owners who are members of the family but not employed in the company
- Owners who are not connected to the family and not doing any work in the company

- Owners who are not family members and do work in the company
- Non-family labourers
- Family-members who are involving in regular activities of the company but not proprietor
- Family-owners who are working in the company

The model has withstood the test of time and shows the relationship between the different dependent sectors. For example, if there is a problem between two owners, it makes sense to check out if the differences can be traced back to family problems. The model also helps different stakeholders realise where they are coming from and can help diffuse tensions. Once the placement of each family member or non-member is clear, they realise their placement, responsibilities, and obligations.

16.5 Types of Family Business

Figure 16.2 illustrates three forms of the family business. First, in a family-owned business, the business is controlled by its ownership size, either by single-family or two or more members in the family.

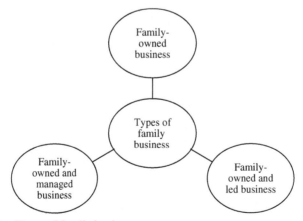

Figure 16.2. Types of family business

Source: BusinessJargons.com.

Second, family-owned and managed business is held by family ownership, establishing business goals, and formulating business policies and strategies. Finally, in the family-owned and led business, the family possesses either majority of shares or in a board of directors' position, influencing the business goals for further developments. In a family business, the first-generation entrepreneur is an innovator concentrating on investing capital and facing uncertainties and challenges. The second-generation entrepreneur joins the business at the middle level and later runs and controls the business established by their former family members.

For any business organisation to succeed, it is imperative to focus on the goal and create value for stakeholders. It can only happen when there is an emphasis on strategic planning. The same is the case for family-managed businesses as well. Here, planning gains even more importance as family members has to be taken along. To reach a defined goal and all the stakeholders being carried along, the company's governance should support growth through an effective board of governors. For any venture to take off, the leader has to be a visionary and should be able to realise the company's vision by carrying the team along with them. This leader can be a family member or non-family member, but the present and future of the company need to have a capable leader. Thus, for a family business to succeed, it is essential to have merit-based leadership, vital planning for strategy, a group of professionals to oversee operations, and family members and owners who are aligned to the company's interests. The same points are encapsulated in Figure 16.3.

16.6 Recent Issues and Challenges in HR Practices in Family Business

For all stakeholders in an organisation to work in tandem, it is imperative to focus on maintaining relationships and keeping people happy and motivated. This is where the human resource function should excel. A family-based firm will have all the challenges that a non-family-based firm will face and issues raised by the family (Brody

Figure 16.3.   Essentials of the family business

& Bogard, 2019). This is hence a field which has to be tread on carefully. Family-based firms face some common problems.

- A lack of professionalism from family members.
- Differential roles and treatment for family members.
- Difficulties in resolving disputes because of emotional attachments.
- Positions are given based on familial ties rather than merit.
- Differing views by family members on the direction the company should take.
- Unclear roles of family members.
- Lack of succession planning as well as a negative perception of family firms by applicants of jobs.

At times, it may become difficult for a family-based CEO to practice human resources objectively and effectively due to the family chain of the successor, role as a parent(s), and relatives (Beurden *et al.*, 2021; Ramadani *et al.*, 2020). It is also quite possible that particular family associates may be believed to be favoured in the firm's hierarchy, managerial level activities, rewards, salary, and benefits because of their status (Eddleston & Kidwell, 2018). In particular, succession planning and its procedures are essential in the family business-facing, as most enterprises do not keep their firm within the family during their subsequent generations. There is considerable concern among non-family workers on an heir's arrival (Tabor & Vardaman, 2020). Most personnel in a family-based company are wary of outside successors as they feel that the "family" feeling will not be there anymore. Most family firms treat their workers also as part of a widened family and make them feel comfortable. A successor from outside the family may not continue to do so. Also, if an undeserving person is named a descendant, the experience of nepotism can weaken non-family workers' commitment to the organisation and become challenging to retain them (Erdirencelebi & Cini, 2021). It is a big challenge to address this concern because choosing the next generation owner/successor in a family business and offering jobs to family members are the principal target of the owners of the family firm. The human resources function in such firms becomes even more crucial as their issues are drawn mainly from the above challenges. Research has shown that family firms tend to use simple, informal and unclear HR practices and criteria in the employment of family members (Rondi *et al.*, 2021).

Good HR practices can bring about solutions to most of the problems. A successful family firm should address various issues described in Figure 16.4 in its HR practices. The family members must learn their family business and be well-experienced in an outside business environment before getting full-time employment (Kok *et al.*, 2003). They should assess their firm from 360 degrees and conduct performance reviews by obtaining feedback from their stakeholders, maintaining internal equity in compensation to all employees at par with market value, and encouraging them to report to the non-family members. The family members should perform their tasks independently without passing them to non-family workers (Eddleston & Kidwell, 2018). Figure 16.5 displays the benefits of the family business and common challenges faced by the HR department in family business worldwide.

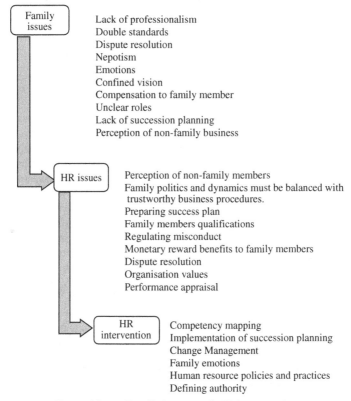

Figure 16.4. Family issues and HR intervention

16.7 Effective HR Strategies/Practices in Family Business in India/Abroad

Hiring, training, assessing, and rewarding talented candidates through a systematic HR process is a vital process to the success of any firm. Growing family firms should be familiar with these HR processes similar to large organisations while recruiting employees from inside and outside the family (Eddleston & Kidwell, 2018). When family members work together in close quarters, the working atmosphere can become more volatile because they are more relaxed, leading to out-of-control emotions and low

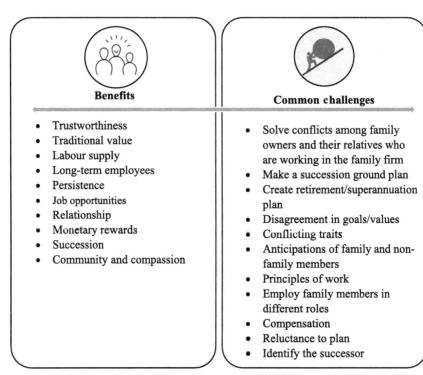

Benefits

- Trustworthiness
- Traditional value
- Labour supply
- Long-term employees
- Persistence
- Job opportunities
- Relationship
- Monetary rewards
- Succession
- Community and compassion

Common challenges

- Solve conflicts among family owners and their relatives who are working in the family firm
- Make a succession ground plan
- Create retirement/superannuation plan
- Disagreement in goals/values
- Conflicting traits
- Anticipations of family and non-family members
- Principles of work
- Employ family members in different roles
- Compensation
- Reluctance to plan
- Identify the successor

Figure 16.5. Benefits and common challenges in family business

employee morale. Family members' livelihoods are frequently linked to the firm's success; thus, they are motivated to maximise profit. The HR executive is presented with various issues that are not prevalent in non-family businesses due to the considerations above.

- Formalise management processes: All businesses do well when they formalise their management processes and create guidelines for processes, whether in hiring, giving incentives, selecting vendors, promoting personnel, etc. This creates clarity and trust and, over time, removes ambiguity and becomes a blueprint for how businesses conduct themselves and are known to all the stakeholders involved (Walsh, 2011). When a family firm attempts to incorporate generally accepted management processes into their day-to-day operations without considering the need to combine the family elements into these operations, often it leads to dissatisfaction, unsuccessful management processes or sometimes, restricts completely to implement the strategies of management. Too often, the attitude is: "We will just have to continue doing it Dad's way until we can figure out how to do it as most businesses do it". This is where HR must step in to persuade the family that processes need to be formalised as it leads to better working culture, respect for the organisation, and growth and revenue for the company.

- Create an engaged workforce: The family business, as all businesses, profits from a happy, productive, and engaged workforce. Such a workforce leads to higher productivity, better revenue, better customer service, better employee turnover, and fewer people taking leave. In a family-run business, the HR function involves managing all employee-related practices. There is more interaction between the family and employees, wherein employees are treated like family. The HR function becomes even more critical here as hiring for new positions within such a setup. There might be pressures on the family to hire people from the extended family or the immediate family. This may or may not fit in with the culture and the job requirements. The approach by the family could be softer and more casual which could hurt the family in the long run. In such a case, a good HR can suggest a systematic way to hire for new positions.

- Make an organisation chart: An organisation chart is a must in all entities as it defines the roles and responsibilities, line of authorities, and division of labourers of the entity. The structure creates a complex family business when two or more young CEOs from a family group work in an organisation. When these young family members work as employees and report to non-family members, they may feel compelled to appeal to their parents if the manager's actions are unsatisfactory. This behaviour may undercut the manager's authority and may subsequently lead to resentment. An organisation chart helps remove these problems. Also, in this way, the roles, areas of work, and responsibilities become clear to everyone in the business. As a result, overlapping roles are avoided.

- Create job descriptions: Job descriptions are one of the essential HR practices. They are a guideline for every employee: what their roles are and what they are not. Furthermore, it assures compliance with labour regulations. Whenever each employee in an organisation knows what they are expected to do, it avoids overlapping roles and responsibilities. This is especially true for family-run businesses as it will help remove tensions within the family regarding authority and the company's day-to-day running.

- Conduct on-boarding and exit interviews: Hiring new employees is a time-consuming and expensive process. Hence, it is essential to get the right talent, nurture it, and motivate it to stay. The culture and work environments of a family business are different from the non-family company. One of the effective HR practices is that HR professionals should orient the new employees about corporate culture, principles, and policies and enter into the family-run organisation and fit into it. These are also helpful to them when they exit. If the new employees are not correctly oriented towards understanding the culture and family business environments, they misunderstand the organisation and quit early. Proper orientation helps them to settle into the company and to be productive. It is also crucial to understand why employees leave the company, so as to improve the conditions and people are motivated to stay and be productive. If an employee is leaving as they cannot work in the family set up, then an attempt should be made to understand the person's trials, and subsequently, conditions should be made better for the next person in the company.

- Effective communication by the manager: Experienced professionals in human resources can train managers to communicate more effectively with their employees. This is especially important in family business as operations tend to be informal because a large part of the workforce is related or has been with the company a long time. HR professionals can help ensure the family does not lose sight that work-hours should be spent working, not resolving family drama. Communication skills are also crucial in dealing with employees who have issues with family members. Family members must be trained to listen to the employee's point of view.

16.8 Succession Planning

Succession planning is of utmost importance in family and non-family organisations as it clears the way for younger people to move into key positions as older people leave. In most family-run businesses, it is paving the way for the heir. Research points to the fact that non-family workers often expect the family successor to non-family externals because the culture in family business goes with family succession (Erdirencelebi & Cini, 2021; D'Amato & Tosca, 2021; Loewen, 2020). Family businesses must dispel fears of workers regarding the transition to another generation's leaders. In a family organisation, the effective communication process, the harmonious relationship among employees and owners, and confirmed successor fitness are the essentials of the succession process. Figure 16.6 explains the various components used for implementing successful HR policy in Volkswagen. How family firms can garner non-family assistance for the family successors' subsequent generation are:

- Fostering familiarity: The employees in a company should be made aware of the succession plan and whether the person joining is from the family or from outside. While looking for a candidate outside the family, the candidate should be familiar with the company's motivations, workings, and culture. The current employees should know that a successor is being called from outside the company before starting the process. This will make them feel valued and trusted (Tabor & Vardaman, 2020).
- Raising the bar: Employees' fears about non-family members can be erased by hiring leaders with good education and a proven track record of success. Similarly, they should respect the leader who is a family member when they have a good education

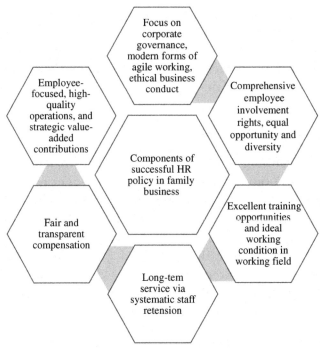

Figure 16.6.   Components of successful HR policy in family business
Source: EXOR (2020); Volkswagen (2020).

and a proven track record. Whenever a new person is at the helm, they will have to prove that they are worth the position by working hard, staying back longer, being involved, etc. (Tabor & Vardaman, 2020).

- Bring in non-family members: After a successor has been selected, the responsibility of training them should not fall only on the incumbent. Non-family managers should also help in the training. These will help them feel valued, prevent attrition, and promote loyalty (Loewen, 2020; Tabor & Vardaman, 2020).

HR professionals of family businesses should engage their employees through regular meetings and communications with all employees, periodical reviews of HR policies and objectives, and fair compensation to family and non-family workers. During the hiring process for the job position, considering integrity is the successful HR practice among all traits of candidates, said Warren Buffett, CEO of Berkshire Hathaway (Schwantes, 2020).

> "We look for three things when we hire people.
> we look for intelligence,
> we look for initiative or energy, and
> we look for integrity.
> And if they don't have the latter, the first two will kill you, because if you're going to get someone without integrity, you want them lazy and dumb."
> — Warren Buffett, Berkshire Hathaway Inc.

Figure 16.7 exhibits the top ten family businesses worldwide and their concise profiles. Table 16.1 describes the effective HR practices followed by these family business companies worldwide (Thompson, 2019) and emerging digital HR practices.

16.9 Conclusion

The family-run firm is like any other business, albeit with some family tensions thrown in. As a result, it is a fertile ground for successors to learn and help the company grow. HR practices in such companies should be based on a culture of transparency, accountability, and trust between members of the family, management, and employees (Müceldili & Tatar, 2021). These will give the family-run business the requisite strength to soar and succeed. This chapter concentrated on the various issues and challenges in HR practices in the existing family business system and suggested effective HR practices suitable for the family business in the VUCA world. The HR practices should be transformed digitally, and suitable measures to be taken for being an effective to suit current technologies amid the pandemic period. The digital transformation of HR practices in family business minimises the need to rely on guesswork in deciding and allows for more accurate decision making. It provides more

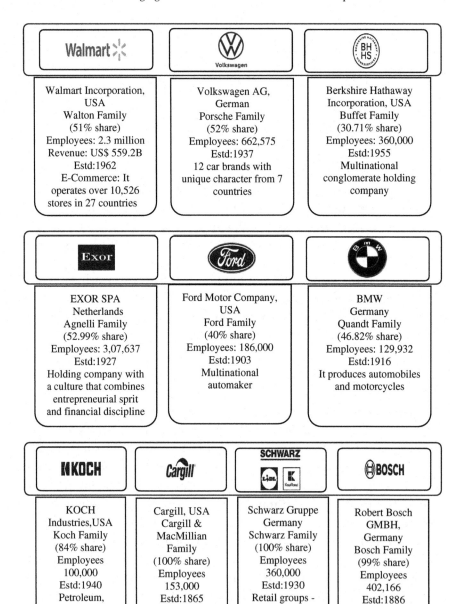

Figure 16.7. Top ten family businesses worldwide

Source: Andrews (2020); Wagner (2021); Walmart (2021); Volkswagen (2020).

Table 16.1.   Effective HR practices of family business firms

HR Strategy	The stratified approach can be followed for programming and controlling the activities in HR. All successful family businesses consider the following components while framing HR strategy. • Corporate Culture • Organisational Structure • Performance Management • Career Development
HR Planning	The HR head can appoint dedicated HR managers at the executive level in each store or branch of the family business. Executive HR managers should consider company-wide policies and interpret them according to their branch location's specific needs for effective HR practices.
Digital HR	Firms should implement HR software, as implementing the software automatically collects data from various family businesses and analyses the human resources data using cognitive technology tools such as Artificial Intelligence (AI) and Machine Learning (ML) programs. Using these data, firms can find the answers to the following questions by deploying business analytics software. • What trends may be seen in the turnover of employees? • How many days are needed to recruit employees? • What level of investment is required to get full productivity among employees? • Which employee(s) in a family firm is/are most likely to depart before the deadline? • What is the influence of staff development and training initiatives on employee performance? The cognitive technologies and business analytics software will help HR professionals to predict the trend, possible changes in the workforce, frequent follow-up of supply and demand of labour forces, employee profiles and their accomplishments, high and low performers information, past details of remuneration, and job enrichment, demographic data, vacancy, on-boarding, orientation and training, employee attrition and turnover rate, employee engagement, and absenteeism.

(Continued)

Table 16.1. (*Continued*)

	The technology-oriented HR analytics tools will help the HR officials to: • Consider a wide range of characteristics, such as developmental opportunities and cultural fit, to better understand applicants. • Identify applicants that have characteristics that are similar to those of the family business company's top performers. • Avoid unconscious bias and provide equal opportunity for all candidates by using a data-driven strategy for recruitment. In this approach to recruiting, one person's position and opinion will no longer influence the selection of candidates. • Allow HR section to be well-arranged and keep informed when there is necessity to appoint by providing analytics on the number of days usually required to select a candidate for particular jobs in an organisation. • Allow family business firm to build better long-term recruiting plans by providing historical data on times of over-hiring and under-hiring.
HR Metrics	HR analytics metrics can be used and measured for effective HR practices. A few examples are: • Time to hire. It is essential to know about the total time/days taken to announce posts and confirm the appointment of applicants. This metric should be supervised by HR in the long run and matched to the preferred organisational rate. • Recruitment cost to hire. The overall amount of recruiting and employing candidates needs to be calculated. This measure is tracked over time to see how much it costs to attract different sorts of applicants. • Rate of turnover. HR leaders should assess the percentage of workers who leave their positions after a year. This measure is tracked throughout time to compare it to the family company's acceptable rate or target set. • Rate of absenteeism. The family business firms should define the acceptable absentee range for effective measurement. It is essential to measure the number of days/hours and the frequency of workers away from their allocated jobs. Continuous monitoring of this metric can later be compared with business goals and its acceptance rate. Deviation, if any, is to be corrected and prevented by the HR leader in his effective practices.

Table 16.1.   (*Continued*)

	• Rate of engagement. Employee productivity and satisfaction are measured to determine whether employees are engaged in their work. Surveys, performance evaluations, and productivity metrics can all be used to examine these. The essential metrics that are monitored during the HR analytical process are: • The data is gathered and compared to understand turnover, absenteeism, and recruiting outcomes. • The efficiency of HR's day-to-day operations and activities are measured using data collected through various branches' software. • This section integrates data from institutional and operational measurements to determine the area it requires process improvement.
Job Analysis and Design	Analysing requirements for hiring through interviews and surveys of both potential recruits and existing staff. Framing suitable HR policies for placing family members in relevant roles and locations.
Establishing Communication	Effective channel of communication between family employees, non-family employees, and managers leads to accurate forecasting of recruitment.
Appreciation	Whenever existing workers innovated and achieved their tasks, they can be appreciated by HR leaders by providing monetary or non-monetary benefits or by words. For example, Walmart appreciates their truck drivers in an important meeting. Officials inform the technology-based action and safety measures taken for truck drivers' benefit to fill up around 60,000 vacancy positions in the trucking and freight industry under the family business (WBR Insights, 2021).

knowledge of reasons for the leaving workers to stay with a family business. It helps create retention strategies, evaluate the workers' behaviour, and decide on improving procedures and the workplace environment. Also, by assessing and comparing the data of present workers and potential applicants, employment may be well suited to the family business' real competence needs.

To implement effective HR practices in a family business, the human resource department should equip skilled statisticians and analytical expertise to manage the large volume of data and take HR-related decisions. Also, data analysis and reporting software should be in place for handling cloud data. Systems should be up-to-date to access quality real-time data from all branches of the family business. HR leaders can use computer data for identifying trends and patterns using predictive analytics, allowing family businesses to be active in maintaining a productive staff. HR leaders of a family business should advance their legacy system to a data-driven analysis system. This technology-based system helps in workforce analysis, recruiting analysis, turnover analysis, compensation analysis, succession planning analysis, generating training reports, talent assessment, calculating human capital return on investment, and improving organisational effectiveness.

References

Advicoach (2018, October 18). Understanding human resources in a family business. Growth Success Team. Available at: https://advicoach. com/blog/2018/10/18/understanding-human-resources-in-a-family-business/

Andrews, P. (2020). Circular simplicity. *Family Business Global, 1*, 14–16. Available at: https://issuu.com/familybusinessmagazine/docs/family_business_global_magazine-pages

Beurden, J. V., Voorde, K. V. D., & Veldhoven, M. V. (2021). The employee perspective on HR practices: A systematic literature review, integration and outlook. *The International Journal of Human Resource Management, 32*(2), 359–393, https://doi.org/10.1080/09585192.2020.1759671

Brody, R. G., & Bogard, K. M. (2019 February). Human resources is a critical part of an effective family business. *Family Business Magazine.* Available at: https://www.familybusinessmagazine.com/human-resources-critical-part-effective-family-business

Castoro, A. & Krawchuk, F. (2020, May 13). What family businesses can learn from the military. Harvard Business Review. Available at: https://hbr.org/2020/05/what-family-businesses-can-learn-from-the-military

Chahal, H., & Sharma, A. K. (2020). Family business in India: Performance, challenges and improvement measures. *Journal of New Business Ventures, 1*(1–2), 9–30.

D'Amato, V., & Tosca, E. (2021). Human resources management and the new challenges in family firms: An Italian case study. In Gnan, L. & Flamini, G. (Eds.), *Designing and Implementing HR Management Systems in Family Businesses*, pp. 42–61. IGI Global. http://doi:10.4018/978-1-7998-4814-1.ch003

Eddleston, K., & Kidwell, R. (2018, December 18). Let's get professional: Family firms need hrm practices. *Entrepreneur & Innovation Exchange.* Available at: https://familybusiness.org/content/Lets-get-professional-family-firms-need-hrm

Erdirencelebi, M., & Cini, M. A. (2021). Human resources management understanding and nepotism in family businesses. In Gnan, L. & Flamini, G. (Eds.), *Designing and Implementing HR Management Systems in Family Businesses*, pp. 183–198. IGI Global. http://doi:10.4018/978-1-7998-4814-1.ch010

EXOR (2020). 2020 Annual Report. Available at: https https://www.exor.com/sites/default/files/2021/document-documents/EXOR_ANNUAL%20REPORT_2020.pdf.

Inc. (2021, January 5). Family-owned businesses. Available at: https://www.inc.com/encyclopedia/family-owned-businesses.html

Kok, J. d., Thurik, R., & Uhlaner, L. (2003). Professional HRM practices in family owned-managed enterprises. EIM and Erasmus University Rotterdam (CASBEC), Zoetermee. Article SCALES paper N200319. https://core.ac.uk/download/pdf/7074518.pdf

Loewen, J. (2020). Four ways to transfer wealth in family business, Professional Insight. *Family Business Global, 1,* 48–49. Available at: https://issuu.com/familybusinessmagazine/docs/family_business_global_magazine-pages

Müceldili, B., & Tatar, B. (2021). Reflections of human resource practices in family business: A qualitative research. In Gnan, L. & Flamini, G. (Eds.), *Designing and Implementing HR Management Systems in Family Businesses*, pp. 1–16. IGI Global. http://doi:10.4018/978-1-7998-4814-1.ch001

PwC (2013). Family firm - The India perspective. Available at: https://www.pwc.in/assets/pdfs/family-business-survey/family-business-survey-2013.pdf

Ramadani, V., Memili, E., Palalić, R., & Chang, E. P. C. (2020). Human resource management in family businesses. In *Entrepreneurial Family Businesses*. Springer Texts in Business and Economics. Springer, Cham. https://doi.org/10.1007/978-3-030-47778-3_7

Rondi, E., Überbacher, R., Schlenk-Barnsdorf, L. V., Massis, A. D., & Hülsbeck, M. (2021). One for all, all for one: A mutual gains perspective on HRM and innovation management practices in family firms, *Journal of Family Business Strategy*, 100394, https://doi.org/10.1016/j.jfbs.2020.100394.

Samara, G. (2020). Family businesses in the Arab Middle East: What do we know and where should we go?. *Journal of Family Business Strategy*, 100359, https://doi.org/10.1016/j.jfbs.2020.100359.

Schuman, A., Sage-Hayward, W., & Ransburg, D. (2016, January 28). Managing the complexity of human resources in family firms. The Family Business Consulting Group. Available at: https://www.thefbcg.com/resource/managing-the-complexity-of-human-resources-in-family-firms/

Schwantes, M. (2020, November 14). Warren Buffett: Integrity is the most important attribute to hire for. Ask 7 simple questions to find it. Inc Newsletter. Available at: https://www.inc.com/marcel-schwantes/warren-buffett-hiring-top-talent-characteristics.html

Tabor, W., & Vardaman, J. (2020, May 15). The key to successful succession planning for family businesses. Harvard Business Review. Available at: https://hbr.org/2020/05/the-key-to-successful-succession-planning-for-family-businesses.

Telford, D. (2020, May 11). The five fundamental building blocks of strong family businesses. The Family Business Consulting Group. Available at: https://www.thefbcg.com/resource/the-five-fundamental-building-blocks-of-strong-family-businesses/

Thompson, A. (2019, February 26). Walmart's human resource management. Available at: http://panmore.com/walmart-human-resource-management-hr-management

Volkswagen (2020). Annual report. Available at: https://annualreport2020.volkswagenag.com/group-management-report/sustainable-value-enhancement/employees.html

Wagner, I. (2021, February 9). Ford employees 2018-2020. Statista. Available at: https://www.statista.com/statistics/297324/number-of-ford-employees/

Walsh, G. (2011). Family business succession managing, the all-important family component. KPMG Enterprise. Available at: https://books.google.co.in/books?id=kWxzMwEACAAJ

Walmart (2021). Company facts. Available at: https://corporate.walmart.com/newsroom/company-facts

WBR Insights (2021). Walmart has the largest workforce in the world: How do they manage all those employees? HR Retail. Available at: https://hrretail.wbresearch.com/walmart-largest-workforce-employee-management-strategy-ty-u

Index

brand awareness, 291, 293
brand consumer, 286
broadcast search, 89
business analytics (BA), 329, 359
business goals, 307
business intelligence (BI), 329
business model, 75
business start up, 254
business's website, 289

C
cash flow difficulty, 307
celebrities, 296
centralisation, 312
change management, 64
characteristics of quality,
    compliance and cost-
    effectiveness, 306
choosing the right influencer, 293
circular view, 346
cloud data, 362
coaching, 18
cognitive technologies, 359
collaborate formally, 311
collaboration, 76
collaborative learning, 260
collective intelligence, 76
communities of practice, 259, 271
compelling vision, 143
competencies, 64, 301
competitive advantage, 76
competitive edge, 330
competitiveness, 54, 88
complicated planning, 249
comprehensive framework of
    crisis leadership, 308
computer vision improvement
    (CV), 227
conscientiousness, 193

consultation, 311
consumer behaviour, 323
consumers' buying decisions, 285
content creator, 290
contextualisation of leadership,
    306
contextual shifts, 312
contingency approach, 23, 26, 29
contingency theories of
    leadership, 311
contingent reward, 196
continuous learning, 110, 313
controls, 298
cooperation, 144
corporate culture, 191, 359
corrective actions, 313
correlations, 198
cost reduction, 93
COVID-19, 156–157, 159, 161, 166,
    215, 301, 315, 345
creative ideas, 97
credibility, 297
crisis, 301–303
crisis leadership, 302
crisis situation, 315
critical, 262
critical reflection, 274
cross-sectional, 48
crowd-based businesses, 77
crowdsourcing, 75
crowdsourcing applications, 76
crowdsourcing framework, 82
cultural diversity, 20
culture, 3, 162
culture of SMEs, 91
curriculum design, 257, 270
customer experience, 289
customer needs, 288
customers, 12

Printed in the United States
by Baker & Taylor Publisher Services